How to
SURVIVE
in
SOMERSET

CHARLES WOOD

HALSGROVE

First published in Great Britain in 2008

Publisher's Disclaimer
Halsgrove have disowned Mr Wood on many occasions in the past
and are more than happy to do so again. The views expressed in this
book emanate solely from the fevered brain of Mr Wood who remains
entirely responsible for them, the Publisher is pleased to say.

British Library Cataloguing-in-Publication Data
A CIP record for this title is available from the British Library

ISBN 978 1 84114 826 7

HALSGROVE
Halsgrove House
Ryelands Industrial Estate
Bagley Road, Wellington
Somerset TA21 9PZ
Tel: 01823 653777
Fax: 01823 216796
email: sales@halsgrove.com
website: www.halsgrove.com

Printed in Great Britain by
The Cromwell Press Ltd, Trowbridge

Naming of Parts

ACKNOWLEDGEMENTS

My grateful thanks to Simon Butler of Halsgrove for the hint he wrote into the corner of his Christmas card. Thanks also to Steven Pugsley and Julian Davidson at that edifice of publishing to let me just get on with it, safe in the knowledge that I've been 'surviving' for years. Sometimes personal experience can have positive effects even if it occasionally cuts a little near the bone.

With nothing being possible without the help of friends I am especially grateful to Andrew, Keith, Jill, Mark, Phil and Tad for pointing my bonnet in the right directions, and to the others, often in the 'Bearin' Up', who might modestly introduce themselves now and again. Huge thanks as well to Atef and Veronika in Abergavenny, and to Luiza and Armin in Vienna for blowing away my cobwebs with their hospitality and giving me space for reflection.

Closer to home, I have to thank my children Lawrence, Maddy, Ez and Felix who have had tough times, and whose support over the years has been an inspiration, I can only extend wonder, love and gratitude. For my lovely Alina, who daily makes my life a joy and who translates my English into English, my words live in my heart. After our exotic travels encountering brown bears, elephants, aggressive monkeys, and 'interesting' cuisines, I have come to appreciate that as long as one has a smile, a pair of wellies and a little green car with the spirit of adventure, it is better to survive in Somerset.

And a mention also for Bilbo the cat for sticking by me and having patience with her varying meal times.

First Musings

"Sumorsaete Ealle"
(The ever-hopeful Somerset County Council motto meaning,
"All the people of Somerset".)

I was penning a cultural book of sorts about Somerset to be ready when the lavender flowered and nasturtiums could be put in a salad, and here I was in Writers' Walk staring at busts in Pushkin Park during film festival week. Perhaps I sought inspiration from the bronze cast likenesses of Alexander Pushkin, Ion Creanga and Mihai Eminescu. All were writers of culture, although admittedly not English.

However, there had to be more for example to Taunton than potwabblers and first class cricket, or indeed to Yeovil than Italian helicopters. Although to be fair, it was a big deal to have just won a contract to build the US presidential helicopter 'Marine One'.

My friend and fellow filmmaker Mark Reynolds was also looking at busts, though not the same ones as me. As chest jutting wasp-waisted girls bum-wiggled passed Mark's gaze, an amply endowed woman with dyed red hair tied back in a bun caused Mark to click his digital camera for the umpteenth time that afternoon. Either in middle age, or just having worked too hard, the woman wore a vibrant pink two piece in a material usually reserved for the making of cuddly teddy bears, all set off by a black patent leather handbag. Only in Moldova. In Somerset even a fashion statement like pink wellies would be kept in the cupboard of embarrassments.

"We're a long way from home." Mark remarked. Somerset was home for us both. Compared to Moldova, squidged as it is between Romania and the Ukraine, Somerset is positively exotic. Mark is Somerset born and Somerset schooled, a secondary education in Wellington being his misfortune. He picked up his first guitar in Somerset and has 'played Glastonbury'. Now living down a secret lane near the summit of Dunkery he survives filmmaking's perennial lean times by being Susan George's gardener. I knew Mark must know a thing or two. Surely he could help me.

HOW TO SURVIVE IN SOMERSET

"What do you reckon to home? Does it feel different coming from Somerset, culturally I mean?" I asked prompting. "You what?" said Mark giving me a sideways look. But battling towards my half century I was welcoming the opinion of a thirty-something. Mark thought for a moment and suggested a beer.

"Well?" I prompted again several bottles later.

"You know you're from Somerset", Mark finally began, "when you turned to drink or heavy metal at an early age and you have nothing to do after 5:30pm. Your first driving lesson's in a tractor. Until you run away, the tallest building you ever see is Debenhams in Taunton." Silence.

"And you're frightened to run away beyond Frome because you think you'll fall off the edge of the world and land on London's lumpy mattress." I ventured. "Then again, it's not recommended to go near Frome, anyway. John Wesley thought it 'a dry, barren and uncomfortable place.' With this coming from a Methodist, the town must be really bad."

Not rising to flippancy, Mark warmed to his subject. "You know why to avoid Bridgwater and you think Bristol is 'up north'. There are places where men are men and sheep are nervous. There's a town called Somerset in Kentucky and a successful punk-rock band called Somerset from Minneapolis in Minnesota. The only all-Somerset band to have ever 'made it' was Racey. They sold half a million, but they were from Weston-super-Mare, which was in Avon at the time, so I suppose they don't count. The music video for Bryan Adams 'Everything I Do I Do it For You' the sound track for 'Robin Hood Prince of Thieves', and number one for 16 weeks in the UK singles charts, was filmed at Kilve Beach.

"You think nothing of paying £20 for a two-mile taxi journey. Takeaways that deliver, what are they? Your neighbours' average age is 76. Pigeons are a menace. Short and choppy on the north coast makes total sense to you; and you can't stand the grockles, despite living off their money."

"Ah huh" I said, hanging on to every word. The one about the grockles, the name given by Somerset folk to describe tourists, was a little near the bone and I gave an edgy laugh before going back to stare at the busts in Pushkin Park.

Chisinau
May 2008

6

LESSON ONE
A LITTLE HISTORY

"Ef you do ax what land is blessed
Wi' works o' natur' o' the best,
I never zeed such 'oodlands yet
Or vields so fair as Zummerset."
(Anon).

Do not be fooled, this is not a book about self-sufficiency. I do not grow my own fruit and vegetables, or keep chickens, geese, or goats. I used to, and it was a very silly idea from another life. Rather, this is just a smidgeon of helpful insider knowledge to those folk who enjoy being a little nosey.

As a beginning some reflection is called for. Somerset is an English county rich of landscape if not of wallet, easy on the eyes even if you have to rub them occasionally.

Extending from Exmoor in the west to Bruton forest on the Wiltshire border, from the Mendips to the Blackdown Hills, Somerset could be thought a welcoming place. Take a stroll on a bright morning as cows mooch in buttercup meadows and bees drone amongst cider apple blossom, and you would rightly think this an idyll of milk and honey; an inspiration for the poetic. However, peer a little closer and you'll discover the need for caution.

There are many dangers. A pheasant may arrive on your lap through the open car window. Alternatively, you could become puggle 'eaded, run down by hunters in pursuit of a rag, stung by a dumbledore, tupped by a hobby horse, consume badger stew or radioactive fish, be bonked by a cricket ball, get lost in a honeycomb of caves, or have rigor mortis at a bus stop.

And then there are the dialect gossipers often predisposed to act a little oddly; characters who seem almost organically grown from the soil, be it upon high moor, hilltop, levels or coast who share tales of red deer, hare and eel.

However, both the places and the people are haplessly submitting to the meddling and uniformity that pervade England today. Progress is beginning to nibble and the cartoon world of Norman Thelwell that had educated Americans for decades in the vagaries of the English country-side is a wisp of itself.

Every move one makes needs to be carefully considered. It is the one rule that should be learned first and foremost. Indeed the first mention I heard of Somerset was in the classroom among a class of impressionable eight year olds. Gathering together at the start of the autumn term with fleeting new form interest we had asked our Latin teacher Mr Athanas, a Greek, where he had been for his summer holidays. We expected to hear about olives and cicadas. "Somerset," he said turning a dreamy gaze to the window, " A lady so pretty that her bottom is pinched by Dorset and Devon. Amor meus Somerset".

And then came my summer holiday. That parent-cosseted summer holiday. As Tom Cartwright wheeled in to bowl over after casual over in cricket's John Player League, I sailed a white wooden toy yacht with canvas sails and metal keel in Minehead's tide filled beach swimming pool, and shed plimsoll sand upon the creaking floorboards of the Plume of Feathers Hotel. Mum sat upon a wind-sanded rug and knitted bright woollen shawls. Dad puffed his pipe filled with Exmoor Gold and bought me two hardcover Asterix books from Smiths for twelve shillings each. And Dad told Mum and me that a bloke called Stringfellow had made the first powered flight in leafy green vegetables. Mum and me looked blank. "In Chard!" he laughed his seldom laugh. Such wonderfulness.

The sun shone hot all day, and rain rinsed the air clean by night as the moon failed to follow our Vauxhall Viva back down North Hill. I heard mentions of Dunster and Stogumber, Glastonbury and Wells, King Arthur and Avalon. Highbridge served me the best T-bone steak I had ever eaten, although the potato croquettes and asparagus that came with it made me sick and I wished for the sturdy constitution of a white faced Exmoor sheep.

Memory is a strange thing. It is selective and prone to exaggeration's inaccuracy. By the mid 1980s I was back and intended to stay, having acquired a new-build of a first time buyer's home. One of an adjoining pair both small but cheap that proved to be the builder's single and only attempt at erection before his divorce.

Early fatherhood had completely befuddled me. Fresh air was good and I craved the excitement of winter wind beside the Severn Sea. That short stretch of coast from Minehead to Bridgwater Bay that is touched by both prehistory and the nuclear age. Picking up and opening the crisply folded ordinance survey, I looked at this and that before putting my finger on Blue Anchor, thinking it good for the day.

It was a time of silliness, when bouffant-haired pop bands with baby gurgle names like Kagagoogoo made insipid warblings with keyboard plinkings on our crackling car radio, and the Wurzels sang of combine harvesters and cider on the ropey CD player. With the music keeping the call of nature out of my ears, my small family and I made the afternoon trip into West Somerset. The word 'west' had acted like a lure and I was snared. To me it suggested mists, freshness and romance, which is odd when really the west is where the sun goes down and the day ends.

I lived in my head, and still do so for that matter, and I have not always been the most practical of people. An idealist, that was me. What I wanted was the country life, a cottage with roses around the door and a cat of character. And also to feel the tingles of nature born of walks on web-glistening mornings, glimpses of deer, hearing wind carried buzzard mews, owl shrieks in dimpsey light and paddles in a sun-spangled sea. And all could be achieved without getting too grubby. I had knowledge of the Mummerset of D.H. Lawrence muttered by gamekeepers distracted from pheasants; the rustic accent seemingly extending from Nottingham to Wiveliscombe. Although looking slightly ridiculous on the page and sounding weird when spoken, I mistook it for the Somerset burr. I still blame the Greek.

Anyway, Blue Anchor sounded nice and I had never been there. Yes, I had passed by on the West Somerset Railway's chuffing steam train donkey's years ago, but at the time I was looking the other way. I had read somewhere that the origin of the name referred to the blue offshore mud hauled up on ships' anchors. But standing there with wind-watered eyes 'blue' seemed a misnomer, a Tourist Board elaboration; a lie of hue. Instead, Blue Anchor was a place of grey, cloying sticky clay.

For a molly-coddled Hampshire-born hog it was also somewhat chilly. Despite local rustic men unbuttoning fleece cotton shirts to expose nipples to snowdrops caught in sunbeams, I was not local nor was I rustic, and the sun that day had business elsewhere. But I was in a stubborn mood and wanted a paddle, albeit in wellies. And I wanted to show my small first-born child Lawrence the grey sombre waves where melancholy can be mistaken as romantic. All-weather suited and bootied, Lawrence kicked against my spine. A-squirm in the pristine blue and white striped Mothercare baby-carry he began to fret and point behind him.

My rust-bucket Citroen was parked beside a desolation of wintering grockle shells, those damp caravans left to storm shake and rancid butter pats. I had acquired the car for a wodge of cash and it proved a drafty cocoon for my scarf-wrapped pregnant wife, who had her head buried in *Homemaking for Paupers*, a book that had a worm-eaten chest of drawers receiving a custard-yellow makeover on the cover. She sought inspiration.

To the right of my son and me, beyond the ripples of the incoming tide, Steep Holm, Somerset's only island, looked sullen. It is a place that rattles if you jump up and down on its spongy top due to the bones from countless seabird generations. Straight ahead of us, the horizon chimneys of industrial Wales belched smoke clouds into a steel sky. A Red Indian might well have read 'Danger' and abandoned madness. Mulishly, I did not.

After several dozen strides of squidge and squelch, avoiding the sand eels, I stumble-sank in boot-sucking gloop. An oblivious wife and the sea were both equidistant behind and in front. Then just to my left, lying on a sand eel cone, was a baby bootie that should have been keeping my son's tootsie as warm as toast. Of course I had to pick it up. As my shoulders went down, Lawrence was flung head first over my shoulder to become sand-plugged in a feat worthy of a baby ostrich. It was one of a few of my life's heart stopping moments. Little legs did air kicks as I gawped. My panicked tug caused a splutter and an ensuing torrent of tissue dissolving tears.

Yanking the baby-carry off my back, I plonked it in the clay. The blue and white had absorbed grey, before I retrieved my bedraggled son and lifted him back from whence he had flown. However, I was stuck fast. My left welly had sunk, swallowed to adhesion, and my left foot popped out as I tried vainly to free myself. Not wanting to put a warm sock onto cold sludge, I stood fleetingly heron-like until gravity lurched my body forward. And that was the start of it.

I returned into the shadows of grockle shells with two blue numb feet each in a sopping sock, a blue numb son in a grubby baby-carry and a soggy bootie in my hand.

"Well, where's the other one?" said my wife rather too calmly. Thunderously she looked at the bootie I held, then at Lawrence's two unbootied feet.

Being beaten on the head by the *Pauper's Guide* in a gale of histrionics and scolding brought a breaking wave of regret that I had given up a salary earned in the exploding petrochemical fields of the Libyan desert. A place of green haze where a man could be hanged for accidentally crashing a lorry; and where I had no appetite for stringy camel served with red-spotted Italian spinach, or oil-polluted fish that could turn you blind.

But my regret was fleeting. There was to be no going back from the Somerset custom of self-employment. And I really-really wanted to be an artist. Nobody had ever taught me, so I would teach myself. Perhaps I could even learn to use a camera. They were the days of a naïve positive thinker when it wasn't cool to whinge.

Indeed, maybe Blue Anchor is an appropriate name after all. In winter anything can turn blue with cold, if not from mud. Even perhaps, a ship's anchor.

I am quite ready to believe that my two wellington boots still remain in Blue Anchor's suction sands, keeping company with forgotten footwear from past ages as far back as the Danes. This was food for thoughts, as I got back into the car.

When having tired of a diet of herring rollmops, the Danes had sailed their monster-headed dragonships up the Severn Sea to become quite a pain. They upset the balance of quiet Somerset life, causing men-folk to hide bread and mutton, daughters and wives. By wading ashore at Blue Anchor the Danes avoided the dancing dragons at Minehead and mud-horses at Stolford that are still around today. Suffice it to say that having found this spot the Danes robbed and burned a small, but not insignificant port close to hand. For a fed-up King Alfred, this was the final straw.

He had come to Somerset to get away from it all; to find a place to retreat. He was possibly the first grockle. Yet upon a small low hill at Athelney Alfred forged the swords for his adventures of creating England and giving the Danes a kick up the bum. Beforehand he had volunteered to be a celebrity chef with the misfortune of apparently burning some cakes. The first time anyone put quill to parchment about this famous event was anonymously in the *Vita S. Neot*, or the Life of Saint Neot to you and me, during the late 900s. Sadly a killjoy number of scholars think it a load of made up rubbish.

They do, however, agree that Alfred built a burh at Waeced, a name that translated from Celtic as the 'settlement beneath the wood'. Before he did so, it was just a little place the Danes did over. The word 'burh' rightly has a chill ring as it describes a town turned into a fortress. Cut timber walls held a garrison with spears and shields that could swarm out like hornets to sting the pesky Danes. However, in the tedium between dragonships, men were much more likely to have waddled out like wasps drunk on cider, bored with playing 'stick the tail on the mud-horse'. Today, with the timber walls long gone, we know Waeced as Watchet. It would be nice to think the modern name is a none too subtle warning to invading grockle shells that come in greater numbers than Danish boats. Sadly, this is just wishful thinking. The town got labelled Watchet after the sky-coloured cloth worn by mariners.

Such salty fellows did prove an inspiration to a travelling poet, who for a short period became the bane of my life. The Tourist Board, the very same that exaggerates the colour of mud, proudly informs anyone interested that Coleridge visited Watchet in 1797, when the idea for his famous poem 'The Ancient Mariner' took shape. There the Tourist Board leaves it.

Gossip has it that on the 13th November a twenty-five year old Samuel Taylor Coleridge arrived at the Bell Inn after dark, having walked forty miles in the day with his friend William Wordsworth, two years his senior, discussing the philosophy of poetry. All the verses that had gone before, they decided, had to go. What was needed was poetry from the heart. Their habit of roaming was scrutinised more than their habit of taking the opium that dream-inspired 'Kubla Khan' on which Coleridge got stuck, never finished, and blamed the 'person from Porlock' for interrupting him. It's not very reassuring to realise that West Somerset's drug problem is now over two hundred years old.

With a threat of invasion looming as Napoleon massed his armies across the Channel, some locals suspected the poets were French spies. A chap from the Home Office, called Walsh, began to follow them around the Quantocks and concluded that they were indeed highly suspicious. As to whether he followed them into Watchet that night can only be guessed at.

The poets 'poetry for the people', however, did not include the child that was once me, a child who would have loved the wandering wunderkinds to get stuck in Blue Anchor mud. Standing as a schoolboy in a cold sweat and wracking my brains, I had stammered out the lines:
"The ship was cheered, the harbour cleared
Merrily did she drop
Below the kirk, below the hill,
Below the lighthouse top."

At the time I had not the foggiest notion that a kirk was a church or that the scene described in verse was in Watchet. All I knew was that for me Coleridge was purgatory.

I wondered if he would have waxed so lyrically, had he seen Watchet by day, or if he had met that respected woman of Watchet, 'Fatty Patty', a prostitute who served Portuguese sailors when they made landfall. There was one occasion, now embedded in local folklore, when Patty was seen beside the harbour wall with her knickers down around her ankles, eating a portion of greasy chips in the company of seagulls. A Roadwater man, who admitted to intimate knowledge, asked her what she was doing. With her mouth full of chips she replied, "Oh, 'as ee finished already?"

Sail on by, you ancient mariner. And now I come to think of it, one small detail of the famous poem left me cogitating; and I quote:
"And now the storm-blast came, and he
Was tyrannous and strong:
He struck with his o'ertaking wings,
And chased us south along."

If the crew had been chased south by the storm-blast, they would have found themselves seeking shelter a couple of miles inland; either in Williton high street or in Washford, waiting for the coming of the West Somerset Railway. Coleridge was perhaps one of those writing chaps who never let the truth spoil a good story. However, I'm sure the Tourist Board is a useful thing.

The *Pauper's Guide* brought me abruptly out of my reverie. The wind gusted to whistle around the grockle shells, causing loud rattles from somewhere unseen. I started the car engine and turned on the CD player. Although I know I would have liked to pretend otherwise, I was being a bit of a grockle myself and it was best to go home. In my heart of hearts I realised neighbours would be wintering me and summering me and wintering me again, before accepting me. What I needed in order to be able to cope with living in Somerset was a survival guide, albeit of a more gentle nature than had possibly been on King Alfred's bookshelf.

What should be in my guide, I was not quite sure. As I drove away I was on the road to find out. I needed more than how to tickle a river trout, how to tease a rabbit out of its pyjamas, how to make painless nettle soup, or how tell the difference between dandelion leaves and sorrel when making a wild salad. I knew that fat hen was the most popular wild plant eaten in Somerset and that lady's smock was rich in vitamin C. Yet there was so much more.

Leaving Blue Anchor behind, a patch of blue in the sky just big enough to patch a pair of sailor's trousers was making the bay look softer and a little kinder in the rear-view mirror. Contrite to my wife and children, born and unborn, as if an albatross hung from my neck, I turned my ears to the music from Nailsea. Tommy Banner, the Wurzels Scottish lead singer, was giving his West Country best:
"I am a cider drinker
It soothes all me troubles away
Oh arr oh arr aay
Oh arr oh arr aay."

Surely, all I needed to do was rekindle a sense of humour, talk to people, and follow the mantra 'Amor meus Somerset'. And if I thought I could do that, I may as well also believe in ghosts, fairies and hobbits.

STRAW HATS AND PIXIE BOOTS

"The brown Barle enjoys his life, and splashes in the sunshine
like boys bathing – like them he is sunburnt and brown.
He throws wanton spray over the ferns that bow and bend as
the cool breeze his current brings sways them in the shade.
He laughs and talks, and sings louder than the wind in the woods."
(Richard Jeffries, *Summer in Somerset*, 1887).

By the time Lawrence got the last of Blue Anchor mud from his ears he had been joined by Maddy, Ez and Felix and our lives became packed in cardboard boxes. Favourite places hid in memory. Ez had been rooting and had found an old colour photograph. "Daddy, is this you?" I glanced at the picture of a goatee-bearded youth wearing a straw hat and suede pixie boots. Leant against a tree beside a river, he was playing a Spanish guitar, and above his head was the shadow of another's hand. "Yes," I replied in answer to my five year old's question as I looked at a past life. An idyllic weekend down from university with a car-load of friends and bottles of cheap wine for cooling in the river.

"You look smiley. Where is it?"

"Tarr Steps. It's a place with a bridge made of big flat stones that are older than Grandad."

"That's very old. Is it a grumpy bridge?"

"I'm sure it is sometimes. If people walked on me every day, I'd get grumpy. Wouldn't you?"

"S'pose. Can we go and see the grumpy bridge?"

"Absolutely."

And so we did. In T-shirts and shorts, my four children, Lawrence, Maddy, Ez and Felix, and I went for an afternoon's paddling in August sunshine. We drove the back way; Dulverton to Danesbrook Water, then to Hawkridge. Before passing the workshop of the antler carver Tom Lock, I slowed down so the children could get a glimpse of his antler chair through his spider-webbed window. Then off we went again, down the steep lane to follow the Barle along where May's bluebells flower.

The ancient steps that day seethed with grockles traipsing over and lolling about them, licking and sucking at ice creams while their kids and dogs went aquatic. The Barle sparkled, at ease with itself. It was hard to believe the turbulent force of the previous winter's storm waters had washed part of the bridge away so that it had to be repaired by marines.

I wanted to find the tree in the photo and that meant a leafy mile, or so, walk away from the chatter-splash of grockles. The up and down path would be fine as long as I was fair in giving piggybacks. At the 'down' places where the path nudged the riverbank dippers sang "sip-sip" and pied wagtails their liquid "tu-reep." We found 'flatties', flat stones to hold between index finger and thumb, and skimmed our 'Ducks and Drakes' until the number of skips became competitive and small tears said it was time to move up again.

It was in an 'up' moment that we emerged from tree shade onto a piece of sunny bracken land to be welcomed by buzzard mews. The bracken made me slightly wary. This was tick country. Ticks are nasty little stinging creatures that can attach themselves to people and make them really quite ill with a bacterial infection called Lyme disease. These blood-suckers can live in self-induced abstinence for up to eighteen years before they decide to bond with someone. If that someone is unlucky enough to be stung, then the tick needs to be removed as quickly as possible. This is done by drawing it gently from the skin with a pair of tweezers and slowly easing it free. As words of warning, the tick should not be twisted as it's being removed, because the mouthparts can break off and remain in the skin. Do not smother the creature with oil, nor squeeze it, otherwise the bowel contents will erupt into the wound in a gush of nastiness. These contents hold the bacteria of disease. All very unpleasant.

My attempt to tell the children to stay out of the bracken fell on deaf ears. Lawrence was leader to the hazelnuts that were ripening in their green jackets. The boys were beginning to stuff their short pockets with the windfall nuts, when Maddy and Ez noticed the butterflies. "Daddy, Daddy, Daddy!" I had never before seen so many fritillaries. And with their numbers only 6% of what they were fifty years ago, I doubt I will ever see their beauty again despite Exmoor being one of the last strong-holds.

The fritillaries were High Browns and they liked the bracken. Some flew fast and vigorous while others sat sunbathing, showing off their outstretched orange wings speckled with black markings. These didn't seem to mind the children getting close. "They're like fairies," Maddy breathed.

"Fairies that live in the treetops on cloudy days. They live there a lot," I said. "Look, the front legs look like brushes to keep their houses clean."

The fritillaries' family name was Nymphlidae, and I thought it high time the children had the joy of becoming nymphs themselves. That meant finding the river. Regretfully, we left the butterflies to their business and headed onwards and down. We hopped a stream by stepping-stones and crossed an iron bridge over to the far bank of the Barle. There I rediscovered the place in the photograph. My straw hat and pixie boots had been from a time long ago. The tree had become lost in tall bracken and guarded by wood ants. The river's shallows were now not for wine bottles but the place to paddle with my laughing children, playing their water games. Then a splash making rings on the water had all five of us seeking shadows. "Shoosh, fish," I whispered, putting a finger to my lips.

"Fishy! Fishy! Fishy!" shouted my youngest, Felix, bouncing excitedly with all his four years. The water was so clear, yet with the reflections of clouds and trees any fish was hard to see. The shadow of a fish is its give-away. And Ez had an eye for it. Soon she was pointing, having realised the black shadow she had noticed on the river bottom was her guide to look above it and see her first brown trout. The tell-tale row of small red flecks were obvious along its sides. Many of the water-skaters and lazily flying midges were on borrowed time, watched from behind sunken stones.

An hour later, having left the ice cream seller by the clapper bridge, still checking the small change I had heaped on his stall counter, four tired children, all with freshly stained T-shirts, and I were driving home. However, not before each had passed my car door checkpoint that searched for stowaway ticks.

"It wasn't a grumpy bridge, Daddy. It was lovely," yawned Ez at bedtime, snuggled like the others under their duvets. "Tell us a story."

"What, the one about the leather dog with happy tail, puzzled monkey, time-patched bears and string-tied hare?"

"No, silly, about today." And I did, but only after she had helped me find the tweezers. I was perhaps the best meal the tick had had in years. And the children's bedtime story? Well, that evolved as it went along, with a few things drawn from what seemed poignant in our lives.

Later I wrote the story down, recalling it from memory and giving it the name, 'The Tree Fairy of Tarr'. It was something that got recorded by BBC Somerset Sound's very own Dame Judi Dench soundalike, Lois Harbinson, a lady who often takes to wearing her own summer straw hat.

The Tree Fairy of Tarr

Where the River Barle cuts, bubbles and ripples its way between rocks and over time-worn stones, there's the old uneven stone clapper bridge called Tarr Steps. Slab touching slab. Ancient. Some say it was built by the Devil himself. Many more think he sunbathes there. But that's nonsense. Absolute balderdash. Here wagtails flit and herons stab, trout swim and snique-snaques cower.

Snique-snaques? I hear you ask. Well, to let you into a secret, they're a sort of fairy thing. Half human, half fish, trout size and not very pretty. Tree fairies turn any person into a snique-snaque if they so wish, but only if a person deserves it.

So, in truth, Tarr Steps is a place of enchantment. A place of mischief. And in springtime just a teeny bit hazardous, especially when the bluebells flower.

What's the danger in bluebells, you may wonder. Pretty things. Delicate. Blue. Even bluer when the sun shines. Oh, but then they are potent. They tinkle the trouble of fairy woven spells. The naughty spells of the tree fairies of Hat Wood, a mere ragwort ride from the old clapper bridge.

Farmer Fumbledumb liked the tree fairies. They rather liked him, too. When he tended his field that lay high above the combe on Parsonage Down, he would cut the ragwort weeds and tie together the stems with red silk as fairy gifts. Horse and hattock!, the fairies would cry. Magic words to make the ragwort fly. Oh yes, gentle Fumbledumb knew to treat those fairies well.

You may think Fumbledumb an odd name. It wasn't his proper one, nobody seemed to remember what that was. It was his crotchety wife that called him Fumbledumb. She thought him clumsy and stupid. And imagine giving presents to the fairies! Silly, silly, man.

Quietly under his breath, so quietly Fumbledumb was sure that his wife couldn't hear, he called her 'Nagglewax' and wished she could learn to be kind. A tree fairy heard him though, as it whisked passed Fumbledumb's open window on a newly cut ragwort stem that trailed red silk. So this mean spirited woman nagged poor Fumbledumb. Nagged and nagged him. Uncaring. Never listening to a word he ever said.

The chicken shed was foxy heaven. A ramshackle mess of bent nails. Fumbledumb's thumbs were black and blue with bruises. Milk pails were spilt. The more his wife nagged, the clumsier he became. Bee stings were sore and lumpy on his arms and neck. He couldn't even manage to drink a cup of nettle tea without dribbling it down his shirt. Laughter was a distant memory. Life only misery. His clumsiness had made them poor; poverty coming through the door as love went out the window.

Fumbledumb yearned for the times his grotty wife had better things to do than nag. Things like taking jars of his honey and muslins of butter to sell at market. It went without saying that she kept the money folk paid, to spend on her selfish self.

Soon in Hat Wood the whispers began. The tree fairies loved their presents of ragwort horses. They loved the red silk. Fumbledumb would get his wish.

On a day of bright May sunshine when not a single new leaf was moved by wind breath and the blue haze was radiant, Nagglewax bustled market-bound across Tarr Steps. Half way over she noticed a tree fairy warming himself on a stone clapper. A ragwort stem with a tattered scrap of red silk tied around it rested beside him.

Wastin' yer toime sunbathin' yer useless good fer-nothin' pigsy, she scolded. Bluebells tinkled. Nagglewax heard. Wha'zat?, she demanded.

Snique-snaque-snozzle, muttered the tree fairy. Flop-a-plop went Nagglewax. It wasn't a great big splash as you might expect, but a trouty one. Yes, Nagglewax had shrunk to the size of a river trout. And where a second before she had legs, she now had a finny tail like a trout.

The tree fairy was roaring with joyous laughter. Snique-snaque-snoo, snickey-snackey-snoo! Horse and hattock! And away it flew back to Hat Wood.

Fumbledumb was surprised he never saw his wife again. Jars of honey and muslins of butter were however found neatly placed on the riverbank by the ancient steps. Her clothes were there, too, but left hugger-mugger in a crumpled heap. The farmer was even more surprised when his hen house seemed to magically repair itself with tiny nails straight and true. His cows were calm and his bees in good humour. After a time he began to remind people that his name was really Tom. Tom of the fairies, they came to call him. Silly Tom, the farmer who grew weeds in his soil. Silly Tom who bought red silk at market stalls.

So if you ever find yourself down by Tarr Steps in the month of May, be cautious if you hear the tinkle of bells, the bluebells of Tarr. Search your conscience before you cross that old clapper bridge. Be not of ill temper, dishonest or unkind. Most of all be sure that you've been thoughtful to tree fairies.

Should you go paddling in the Barle, look carefully where the waters eddy. Stare behind and between the rocks and stones. Gaze through reflections. You may find a snique-snaque, maybe even Nagglewax herself.

LESSON THREE
BELONGING

"Townfolk know pleasures, country people joys."
(Minna Thomas Antrim, American writer and epigrammist, 1950).

"Of Somerset maidens and Somerset men
I could talk and could praise 'em again and again,
They're all wide awake folk, kind thoughted indeed,
Good-hearted and friendly and helpful in need.
The Somerset breed
Is ne'er full of greed
But good-hearted, friendly and helpful in need."

(Anon)

After a couple more ill judged prods of the map, I closed my eyes and let my finger land once more. Practice made perfect. I landed with a heart transplant, together with my kids and a hatful of woes in the Taunton Deane town of Wiveliscombe. Perversely, the place was oddly quiet about its own organ removal. The organ taken from a town chapel in 1900 was, however, nothing to excite Josephine de Beauharnais, or the likes of me. This one was musical and was once in the house of French Emperor Napoleon Bonaparte, lent to him by Spencer Percival, before he became the only British Prime Minister to be assassinated. Bizarrely, the organ is now in Australia.

Over previous centuries Wiveliscombe had gone through a few changes of spelling, like Weevilscombe and Weaselscombe, both possible epithets to infestations. There is an odd logic to calling a place after little bugs who ate the barley crop, or furry rapscallions who snaffled the rabbits that left human families with rumbling tummies.

Wiveliscombe was finally settled upon, when things got really bad. Called 'Wivey' by locals, it was the most poignantly appropriate of places for me, because the name means 'wifeless combe', and wifeless was what I was.

Still a romantic, I now bordered on being silly. What I put my finger on was a brewing town that, natives still giggle, once had thirty pubs. Bliss, I thought, I liked pubs a lot.

There was even advice to hand at the White Hart of how a chap can tell if he has had one too many. The pub gave out large luggage labels to regulars that said: "He is not drunk who from the floor can rise and drink, and ask for more: but drunk is he who speechless lies without the strength to drink or rise." I am guessing that the labels were only there to help the literate.

As for my family and me, we moved into an old thin barn pretending to be a cottage with a blue, warped front door. We inherited the ghost of an old Pole and the demijohns of an alcoholic. The cottage was like an inverted Tardis; looking quite big from the outside but tiny on the inside. The building had been the hay store for the horses serving the defunct 'Anchor' pub over the garden wall where families of grey squirrels now chitter and squabble, building dreys in the eaves.

A hundred or more years ago, someone filled in the two large openings in our thin barn, meant for shoving in hay bales, with a single course of bricks. Then they bunged in some windows and a few wooden-slatted internal partitions, and said "Hey presto, a cottage". Maybe this started the trend that has grown in sophistication and continues across Somerset today, benefiting the wealthy to the detriment of owls. Not that anyone who ever lived in my cottage was ever wealthy. However, as with the design of Yeovil's helicopters, a trend has to start somewhere. Behind the blue warped front door with its appealing character, we moved about in chilled rooms and slept between damp sheets, until installing rudimentary central heating made even our piggy-banks cease rattling.

The surrounding hills hold Wivey like a cup of wonders. Buzzards young and old gather to inhale mists and to worm-tug in winter fields. Worm-tugging brings audiences of lapwings that 'pee-weet' approval at any worm determined enough to keep a grip of this mortal coil. Some become really quite elastic. Not all worms however, are in the fields. There are many that although safe from buzzards, wriggle for my entertainment.

If visiting friends asked if there was anything out the back of our cottage, I said "yes," and smiled at them thinking myself a clever-clogs. Invariably they would try the question again, wanting me to elaborate. And again I would give the same reply, "yes". This could go on for a while until I sensed irritation. Then I would explain 'yes' is the Somerset word for an earthworm. Through the back wall of the ground floor is nothing but Somerset soil and lots and lots of earth enriching worms. The building was dug out of the side of the hill, with the level of our neighbour's garden being just below the upstairs windows. Through them came a nasty niff.

The neighbour's black miniature poodles did lots of what their name suggested. When squatting bottoms on the grass, or even thinking about squatting bottoms, they bark at any signs of life that we might show whether dressing gowned or boxer shorted. It's been somewhat annoying, and for a time was not helped by Maddy holding her favourite doll to her chest whilst shouting, "Poodle-bums! Poodle-bums!" out of the smallest landing window. The doll was a moderating influence. When teenage consigned it to the 'pit' under the bed the language became much worse. Proof that Somerset youth was adding little to a rich heritage of dialect.

However, if the pedigree poodles were a pain, they were not as bad as the bin-bag ripping mongrels slipping through the garden gate if either postie or parish magaziner had been too rushed to click the latch. Help was at hand through chilli balls made by chopping up red chillis and covering them with melted cooking chocolate from a stove warmed saucepan. When set, the balls could be lobbed at a pooch for a charade of "Puff the Magic Dragon". One greedy off-the-leash 'Westie' was magnificent. After several performances our rubbish remained intact for Tuesday's dustbin men.

As with many a Wiveliscomber, the poodles' mistress makes the weekday Taunton commute. The poodles, left at home, have a dippy, middle-aged dog-walker. One day she found young Dan, the painter assigned the crappy job of leaping over the garden wall to slip and slide whilst filling in wall cracks and brushing Weathershield over our badly worn pebble-dash. The dog-walker asked Dan why he bothered doing such a good job given that it was just an outhouse. Dan said it wasn't, it was a cottage and people lived in it. This was news to her. For several years she had come to take the poodles walkies and always thought they had been barking at rats.

Soon the poodles had reason to raise alarm. Nature has a way of letting you know when things need to be addressed. With a winter night's deluge came a great seepage of sewage. An unwanted backwash lifted drain gratings and bubbled up between the hallway floor bricks. It was not good. Hurriedly rolled towels became pungent and inadequate dams as newly laid sitting room carpet squelched under small feet when Ez and Felix rescued their teddies. Outside the blue warped front door snails sought doorstep sanctuary threatened by the unconfined evacuation flowing by. A panicked torch beam fell upon two hedgehogs snuffle-gargling criticism. With disintegrated tissue impaled on their spines, they paddled against the stream in their own search for higher ground and the sympathy of fellow night creatures.

Daylight brought trepidation and thoughts of whether my daughters' veggie diet would be as beneficial to the garden roses as the horse manure. Looking like the River Parrett at a Bridgwater low tide, a grey silty sludge ran through the front garden, engulfing the bottoms of rose bushes, bird table, and cobbles, to end its journey in the street like a miniature river delta.

Later, I was formally introduced myself to the poodles by giving an apologetic knock on their mistress's front door. She was slow to admit ownership of a forgotten drain, which together with an entanglement of tree roots were the culprits of blame. It was not the best way to love one's neighbour.

Beyond our blue front gate the small street, without the sludge, is full of old world grace and charm. A short cut for tractors, horses and the tyred and soled school run. At the top end teenage pupils loiter, braving the gloomy shadows of 'Drain Steps', a narrow alley dripping with pigeon poo. There they eat chip shop chips from greasy paper, snatch a dog-eared fag, or maybe have a snog. And risking bruised butts, sometimes conceive during lunch break. On wet days the steps are potentially lethal. I wound up my eldest three children, Lawrence, Maddy and Ez, and gave them a push in the direction of the secondary school at the opposite end of the street, and wished life could work like clockwork.

Felix, on the other hand, I personally walked to the primary school and would tell him at the school gate to be good. But if he wasn't, what could they do? I remember the Headteacher, Tony Halstead, having an occasion to delve into the past by leafing through the school discipline book used by Victorian and Edwardian teachers. It was proof that children had never been particularly well behaved. The book was a fascinating insight. Children were caned for things like indifference, sulkiness and throwing stones.

A lad called Bartram "interfering with a horse" was Tony's own particular favourite.

And whatever the misdemeanour the children were caned for, they had between one and six strokes. Nowadays when children are badly behaved, teachers talk to them very nicely and speak to their parents and explain this is not acceptable. In the old days they were beaten senseless. Tony wasn't quite sure which is the best. But at the end of an Easter holiday he wished he had the power to discipline wildlife.

On the last day of the holidays he received a phone call at home. The school boiler wasn't working. Which sounded fair enough, he thought, because that often happens. However, the reason this time was that jackdaws had moved into the chimneys. Tony's immediate reaction was "no problem" and everybody came back to school the next day. Felix was among all the children who thought the news was wonderful. Despite being told the school couldn't use the heating system they were perfectly happy. A vote was taken and they said, "OK, we'll leave the birds." Tony thought that was very laudable.

Unfortunately, the weather changed. The following day it was freezing and the school had no heating. Consequently, he rushed out and bought fifteen fan heaters and plugged them all in. The school warmed up, but the lighting system gave out, because there wasn't sufficient power. Following that, the school discovered that the jackdaws were in for six weeks. Two days later rats appeared on the scene. And just as Tony was sorting the rats out with the pest control officer, so squirrels were spotted moving out of the dining room roof. It transpired after a head count there were eight squirrels in the roof. They had had obviously decided that this was the place to be because the word got out. Soon the school had starlings in there as well. So in the space of four days, the school had gone from jackdaws and no heating, to squirrels, rats and starlings. It was probably the most interesting week of Tony Halstead's career. For Felix it was a whole load of fun.

Back home, the first person to call on me was Kate from a few doors down. She lived with cats and a husband who sold baked potatoes, and had followed the postman up the garden path. "Do you want that CD?" she asked, pointing at the freely delivered AOL CD in my hand. Obviously she wanted to add it to the collection already in hers. "Only it's the birds. Blackbirds especially. They eat all my goozegogs and raspberries." Tripping over her tongue with excitement she told me that she had had a brainwave to thread the CDs onto a string, then hang them across her allotment. Confidence oozed from her that their shiny rattle would scare away the unwanted birds. After telling me that her idea was "absolutely brilliant", she stopped herself in mid flow to stare.

You all right? You look a bit funny. Your hair's all sprutty and patchy."

"It's stress," I said, figuring that wasn't too wise to get into a convoluted chat about alopecia and heart transplants.

Soon afterwards, David, the local postmaster, offered me a punnet of raspberries from his garden. His face had a familiar look. A long bearded likeness had gazed at me from a Victorian sepia photograph printed on a book sleeve. David bore a striking resemblance to the gentle and self-effacing naturalist and explorer Alfred Russel Wallace, who but for want of a patron would have beaten Darwin in getting his theory of an origin of the species into print first. Behind the post office counter David went about his work with the same meticulous care as Wallace would have mounted a rare specimen of butterfly. And as Wallace gathered bugs, David gathered gossip and conveyed it to others as help.

It has to be said that to begin with, I did attract a few glances from the gossipers, and I earwigged a few whispers, "...the new bloke in the cruddy corner cottage .... first the old Pole, then the alcoholic, then him ... looks after four children all by himself ... odd looking". After a week or so the dumpy lady behind the counter in 'Carousel Pig' told me: "We know all about you." I think I went pink.

Being fair though, the people of Wivey do have good cause to be on their toes nowadays when newcomers appear fresh into their midst. Back in 1963 they were told off by those 'with a need to know', for not being vigilant enough. That was when the 'Great Train Robbery' gang holed themselves up at Combe End in Huish Champflower, a mile or so away. They came into Wivey to do their shopping and spend some of their £2.6 million ill-gotten gains, and probably struck up some fleeting friendships. Neither Ronnie Biggs, Charlie Wilson, nor Buster Edwards ever seems to have been told, "We know all about you." Ask anyone in the town who remembers the 1966 World Cup Final if they remember the train robbers, they say "Who?"

Trying to find a reason why the infamous band came to choose Wivey leads to pure flights of fancy; but folk swear that there is a map pinned to a café wall in a remote souk in the Atlas mountains of Morocco. Wiveliscombe is marked on it in as prominently as London and Bristol. Perhaps one of the robbers had sought seclusion to ponder and plot, and over a cup of thick coffee saw before him the inspiration for the perfect hideaway.

Indeed, ten years before the train robbers did their deed at Bridego Railway Bridge, outside Mentmore, Wivey was hailed as being 'a centre of international espionage'. It was a tabloid affair that could surely have had Howard Hawks vying for screen rights and casting Humphrey Bogart for a last swan song, capitalizing on the Morocco-set 'Casablanca'. The plot scenario involved a Czech spy called Vavru Hagju who was encouraged by a British delegate to the UN Sir Gladwyn Jebb to continue espionage activities. These had begun in Wivey, where Vavru came to visit his wife living in a local foreign workers camp. All very film noir.

So getting the gossipers started is better than an evening with the telly. What you get is local knowledge. The sleaze is most entertaining as long as your own family is not involved. There was the time when a cuddle of women in the street were laughing that, "Mr. Drippy got a stiffy." And the remark, "We should tar and feather them", was met with much agreement. Infidelity had been discovered by an 'on duty' fireman. I gleaned that the gist was something to do with big toes being stuck in plugholes.

But what was beginning to concern me most was a need for earplugs in my lugholes. Twice a week, and sometimes more, comes a cacophony of sound. Wednesday evening is just a practice for what is to come on Sunday morning, when the prolonged clanging only dies away when Missus-Somebody-or-Other's church-bound staccato of heels sounds like a frantic yaffle. The bim-boms tinkle glass and sway the spiders; and Saturday night hangovers refuse to be molly-coddled even under a pillow mountain. The gull that sits on top of the tower's flagpole knows that to cry is futile and wings it to the coast, or at least to Milverton. And the rooks give up their game of weathervane roundabouts and take their caws elsewhere.

Eight church bells have never clanged so loud as from the tower of Wivey's cathedral-sized parish church, if you happen to live within fifty yards. 'Health & Delight, good ringing yield' and 'From lying lips and slanderous tongue, good Lord deliver us' are individual inscriptions upon a couple of the bells. Although that didn't mean, said the man in the post office, that the Wiveliscombers were particularly God-fearing. "We're all trying hard to get bad reputations – it's far more interesting." With such worthy sentiments I yield to the view that our bellringers should continue practising towards prowess, and say to myself 'bring it on'.

The cottage was rattled and was seeking attention, as were the rest of the needy in my care. The children needed feeding, the roses around the front door needed extensive pruning, aphids needed to be encouraged to go elsewhere to avoid genocide, roof slates needed rejigging, and I needed to introduce myself to a brindled cat of character that I had chanced to see through the raindrops that ran down the bedroom window. It was sitting in the church graveyard having joined the mourners at a burial service. A lady holding a large green umbrella printed with the words 'Body Shop' sheltered the sensible cat interested in the big wooden box that had been lowered into the hole in the ground.

Making an early offer, the cat agreed to adopt me as long as I fed her. I apologised that I was unable to buy mouse flavoured cat food, but opened doors for her like a true gentleman. We were her third household in the street. When her people moved on, she stayed behind becoming known to locals as 'Bessie the Wall Cat', a friend to passers' by and to those who had passed on. She continues to lie on her back, legs akimbo, in patches of street sunshine, waiting for somebody to tickle her tummy, attracting comments like, "Bessie, you're such a tart."

Cats are important characters of Wivey that live in and out of other peoples' houses to enjoy a varied diet. Fresh trout, ham on the bone and roast chicken can all be available for the quick-witted puss in a snatch a grab. Others though like to linger. Take Bessie, for instance. If it is wet and I am out, she will go and find her brown paper bag next door to sleep the day away in. Or, if feeling peckish, she will wander two doors down for a snack and an Aga-side siesta. Sometimes she will bring things of interest to show me like a goldfinch left by the warped blue front door. A large rat banged against the window of the study will quickly get my attention.

I mentioned the rat to Jill next door, the lady with the brown paper bag, and she told me a tale. A procession of rats was seen going in and out of the local cider factory before it burned down nearly forty years ago, and they were led in by a gurt rat. On the way out the rats were all obviously pissed and unsteady on their paws, all apart from the gurt one. Maybe Bessie had collared the teetotaller's relative and had come to exhibit her prize.

Yet, as loveable as she may be Bessie is not Wivey's most notorious mog. She has a namesake, a tomcat called Thomas Bessie who roamed the town streets in the 1880s. While still in kittenhood, TB appeared to be normal, but later developed fur-covered pigeon-sized wings. In 1899 an opportunistic Wivey photographer, Mr G.W. French, managed to get TB to pose on his studio couch for "a contemporary article in the *Strand Magazine*," ensuring the tomcat entered the new century a star. Thirty years later, long correspondence still appeared in the national press about winged cats in Spain and even a Darwin-inspired theory about the evolution of a new variety of species. Cats seemed to be mutating to be able to chase things on the wing. A logical train of thought, as bats are really flying mice. Such is the progress of the world outside Somerset.

At home, and aware of the Thomas Bessie story, I provided my Bessie with the alias of 'Bilbo'. There had been some larder adventures in the street. And a new name, I hoped, might prevent confusion should a neighbourly boot-up-the-bum send her airborne. By the cat's thoughtful introductions, I began to enjoy the benefits of the spring that followed my second Wivey winter.

Stevie from the allotments had offered to help me in the garden. Describing it as a "rare cummel", it was a kind way of saying that it was a bloody mess. While disentangling the garden undergrowth, he came and tugged me by the arm. "Aay voun' u kuud-leez nas wi vaaw'ur ai'gs een un." On pulling back a piece of wall ivy, there was little doubt what Stevie was on about. There was a wren's nest with four eggs in it. Way to go, I thought.

When the squirrel in our roof nibbled the last snowdrop, and the mice began on the primrose petals, having been left to their own devices because the cat snoozed, sated by salmon in sachets and kitchen grabs, I was invited to the pub. The invite came one Wednesday with a warning: "Don't bring a book with you; they'll think you're trying to show off. "So making do with the local knowledge that I had managed to memorise, the habit of trudging up the hill began. On my way up I passed Max the taxidermist from 'Heads N' Tails' coming down. He was carrying a stuffed kingfisher perched on a twig.

"Cat kill," he said. "Not to worry, it wasn't your rat catcher."

How did he know about the rat?

LESSON FOUR
BEARIN' UP

*"Few things are more pleasant than a village graced with a
good church, a good priest and a good pub. "*
(John Hillaby, writer and walker).

The Bear Inn had been renamed by the bar room grumblers as the 'Bearin' Up'. Inside fingers may scratch at a nicotine patch, while outside ash-powdered feet shuffle on the street pavement or upon the cobbles in the pub alleyway. The smoking ban has bitten the countryside, and possibly folk will be told to sweep up the leaves next.

I was glad to have known the warm fug and smoky wreath that once hung heavy. In a bar filled with bibblers, those local chaps who enjoy a pint or two, there were farm workers and plumbers, butchers sons and 'sparkies'. And there was always one 'builder'. Timmy was in full flow. Part man part wiry woodland elf with plaster dust in his grizzle-beard Timmy did 'a bit of this and a bit of that' and was always ready to 'have a go' at anything building related so long as a right angle was not essential.

What had set him off was the thin packet of Nobby's nuts. "How much be they? Bugger me! Why haven't you got any porky scratchins'? 'Ere, does any of you lot remember Manley Branfield's uncle. Used to come out from Minehead in a motorbike and sidecar and buy pigs and take them back in his motorbike and sidecar to Minehead to rear up, and fatten for the kill, years back. The pigs didn't mind ... the sidecar I mean!"

I made myself heard for the first time when I told Timmy that bacon was something of a Somerset word. The Normans had no use for the salted pig flesh, so they let their serfs give it a name. They called it 'bacon', from the Anglo-Saxon 'becken' meaning a beech tree, because the flesh of pigs fed on beech-mast is firm, and tastes good. Timmy mulled this one over and realized this was probably why he had never had a decent 'fryup' for breakfast during his several 'hollerdays' in France.

Earlier Timmy had come to cast an eye over why raindrops ran down walls inside my cottage. He wrinkled his brow and scratched his balding pate at my shaly roof slates. He informed me that the slates were from Okehampton. Not the one in Dartmoor's dismal dankness but from the defunked quarry a mile or so away beside the Watchet road of the same name. "They're like blottin' paper and when they're full, they're full. A lot of Wivey's still got 'em, but with people with posh voices comin' here and buyin' up and doin' up property an' all they be getting rarer," he confided.

Timmy did not speak much of grockles and even less of emmets. When he did, he spoke his mind, never admitting that we needed them. Although the Somerset word for ants, 'emmets' is the collective name given to the grockles who come by the summer coach load heading for Butlins. Like ants, they are attracted to jams as happened in Wivey before the bypass.

For a time, a few years ago neither grockles nor emmets wanted even to show their faces. They were put off by 'foot and mouth'. In Wivey, as elsewhere, cows and goats lay on their backs and stuck hooves skywards out of open topped lorries. Now, despite the smell of char-roasted meat having drifted away on the four winds, wallets, purses and credit cards have still not returned in their original numbers. Things have never been helped with Wivey being off the beaten track, but we felt we were getting poorer, or as one BBC commentator put it, "living in economically interesting times." To be fair, these times began some while ago when the Exmoor humourist and B&B owner, Norma Huxtable, became anxious and took to hiding her cash tin down a rabbit hole.

The worry for Timmy though was his nuts. The cost of living was soaring; and brack, the cheap pork fat strip once bought from the award winning 'Thorne's the Butcher,' that made dripping toast fit to fill Timmy's tummy, was harder to come by.

"They'll be coppicing Nynehead woods again to breed crows behind the can of peas, that's what I think." mused Timmy. Men at the bar nodded, staring into their pint glasses. I mouthed, 'What?' This was education. I did know that from Nynehead to Wivey was a short flight away for a fleeing crow, or an up and down drive passed woods with hazel dozing dormice and reclusive crested newts. What I learned was that the can of peas was not off the shelves of the Co-op, but the lovable name given to Nynehead's 'Cairn of Peace'. Erected to commemorate the village hosting the World Ploughing Championships in 1971, these days it's a rendezvous for amorous couples who raise furrowed brows.

The need for crows was easy to explain. When times got hard they were bred for food. The children's nursery rhyme 'Four and Twenty Blackbirds Baked in a Pie' comes to mind. Although a king in his own domain, Timmy had parted from his spouse, so the only thing set before him in this wifeless combe was another packet of nuts. "Chickens are easier to pluck mind, far less finicky." Timmy reflected as an afterthought. I presumed he meant, easier than blackbirds.

"But there's no harm in supplementing our larders, is there?" said a muffled voice that spoke from inside the raised collar of an oversized gannex. Goodness knows who it was, but he could easily have had a brace of pheasants inside his coat.

Looking around the bar, a few rueful smiles may have betrayed a willing poacher or two. "Remember thems that went up Baronsdown? Bloody 'ell they was dumb uns," said a moustache and stubble called Bugsy. The smiles about him suddenly became nervous.

Baronsdown is a red deer sanctuary near Dulverton owned by an organisation called 'The League Against Cruel Sports' that buys up parcels of land in the area and fast tracks its townie officials to become Labour back benchers in the Houses of Parliament.

As an organisation the League is well connected and Sir Paul McCartney, the ex-Beatle, bought a conifer plantation alive with deer and adder at Upton on the Brendon Hills for the League's purposes of preventing hunting with hounds. Sadly, some of the League spokesmen are only pretend wildlife experts. One went on record saying the white hind of the Quantocks was "poached for the price of her antlers". That particular fellow was unavailable for further comment as he headed for the backbenches, when country folk informed that female deer do not actually have antlers. Those desiring high office often have such special qualities.

At Baronsdown the land is unfenced, and deer come and go at will, but because they are fed hay, silage and concentrates all year round, they converge there in such large numbers that they fall over each others' legs. For several years, locals have been concerned about the health of these deer. When a case of TB was confirmed in a five-year-old stag near Baronsdown, people became afraid that it would slowly work its way through all the wild red deer on Exmoor. Baronsdown was high profile and all ears in the 'Bearin' Up', including mine, turned towards Bugsy.

"Old Ned and his lad were doin' a bit of poachin' up Baronsdown and they are dragging this stag back to their truck after havin' a successful time of it," Bugsy went on. "As they go they meet another bloody poacher, who's pullin' his deer along, too. The other bloke goes and shouts to them, 'Oi! I don't want to tell you how to suck eggs, but I can tell you that it's much easier if you drag the stag in t'other direction. Then the antlers won't dig into the ground.'

The bloke then goes on his way leaving Old Ned and his lad to get on with it. And they do just what he suggested. Some considerable time later the lad says, "Dad, that bloke was right. This is an awful lot easier!' 'Yeah, son, but we're getting further and further from our truck.'"

Bugsy burst into a roar of laughter. Oh, it was one of Bugsy's jokes. The relief was palpable because you never knew nowadays who might be listening. Phil, a former boat builder turned case maker for grandfather clocks, put down his copy of the *Independent*. He took a sip from his pint of Tawny, gave an exaggerated blink and smiled with his eyes. For such a thin man, Phil had a voracious appetite for food and had a particular penchant for venison and pheasant casseroled by his lawyer wife.

"Like your car, Bugsy!" Phil called through the fug. Bugsy has a Jag, and if the truth be told he has a jumble of them all in bits and bobs and odds and sods, gearboxes and camshafts, sprockets and bonnets. The car that Phil referred to was an XJ6 with a paint job. And what a paint job it was. A motorised sweet chariot emblazoned with a Cross of Saint George and red roses roaring a fanaticism for the English rugby team. It gets Bugsy in free into the 'players car park' at Bath's Spring Gardens. He still chuckles about putting a scribbled note on England captain Phil Vickery's windscreen telling him "to get a decent car."

A proper Jaguar wheeler-dealer Bugsy rescues rusting hulks from around the country, piles them up in a farm yard and turns them into pristine motors with such love and affection that they could just have rolled off the Birmingham's Castle Bromwich production line in a time warp. Bugsy has become almost as great a legend in the Bearin' Up' as Joel Garner, the great West Indian and Somerset fast bowler whose Jag Bugsy has the privilege of servicing.

"You gone and got yourself another heap of Volvo, Phil?" called Bugsy in a voice louder than a 1940s' XK120, the noisiest Jag ever.

"Yep".

"You should have got yourself a proper car, dinnum! What d'you reckon Chazzer, you still got that bit of old French rubbish?"

From that moment I knew that I belonged. One day I could say "Tata, Bugsy. You off for an Indian takeaway?" But that was the future. When I eventually poddled homewards down Wivey's hill, the clappers from the evening's bell practise had long been muffled to silence without my hearing a single ding or dong from lying lips and slanderous tongue.

LESSON FIVE
DIALECT DELIGHTS

"Dialect words those terrible marks of the beast to the truly genteel."
(Thomas Hardy, writer and poet)

I was quick to learn that in Somerset 'yes' was an earthworm and 'aarr' meant yes. Hearing Terry the roofer boast that he'd done a "praper job" with my ridge tiles, I was curious to know whether Somerset dialect was also one of his strong points.

"Dazzy-snoo. An' by the way yer slates are all to lippets."

By the creasing of his laughter dimples I hedged my bets whether Terry carried the wisdom of age or was just taking the piddle.

"One, two, dree, vour, vive, zix, zem, eight, nine, taine." Now he was just showing off.

But it was an insider job that really showed up my ignorance.

"We both want a 'lappy' from now on," said Maddy when she and Ez came home from school one day having been told by the big-bummed dinner lady, to "clack it inter thee."

My first instinct was to think the girls wanted Macbook laptops as fashion accessories. They soon shot that idea down in flames with, "Dad, for God's sake!" in stereo. All they wanted was to start having daily packed lunches after being caught prodding lumpy semolina and told to eat it up. So I sympathised, reasoning a small amount of research into some of the interesting words appearing outside pub quiz nights might not hurt.

Take 'Yeow' for instance. This isn't a moan of pain from a farmer accidentally sticking a pitchfork through his welly, but merely the thoughtful use of a monosyllable to say that in Somerset, as elsewhere, a lady sheep is called a ewe.

If, however, 'Lamb's wool' is mentioned in a hushed tone, it will have nothing to do with a yeow's 'little un', but instead is a drink of mulled cider with spiced apple; and much more exciting to look at than a woolly buttercup leaper, albeit not quite so cute.

Any young farmer saying "snuddle" to his girlfriend, doesn't mean he's after some heavy petting with snogs and cuddles behind his tractor, but merely that his field corners were difficult to plough. I told Lawrence this pearl of wisdom, and he saw fit to whisper it into a girl's ear at the

Rugby Club's New Year party. By morning he still had a red cheek from the slap. Proof that some meanings are hard to grasp.

Obviously, if a chap says 'Art'noon', don't glance at the watch naively hoping that the mad club of landscape painters are coming out in the midday sun. It's merely a wish for pleasant times before tea. Should twitchers be out and about afterwards staring through binoculars at 'bum-towels' and 'dish-washers', the long-tailed tits and pied wagtails would be right to object to such name-calling.

'Bibblers' and 'guddlers', some sharing bar stools with small dogs, are chaps found in the Bearin' Up. It is accepted that a bibbler tends to sit and cogitate, so doesn't drink quite as much as a guddler who is, more often than not, the cause for many a descriptive word.

"Dough-knee get 'ammered. Woe betide you, if you dare get puggle 'eaded," a wife might warn prior to the Bearin' Up opening on a Friday evening.

"Cordin eye, stimey wenoam," is something bibblers mutter between themselves after watching the third calamity off a barstool.

The guddler's excuse could well be, "tis tarble narry," as he blames the barstool before sighing, "my azwell gwoam," when the landlord refuses to serve a single drop more cider.

Should a guddler start to dribble and babble incoherently, he is said to 'dwally'. In the Bearin' Up, the assistance of the landlord is sometimes called for: "Here Jim! Let's take th' old fuller home and put-n to bed; tidn no good to let-n bide here an dwally all night." The words need no explanation.

Let it be said, those Somerset folk who don't want to learn something for themselves won't let that 'something' enter their heads. They are stubborn like that. However, the bibblers in the Bearin' Up have been known to cogitate over the need for some understandable qualifications. For example, when a field needs a good going over, it might be necessary to call upon someone able to do a 'praper job'. Here it would be best, the bibblers say, to give the local zoologist a shout. And, if the zoologist does not want to break into too much of a sweat, it may be necessary to invest in a new issue of shares. This might appear nothing other than modern commercial sense. The sort of thing attractive to banks and brokers possibly imagining great potential in a rare badger sanctuary, or a new breed of giant rabbit.

Yet even in the Bearin' Up some bibbler word or other can cause head scratching, and explanation becomes necessary. In the old dialect way of speaking a 'zool' means nothing more than 'plough'. And of course the 'gist' is the grounds for using it, which is obviously the field that 'needs a good going over'. So in simple translation, 'zool-o'-gist' means 'plough of the grounds', and to do the best possible job, it may be necessary to replace the ploughshares to get nice straight furrows. For those not on a bibbler's wavelength, trying to understand things has the habit of causing muddle.

Shakespeare, particularly, gets them debating. In trying to protect his blind old father, the Earl of Gloucester, from Oswald the Steward, Edgar, disguised as a peasant, challenges his adversary in the following terms:

'Keep out, che vore ye, or Ise try whether your costard or my ballow be the harder.

Chill be plain with you.'

(*King Lear*, Act IV, Sc. 6)

Edgar's speech is more or less pure Somerset dialect but scholars still quibble about what 'che vore ye' means. Some say it's 'I warn you'; others, 'I warrant you' and this leads to boredom. Historians like to argue that the once hunted wild pig, with its characteristics of noise, speed of trotter, and impetuous nature, was the reason for giving the name 'boar' to the peculiar head of water in the River Parrett. The phenomenon that reaches two feet on some spring tides, can be seen downstream and at Bridgwater. However, Dr Johnson said that 'boar' should be spelt 'bore', like the hollow in a gun-barrel, and because this was what he put in his dictionary, folk assumed he must be right. Personally, I think the Bridgwater bore is a film 'anorak' I know.

If intellectual clever-clogs have dialect trouble, what hope is there for lesser mortals in a Somerset game that has been played for years? It's been a game of sounds, and observation, and nods backwards into history.

What is remarkable is how little the old speech has changed in the hidden bits of the county. Remoteness has saved modern meddling with a simple language of country life that even today shies away from change despite the M5 and the A303, Virgin Rail and South West Trains, the internet, and frequent cross border tractors. As a rough rule of thumb folks' prattle sounded different depending on whether they were east or west of the Quantocks. Indeed, the 'easterlies' were accused of speaking 'Deb'n'. Those living middle-for-diddle on the Quantocks could choose either way, so took it upon themselves to translate.

As far back as 1875, the Victorian writer Frederic Elworthy commented that he met an eighty-year-old Quantocks woman who had lived within four miles of the sea, yet had never seen it. In such circumstances, dialects could change within a couple of miles. He wrote somewhat patronisingly: "The peasantry, who are the true repositories of verbal treasures, are shy, and not easily drawn out by any one they look upon as a 'jin-l-mun'." Today, it would be foolish to call anybody a 'repository' for anything; especially if that 'anybody' is 'a peasant' driving a JCB. Hackles would be raised. And it's hardly unsurprising that folk are still 'shy and not easily drawn out when the only 'gentlemen' they have the misfortune to come across drive Range Rovers at speed, or send them nasty letters about bank overdrafts.

The pronunciation is an ancient one where S is often, but not always, sounded as a Z; F sounds as a V and vowel sounds gain an R. Words with 'ea' in them like beat, heat and neat are pronounced with two syllables, for instance Be-At. It's really quite simple. It's the sounds and words of the court of King Alfred.

The dwindling numbers that are spoilt for choice in finding a Sunday pew may not realize the Lord's Prayer is nearly pure Somerset. Of the sixty-nine words known off by heart, sixty-four of them are Anglo-Saxon. With the wooden pews often being so uncomfortable to perch on and heating costs rising, there is a danger of the less hardy in the community catching that nasty problem 'Pew Moanier'. A thick overcoat trick is recommended; if not for cladding, then definitely for padding. As George from down the road once muttered his wife, Madge, always appeared to have larger breasts on Sundays. This was because she always tucked a small pillow inside her blue 'Debenhams' coat. "Aay zeed Madge, u-rig'd aewt een arl ur duuneens. Vicuur's droaneen u-nuuf tu zain un'eebaurdee tu zleeup. What George meant was, "I saw Madge dressed in Sunday best. The Vicar's droning is good enough to send anybody to sleep."

Many dialect words fall straight out of Chaucer. He uses the word 'mell' in the *Plowman's Tale* meaning to meddle which is still in dialect. The word 'alost' in dialect is the Anglo-Saxon 'ylost'. Curiously, this word is still used by a gamekeeper to his dog to seek out a pellet-peppered fezzie.

I find it interesting to take a peek at some early history, and I'm sure this will receive bibbler support. Over the centuries Somerset has been home for Brython and Belg, Roman, Saxon, Viking, Norman, and more recently Pole. Celtic, Latin, Danish and French were pains to get the tongue around, regardless of rewiring the brain. However, it was Latin that was most avoided. Here I have to hold my hand up as I did my level best to avoid it, too. In olden times Latin was just for monks and for the small number of people they taught.

And there was much to take in. Even today Somerset dialect creates a bit of fog among the uninitiated, so be wary. Despite vain attempts to the contrary, Latin has wheedled its way in, like it wheedled its way into the mind of Mr Athanas, my Greek Latin teacher with all his amor meus Somersets.

At their school, my children googled 'Romans' and learnt that Britain was occupied for over 300 years. Cultural change was legion. Although Costa del Crewkerne may be an exaggeration, villa building in Somerset was prolific and the Romans did their best to be influential. Even going so far as inscribing ancient standing stones, like the Caractacus Stone on Exmoor, in Latin. This was a complete waste of time, because Exmoor ponies only see fit to use it as a bottom-scratcher and the locals tend to ignore it.

Yet Latin was insidious. A Somerset 'chapper' will use words of Latin origin and not know it, as he will pronounce them wrong and use them in the wrong sense. By saying, 'Sright nottlin, sno. Spec me rumatics'll zoon be yer' he means 'It's really cold, you know. I expect my rheumatism will soon be here'. The sentence has the Latin word 'specto' in it that means 'to look'. One can never be too sure when Latin will creep up by chance and bite. This is not ignorance, but a fact of life.

However, as a general rule, with Latin consigned to a black hole, Somerset dialect is a mish-mash of the options that were left. So let Lieutenant Colonel J.A. Garton provide some further insight, published in the Cider Press over a quarter of a century ago:

"Many words, thought to be wrongly pronounced by the countryman, are actually correct, and it is the accepted pronunciation which is wrong. English pronounces W-A-R-M worm, and W-O-R-M wyrm; in the dialect W-A-R-M is pronounced as it is spelt, Anglo-Saxon W-E-A-R-M. The Anglo-Saxon for worm is W-Y-R-M. The verb To Be is used in the old form, I be, Thee bist, He be, We be, Thee 'rt, They be. 'Had I known I wouldn't have gone', is 'If I'd a-know'd I 'ooden never a-went'; 'A' is the old way of denoting the past tense, and went is from the verb to wend (Anglo-Saxon wendan). Infinitives are often formed by the addition of y; 'I can thatch' is 'I d'thatchy'; 'I must go and milk' is 'I must milky'.

"When well spoken, the dialect is pleasant to listen to. It is well suited for expressing the subtle humour and simple philosophy of the lovable people who use it, and in whose minds and speech, treasures of the past which would otherwise be lost, are preserved."

What a load of romantic twaddle. The life of the Somerset farm labourer was nasty, brutish and short, and spent in abject poverty. In 1778, S. Richardson noted that in Wellington, he and his riding companion "were immediately surrounded by beggars to such a degree that we had difficulty to keep them from under our horses' heels." And, the first sight Queen Victoria had of Somerset was as a baby, spending a night at the George Hotel in Ilminster. It was enough to traumatise her. From then on, throughout her life, whenever she had to drive through the county, she did so with her carriage window blinds shut.

Hers was behaviour enough to give a chap a complex and I speak from personal experience. Whilst in bed on a Taunton hospital ward, with swollen knees, I was getting on well with my neighbour who was in for 'ticker trouble'. He had a drag n' fry that he towed to country shows, like at Dunster or Shepton Mallet, so he could not help his diet of sizzling fatty food. Across the ward was 'The Major', a retired officer less important than J. A. Garton, the Lieutenant Colonel.

The Major was our entertainment. During visiting hours his wife, togged in blue jodhpurs and hacking boots, brought him gin disguised in mineral water bottles. Looking dolefully at me and drag n' fry, he said, "My dear, I hate having to mix with the commonalities." She commiserated. However, what could be done? Watching my 'betters' enjoying themselves was the only hobby I could afford. Occasionally, I see the Major's wife still dressed in the same garb with a little more hay attached, hurrying about in Wivey, too fast for me to take the opportunity to ask after her husband's health.

So here I feel the need to raise a little cautionary tale about elocution. 'Colonel G' pointed out that polite English, spoken with 'a plum in the mouth', pronounces W-A-S-P wosp; and I feel forced to admit that this is the way I say it. The Anglo-Saxon word is W-O-P-S. My children have grown up in Somerset, knowing the small black and yellow jam buzzer as a Wopsy. And I feel duly proud of their sponge-like absorption of things local. Recently however, my daughter Ez, now eighteen and back-packing Australia, admitted that she had gone through her childhood thinking that 'whoops-a-daisy', that I said when she bumped herself on this or that, was actually 'Wopsy-dazy'. It had worried her that I might punish her clumsiness with a flick about the head with a rolled-up copy of the *Independent*. With the truth having dawned that Ez feared being bashed like a wasp, I felt humbled that she continued to love me.

Dialect can be charming and expressive, shedding light on the kind of life Somerset folk can still lead despite so few folk knowing how to speak it. However, my mind returns to Stogumber and an end of season cricket match, where the ups and downs had already been decided, and the evenings are drawing in.

"Thee's knaw'd Jarge, me gurt zow had taine young 'uns yesday," were words overheard in the before tea session as the Wivey ever-so-slow bowler and a teammate conversed, while the ball rolled gently between them over the rope. Seconds later the puffing, sweating, swearing Wivey captain collapsed exhausted beside them. The ball had beaten him, too.

"S'getting dimpsey so you d'mind y'doan go vallin auver," the ever-so-slow bowler advised. Adding, "Zit down and bide a bit."

"Dazzy-snoo don't look viddy," mumbled an aged concerned voice from behind the boundary at the Wivey captain's wobbly state.

"Mind tae shut the git, alse the hoss mid geet out," the ever-so-slow bowler soon commented as he watched a teammate retrieve the cricket ball biffed into an adjacent field.

"I be in tarble pain, me veet be killing me," he later said standing outside the pavilion, holding a cup of tea in one hand and clotted cream scone topped with strawberry jam in the other.

The icing on the cake were those rounds of "Closer to Home" during the pub quiz night at Luxborough's 'Blazing Stump'. Here Chris-the-Communist joined forces with old George-the-Colostomy-Bag, Martin-the-Scribbler, Pam-the-Art-Shop, Piers-the-Solicitor, and Steve-the-Unemployed to give options of meaning. Sitting across the flag-stoned floor on the opposing team, it was Miles and Steve who fooled us most. They were undeniably the best fibbers. The following words, some of which sneak themselves here or there into this book, are just a selection from the many whose meanings I only ever guessed at:

Aarr: Yes
Addle: A pus-filled swelling
Aggy: Gather eggs as in "I be gwain aggy"
Alice: Ulcer, so be careful when christening your daughter
All to lippets: Fallen to pieces
Amper: Pimple
Ann Summer: More handsome, and nothing to do with sex aids
Ass backwards: Back to front
Ballyrag: To scold, tell off especially with foul language
Baven: Faggot of unprepared twigs and branches
Begrumpled: Offended
Benapt: Left high and dry by the tide
Betwaddled: Confused
Bibber: Shiver
Bibbler: One who enjoys a pint or two
Biddle: Beetle
Bim-boms: Church bells
Bloody-warrior: Wallflower
Bog baler: Long-handled scoop for emptying outdoor toilets
Boggler: A horse given to stumbling, but not falling
Bucket and chuck it: The outdoor toilet
Bull-beggar: Hobgoblin
Bum-Towel: Long-Tailed Tit
Bunches: Word of exclamation like rollocks
Caddle: Confusion, muddle
Chapper: Fellow, chap
Clinkerbells: Icicles
Cleeve: Steep slope
Colley: Blackbird
Crousty: Ill-tempered
Dabster: Expert
Daddicky: Rotten

Daddygranfer: Woodlouse
Dang I: Well, I'm damned!
Daug-tuy'urd: Knackered
Dazzy-snoo: Definitely
Deb'n: Devon
Dewbit: Breakfast
Dimpsey: Half lit, at twilight or dusk
Dinnum: Didn't they
Dirsh: Thrush
Dish-Washer: Grey wagtail
Down-Come: A fall in income
Draffit: Vessel in which to collect pig swill
Drang: Alleyway
Driggle-Draggle: In a slovenly manner applied to a woman's dress.
Drowner: Employed to cut osiers in the dykes of Sedgemoor
Drowning the Miller: Pouring too much water to make the tea too weak
Emmets: Tourists in large numbers
Emmet-batch: An ant-hill.
Evet: A lizard.
Farty: Forty
Fezzie: Pheasant
Gallybeggar: Bugbear, hobgoblin
Ganny-cock's Snob: The long membranous appendage at the cock-turkey's beak
Gawk: Stare
Git: Gate. So don't be alarmed if anyone says they're off to hang one
Goozegogs: Gooseberries
Grockle: Tourist
Grockle shells: Caravans
Guddler: A heavy alcoholic drinker
Gulch: Swallow fast
Gurt, girt: Great
Hayty-tayty: Seesaw
Hellier: Roof tiler
Hoon: Throw with vigour.
Horse-stinger: A dragonfly.
Hully: A peculiarly shaped long wicker trap used for catching eels.
Hunky punks: gargoyle
Jack-o-lanterns: Will-o-the-wisps, the souls of unbaptized children
Keffel: A bad and worn out horse.
Kern: turn from blossom to fruit
Lants: Sand Eels

Larn: Teach
Maized: Mad, insane
Mower: Moor
Mud horse: A type of sled with a ski-shaped base and wicker basket used on the Somerset coast for fishing
Mugglin: Struggling
Narry: Narrow
Nestle tripe: Runt, especially of pigs
Nottled: Really cold
Numbriller: Umbrella
Pew Moanier: Pneumonia
Pixie led: Simple minded, crazed
Praper: Excellent
Puggle 'eaded: Drunk. Cider drinkers can often be recognised by their rosy faces and inability to articulate. They are then considered puggle 'eaded
Rampin: Raving mad
Ruckles: Peat stacks
Scollared: Taught
Smeech: Smoky smelling
Sumshus: Lovely to eat
Tarble: Terrible
Teetsy-totsy: Cowslip
Thunder box: Toilet
Trow: Sailing barge designed for use on the River Parrett
Unket: Uncanny
Viddy: Right
Wopse: Wasp
Wontwiggle: A mole tunnel
Yes: An earthworm
Zummat: Something
Zummerzet: Somerset
Zyve: Scythe

The Numbriller
An exchange of words to end a romance:
   "Better take a numbriller, 'tis going to rain." I says.
   "No, it ain't," she say, "and I shan't."
   "Ave it your own way," I says.
   "No, I won't she say.
   "We'll wait and see then," I says.
   "No, we won't," she say: "it ain't going to rain."

So I just stands and looks at her without a word.

"Can't yer say something or do something?" she went on. "I say it ain't going to rain; now then?"

"Well," I says, "you won't 'ave it my way, nor yet your own way; nor even wait and see the Lord's way: what is there for I to say or do?"

"Bunches!" she say, "and if you can't say something or do something we shan't suit."

"Very well," I says, and leaves 'er door, and goes off home.

There you might suppose was the end, but not a bit of it. Ten minutes later she come down to my door, and t'was raining then: and she say, "You was wrong: 'twas not going to rain when you said 'twas: it comed on after."

"'Tis what I meant," I says.

"No, you never," she say: "and 'tis not what I call rain even now – 'tis but a smizzle. You say, "Tis going to rain': you never say when, or 'ow long, or 'ow 'ard and that' – you never say nothing. If you'd a' said 'twill be going to rain, 'twould ha' been some sense to it. But to say, "Tis going to rain,' and 'twasn't going to rain when you spoke it, and didn't rain for long after: and it ain't what I call rain now: 'tis but a smizzle. And you say, 'Better take a numbriller': now a numbriller is for rain, and this be only a smizzle. There be rain and rain, same as there is men and men; but there aren't numbrillers and numbrillers, but just a numbriller; and a numbriller isn't for smizzle, and you say 'take a numbriller' – where's the sense in a numbriller for smizzle? Drat the man! If you can't say something or do something, you won't suit – "

That was the end. If you go courting, seems to me you'm courting all sorts of things you'm not wanting.

(Rev. Alfred Percivall Pott, 'Somerset Neighbours' 1921.)

A Matter of Content
'I've a-heard the wold volk zay as how thur wur a man what eat a caaf at a zitten. To make ut a bit more taasty like, they had un made up into pies. Thic man eat two ar dree o'theaze yere pies an' then a-didden zim to be geten on vury well, zo they ast un if a-wur stooded. No, a-zed, a-wurden stooded, an' the pies was vury good, but a-thought 'twur 'bout time a-started on thic thur caaf.'

A Christmas Story
There is an old Somerset superstition that when sheep turned to face the

east on the stroke of midnight of Christmas day morning, animals were given the power of speech until the strike of one. With that in mind one anecdote continues to get repeated over the years:

'There were an old farmer had an ox that were al'as okkud, an'one night 'e say to it,

"Thee girt stoopid fule. I'd a-like to know who taught 'ee to be so okkud. I'd larn 'en."

The ox turned round, "Why. 'twas thee, thee stoopid girt fule."'

LESSON SIX
FOLLOWING THE BONNET

"Truly a week of English summer in the hills and plains of Somerset is a rare a piece of enchantment as any man could wish; we may ride in our 20th century cars through country that has not been spoiled in a thousand years."

(Arthur Mee, 1940)

"In my beginning is my end. In succession
Houses rise and fall, crumble, are extended,
Are removed, destroyed, restored, or in their place
Is an open field, or a factory, or a by-pass."

(T.S. Elliot, 'East Coker', 1944)

I was being driven on the wrong side of the road through a Romanian ghost town and there were no signs, nothing to say that anything was out of the ordinary. We were on the left, which is all well and dandy between Wivey and Taunton, but was certainly peculiar in Orastie, a place the size of Chard. No traffic, however, came towards us. It was very hot. Fumes from a small stretch of asphalt resurfacing work carried out by four grubby sloth-like men and a couple of small oily steamrollers filtered into my nose, adding to the reek of warm sheep's cheese sandwiches. I yearned for Somerset cheddar. I yearned for Somerset full stop.

As soon as the town was behind us we found the missing traffic. It was in a static jam miles long. Bonnets were open and families picnicked on stinky cheese. Opportunistic children peddled bottles of iffy water plundered in hundreds from an overturned truck in a ditch the opposite end of Orastie. Lone men paced up and down ranting the unintelligible into mobile phones as others snoozed. And they may still be snoozing now.

In Somerset this just would not happen. There would always be leafy lanes around the problem, as long as one remembers the rural code that tractors, cows, sheep, and the aging population don't do reverse. Delays can also be caused getting stuck behind bouncy zigzagging squirrels, while the squished ones hint at impatience. However, whatever the pitfalls, the best way to see things whilst having some time on your hands is to go by lane and follow your bonnet, for as I used to tell my children, Somerset is "very shneaky-shnoodle." Hidden.

42

Trying to take it all in from the M5 is just not good enough. The motorway cuts a swathe through Somerset, fast-laning carbon perfumes into Devon and Cornwall. Few travellers in tin cocoons feel the need to stop for anything other than a pee. However, thousands upon thousands do slow down to rubber-neck when passing Bridgwater.

Standing in the company of pylons that have stepped boldly out of Hinkley Point nuclear power station, and surrounded by an acre of reed beds to deep to wade across, is a giant officially called 'The Willow Man'. At over thirty-nine feet high it had a predecessor that some arty-farts hailed as the 'Angel of the South', Somerset's answer to Antony Gormley's ethereal 'Angel of the North'.

Caesar claimed that ancient druids made immense figures of wicker-work filled with victims and burnt as a sacrifice. Although this may account for the sinister reputation of giants in fairy stories and legends, the one beside the motorway was part funded by Sainsbury's supermarkets without fear of losing its customers. Created by sculptor Serena del Hey, the first willow man was unveiled in 2000, but burnt down the following year. After the attack, Serena said she did not believe there was a link between the fire and ritual burnings of wicker figures at Glastonbury Festival. She made no comment that the jealous rivalry of other supermarket chains might have been involved, or that people were influenced by the DVD of Christopher Lee cremating Edward Woodward trapped in 'The Wicker Man'. I don't think she realised that some scenes of the film were shot at Wookey Hole.

Serena remade her sculpture in three weeks with steel wire interwoven with willow. With its stout legs and small pointy arms, the sculpture quickly became a distraction from Bridgwater's sulphurous pong, forming an uneasy alliance with a nearby camel that had until then been lonely in the job. Happily, the camel was not unloved. The BBC radio presenter Terry Wogan often made mention of the sentinel beast on his morning show, and ensured its ongoing national support. What people often fail to grasp is that the camel is more than a papier-mâché carnival castaway. It's iconic. Perhaps for years it has tried to hitch a lift away from Bridgwater only to meet with failure for want of raising a hoof.

When Bridgwater's cellophane factory closed in summer 2005 and its chimney grew cold, there was no longer a need for drivers to wind up windows, turn off ventilation fans and push harder on the accelerator. The wafting stench that for years blighted the motorway had suddenly gone. Such freshness of air meant that the camel could have a lick of paint and a baby. I am anxious that they will both stay, happy together watching the passing flow.

And when I say Somerset is shneaky-shnoodle, I certainly do not mean that some things are not on the ordnance survey map. Like for instance, the railway bridge over the M5 that links the arms factory in Puriton to Dunball docks. This is completely missing. However, that is just official secrets. No, what I mean is hidden like the finest skull of a great cave bear ever found in England. This is now in Taunton Museum having been discovered in 1824 by William Beard. It was in a cave under Banwell Hill, near his father's farm. But let me give a better example.

South of Wincanton, a place John Wesley called "one of the dullest places in all of the county," is Templecombe. It was occupied by the idolatrous Knights Templar who occupied the manor in 1185 to breed horses for the Crusades. Just a few walls are all that remains, yet one holy relic, unique in Britain, has survived the Templars by centuries. During a gale in 1951, the ceiling of an outhouse collapsed, revealing a wooden panel with a face painted upon it.

Cleaning discovered the face to be a thirteenth century portrait of Christ. He is shown without a halo, the way the Templars worshipped him, and bears a striking resemblance to the famous Turin Shroud from which the painting might have been copied. The painting now hangs in the church. Once you have asked for the church door key from the nearby pub, Christ will be seen gazing down with a sublime if somewhat bemused look upon his face. Being in the dark for an age can have that effect. However, Templecombe does not immediately come to mind when thinking of interesting places.

Off the beaten track, they used to call it. Really, it's just the fault of progress, despite the history that lingers. When the ancients erected their stone circle at Stanton Drew, it was possibly the centre of a Neolithic metropolis. And if you needed to be buried, then why not in Nempnett Thrubwell? You would have been away with the fairies. There is an extensive oval barrow in the parish, having the wonderful name of 'Fairy Toot'. Wade and Wade mention it in their 1929 book *Somerset* as "a remarkably fine tumulus of masonry, said to have been one of Britain's best." Compton Dando has a Roman god as a corner stone holding up the church and healing waters are said to spring from the ground from Doulting Well, near Shepton Mallet.

A boy from Somerton called Ina was chosen to be king in much the same way as the Dalai Lama is chosen today. He was looking after his father's oxen when he was taken from his father's Somerset farm. A hundred years before Alfred, he had supremacy over all England lying south of London and was the first king to give rights to Welshmen.

And how could I forget the phallic chimney on Aller church. It sticks in the memory more than the fact that the church itself marks the spot where Alfred converted his defeated Danish enemy Guthrum to

Christianity. However, with one thing and another, much of what is visual and interesting in Somerset's backwaters has tended to become a bit overgrown.

Nowadays one snaggles goosegrass and nettles on the wing-mirrors brushing past bracken fern, cow-parsley and dog-rose along tarmac winding miles, some with grass and moss growing in the middle. To do so is to discover quiet parishes and perhaps a church with a difference. Superstitious sailors scratched outlines of their shoes in the lead on Dunster's church roof for good luck, before setting sail from the Horn. Having seen the scratchings for myself, I wonder what 'WB' was like as a man in 1761, or who the caricature was of a man with a pipe and a tricorn hat?

St Mary's church at Orchardleigh near Frome is a rare gem. No other among the rest of the country's ten thousand or so churches is like it. Sitting at the edge of a lake and ringed by a moat, it is often referred to as 'the church on the island.' Its remoteness means there is no electricity supply, so services are candlelit and the organ has to be pumped by hand. Unsurprisingly, there is a scarcity of invading church mice. This would have been a better place for Wulfic to choose to spend a life devoted to prayer in a hermit cell. In Haselbury Plucknett he got bitten on the toe by a mouse during meditation, so he took to wearing rusty chain mail rather than dressing in horsehair.

The Mendip village of Hinton St George is still noted these days for its Punky Night on the last Thursday evening in October that stemmed from an annual round-up by wives of drunken husbands failing to find their way home after the nearby fair at Chiselborough. It's a tradition that gave America the delightful inspiration to hollow out and carve pumpkins for display as Jack-o-Lanterns every Halloween. Wives and children in Hinton have always used mangold-wurzels. It's typical of the Yanks to borrow things from others and make them bigger.

However, seek out the Somerset villages and there will be found many a home of a worthy, pirate or promisor, chiselled memorial, stone carved creature or hunky punk. When it comes to details, instinct will possibly hold you in better stead than word of mouth. Folk can be full of yarns that mislead the gullible. Sir Francis Drake, for instance, never did fire a cannon ball from his ship to land in Monksilver at the feet of his beloved Elizabeth Sydenham. That's silly. What actually persuaded her to stop her getting wed to another suitor that day was a meteorite weighing hundreds of pounds falling with a flash of fire from the sky. It was the original wedding crasher and just one of those things, believe it or not. Yet it gave the chance for Elizabeth to change her mind and instead marry Francis in 1585. So, before anyone decides to take the plunge, I advise they first seek guidance from heaven.

And then there are the likes of Ruth Tongue. She claimed to be born in Cheddon Fitzpaine between midnight and cockcrow on St James' Day morning. This made her a Chime Child credited with the power of seeing spirits. Or perhaps she just flirted with her imagination, as in her load of rubbish about the Wellington Monument.

Apparently her housemaid confided that when she was just six months old, she had a massive tapeworm with forty mouths. She was finally cured of the monster by being strapped to a board, and carried around the monument every day for three months.

To believe such things qualifies one to charge windmills, and Somerset has a few of those with Stembridge Mill in High Ham being the prettiest. Although impressive, they are not quite as outstanding as the multiple column inches in rural corners were a man had the time to admire his folly.

From Dunster to Bruton, Willett to Burton Pynsent, folly building had distracted local worthies from their idleness, and dot the Somerset land-scape in profusion. Although one structure is now in a worse state that most. It was a folly built in the eighteenth century by Lord Egremont, a romantic and retro idealist. He believed that gunpowder was so monstrous an invention that it would soon be outlawed from use in warfare. So unshakable was his belief that the world would agree with him that he built himself a giant medieval-style castle near Spaxton, ready for the fashion of bow-and-arrow wars to return. They did not and these days only a few of the castle's stones remain.

Happily 'Jack the Treacle Eater' is still complete, one of four follies in Barwick, just south of Yeovil, that were bought by South Somerset District Council for the cost of a 'fiver' in the early 1990s. It had proved a novel look out tower for the village's Prisoner of War Camp housing Italian and German prisoners during the Second World War. Consisting of a winged Mercury statuette on top of a turret over a small archway, it commemorates a local runner with the stamina to carry family messages to London. He was an athlete said to have trained on treacle.

Agreed, there is something gloriously old fashioned about a folly, but build them too high and aeroplanes can come to a sticky end as happened at the King Alfred Tower, a triangular effort near Bruton, with a circumference about the same as its one hundred and sixty foot height. Made of over one million dark red bricks, all locally fired at Hilcombe, the tower was designed in 1765 by Henry Flitcroft, much to the regret of the families of five American airmen. The men died in July 1944 when their Noorduyn C-64A Norseman, a Lysander lookalike, flew into the conical roof of the turret in thick fog.

For obvious reasons they were unable to appreciate the view that the great twentieth century diarist James Lees-Milne described from the top of the tower. He wrote, "the panorama embracing Salisbury Plain, the Blackmore Vale bounded by the Dorset Downs, and the levels of Sedge Moor is one of unending trees and fields of English green". Johnny Depp and Juliette Binoche came to Bruton to film 'Chocolat' in 2000, the event it's now said led to Depp falling in love with Somerset and buying a home in the county.

From one of Somerset's newest inhabitants one can find signs of the oldest by leaving Bruton's highs to search the lows between Westhay and Shapwick. The Sweet Track would be folly to follow if searching for a bar of Dairy Milk or a jelly baby, it's mud that makes it sticky, not sugar syrup. Named after its discoverer, Ray Sweet, a peat digger who found it in 1970, the track has been claimed to be the oldest road in the world. Built by people tired of paddling in brackish water and getting peat stuck between their toes during the thirty-ninth century BC, the track consisted of crossed poles of ash, oak and lime that were driven into the water-logged soil to support a walkway. This mainly consisted of oak planks laid end-to-end for nearly one and a quarter miles through the damp quiet of the Brue valley.

Perhaps it's a subjective thing, but Shapwick's peat bogs and heath-land appear at their best in spring, a microcosm world of froglet and snail, and of coot and swan. Bulrushes grow tall above sphagnum moss, and flowers open yellow. Marsh marigolds crowd the shallows, flag-iris hang out pennants, and teetsy-totsies always seem demure in the meadows. In the distance across the beds of reed and sedge is Glastonbury Tor. I feel it's sensible to get your bearings, otherwise you could easily get lost.

The County Council has not helped. There used to be a a signpost on High Ham village green that read "Beer" in one direction, "Stout" in another and "Pedwell" in the third. Naughty village lads naturally altered the word to "Peedwell" so regularly that the Council took the signpost down.

Amongst the Somerset lanes one could easily find oneself becoming a foreigner within a few miles. A lady in Stoke St Gregory remembered a farmer from the village chastise his son for becoming engaged to a Glastonbury girl, "What 'ee want to marry a furriner for, ther'er perty 'o bonny lassies in Stoke." Similarly, when a farmer from Street courted his wife-to-be, before folk decided to shorten Pitney Lortie to Pitney, the village lads used to lie in wait for him as he entered the village, as they didn't like a foreigner marrying a Pitney girl.

It was a different world before the laying of tarmac. A notice, printed in tattered yellowed copy of the *Taunton Courier* from as far back as 1814, was found a while ago in a Pitney attic. A "Light Post Coach," it said, set out from the Angel Inn, East Street, Taunton every midnight for Bristol, Bath, London, Birmingham, Liverpool, Manchester, Coventry, Leicester, Nottingham and all parts of the North. Also every morning at eight was a coach for Exeter, Plymouth and Falmouth. "Cheap and expeditious travelling," the notice called it. Better, surely, to run more buses. More recently, a friend of mine was being nagged by his wife to take her for an expensive evening out as a birthday treat. So he took her to the petrol station with him. Somerset life is becoming increasingly tough on the wallet.

Before the days of Tesco, folk tended to grow their own vegetables and fruit, especially strawberries. There was even a 'Strawberry Train' that used to run on the single line Cheddar Valley Railway. Sadly, it became a casualty of the by-pass that now runs along where the tracks used to be. Axbridge folk grew strawberries along the hillside adjacent to the line, and every day they took them to the station in prams, wheelbarrows, and anything that could carry baskets tied five together on a stick. The prices ranged from fourpence to one shilling per pound and the growers acting as Agents "waved their telegrams with their day's prices across the gardens like tick-tack men."

The by-pass also brought other casualties. Saddest were the pet dogs and cats who had previously seemed to know the 'ups and downs' of the trains. The year after the road first opened in 1966 their losses were high.

Cynics would say this was unfortunate but not surprising, as we often don't pay enough attention to people, especially those of whom we should be proud. John Speke, discoverer of the source of the Nile is buried in Dowlish Wake. The first Speaker of the House of Commons, Sir Thomas Hungerford, built the castle at Farleigh Hungerford.

A man with the little known name of John Henry Brodribb was born in Keinton Mandeville. He became famous throughout England as Sir Henry Irving, the greatest actor of his time. The man who may have written the music to our national anthem was born in Wellow in 1563. He was John Bull. An air without words was in a manuscript of his found over two hundred years after his death. The comic actor and writer John Cleese was born in Weston-super-Mare in 1939, and actress Jenny Agutter was born in Taunton. And these are just a few whose lives are compressed into a line.

Some are deserving of more. William Edgell died in Midsomer Norton 1940 after a life spent trying to honour a promise that he made to his father. This wasn't any old promise like feeding the cat, being teetotal or always having a bet on the Grand National. No. William's burden was to do all he could to prove his father's pet theory that the earth is flat. He did his best to defy the Universe, spending night after night watching the sky through a steel tube in his garden that pointed at the Pole Star. And he studied it until he was sure in his own mind that all the astronomers were wrong. By his calculations the star was only five thousand miles away and the Sun only ten miles across. Safe with this knowledge, he went to his grave.

As Midsommer Norton could inspire 'Flat Earthers', so East Coker provided inspiration for writers.

Robinson Crusoe would never have been on a child's bookshelf but for another William, this time called William Dampier. East Coker, not too far from the Dorset border, is where he grew up. After leaving Yeovil Grammar School he went on to pilot the ship that not only found, but also ferried home shipwrecked Alexander Selkirk from a desert island. Daniel Defoe immortalised Alexander's story by writing the famous book.

It is fair to say that William had rather a full life. He was a blend of hero and villain, scholar, buccaneer and explorer. An orphan at sixteen, he sailed west to Newfoundland, east to the Dutch Indies, came home aged only twenty-one to fight against the Dutch and then began a career of adventure around the globe, making a general nuisance of himself.

He joined a gang of pirates who played merry hell in the isthmus of Darien, the narrow strip of land that lies between the Caribbean and the Pacific Ocean, capturing towns and ships. And despite periods of terrible privation he was one of the first Englishmen to touch the coasts of China and Australia. Nelson bade his midshipmen to study William's discourse on 'Winds, Tides, and Currents'. The British government was so impressed that eight years after William's initial return in 1691, it gave him a ship and sent him back from whence he had come. He found the southwest and north coasts of Australia 'horrible', with 'barren shores, savage men, and terrifying kangaroos'. It was all very different to South Somerset, and mellowed by age, he was happy to leave any further exploration to Captain Cook.

If William was East Coker's most famous son, then the American author and poet Thomas Stearns Elliot, who became a British subject in 1927 and received the Nobel Prize for Literature in 1948, must come a close second. T.S.'s ashes are buried in the church with those of his ancestors.

At the time William Dampier was on his adventures, Langport was just that, a port on the River Parrett once with thriving docks and dives for the sailors, despite being over twenty miles from the sea. A fund exists in the local Nat West Bank, the successor of the famous Stuckey's Bank founded in the same building in 1770, "to pay for the basic accoutrements of a bride's bottom drawer."

The conditions of the 'Annie Tite Fund' are that an appellant "be borne and resident in the parish and proven of virtuous or good repute." In other words, she had to a virgin. No doubt, this was intended to restrain potential sailor charmers from over-amorous embraces and maintain a sense of civil decorum. Not wanting to cast aspersions at the young ladies of Langport, but none ever made a claim. A decision was taken in recent years to use the fund as a bursary for local undergraduates of both sexes to buy books to help their studies at university.

A few of the books will surely have been written by Walter Bagehot, that famous son of Langport, born in 1828. Walter became a journalist and edited the *Economist* for seventeen years and left a classic book on the English Constitution. He threw his ideas out "like fireworks," and his newspaper articles grew into books that were translated into leading European languages and accepted as university textbooks. It's safe to say that his views of finance influences governments. Where would we be today without him?

Personally, what I like best about Langport is in the medieval stained glass in the church chancel. Among the soft blues, greens and reds is a little pig with a bell around its neck. It's so sweet.

And that just about sums things up. Even the smallest details matter. To find them, I follow my bonnet and hope for the best, although that can be subjective. Maybe there are some things that touch everyone. If they do, then in Somerset they are likely to survive.

LESSON SEVEN
DISAFFECTION

"Life went a-Maying
With Nature, Hope, and Poesy;
When I was young!
When I was young? -Ah, woeful when!"
(Samuel Taylor Coleridge, 'Youth and Age').

"Swimming pools and chandeliers
Kinda things we don't get around here.
NFB. Why don't you write it down for me? NFB."
(Peter Bruntnell, singer/songwriter).

"The grove at the village well" sounds much better translated as Nempnett Thrubwell, a sleepy Somerset village with no pub, or shop or traffic cop. Immortalised in the song 'Down In Nempnett Thrubwell' by the Wurzels, it was written by Adge Cutler before his death in 1974. It was a wonderful place, if you believe Adge. Frogs were as big as dogs that harmonised in song and all the fleas wore hobnail boots. One could see rabbits as big as sows, hens the size of cows, and pigeons pulling the ploughs. The sun shone and you can even hear the grasses grow. And it never rained.

Sadly, the clouds now gathered. Not the kind that poured hailstones "the size of walnuts" to break windows throughout Beckington in 1916, nor the silk sack kind that billow white against Adge's blue Somerset heaven, but dark with a touch of threat. Late and still talking, Tom, Cloe and Lisa plonked themselves down amongst the other FE students, a cultural mix of emo and greebo, chav and prep. Motivated more by fashion and social networking than the academic muddling that had recently become my responsibilty.

"It's crap, innit?" said Tom.

"Yeah." said Cloe and Lisa together.

"What's crap, Tom?" I asked, raising my voice a tad to make myself heard.

"This room."

"This college? This workshop?"

"Nah. Somerset."

I feigned a sympathetic nod.

The Saxons named this nirvana the Summer Land and it had just been reduced to a four-letter word. A land to which, Ptolemy wrote, the god Hercules sailed in a golden bowl and where some claim Exmoor ponies are descended from those owned by the Roman legions. Jesus is said to have lived in Glastonbury with his uncle, Joseph of Arimathea and the Vikings were finally converted to Christ in the wetlands. Oh, how I loved the rich pastures and water meadows, rolling hills, still rivers and shady forests and the thought of Nempnett Thrubwell.

"Watchet's really crap," said Roddi, a Welsh lad whose parents, he often laughed, turned left before the Severn Bridge, because they could not afford the toll. "Nowhere to go, no places to hook up except for the shelters. Idiots tell us off for being furtive and disaffected, but we're not. We're just bored."

So I listened and I gleaned, and my chipped spectacles lost their tint of rose. The ammonites at Helwell Beach that have been there for millions of years became a secondary thought.

I asked what a hook up spot was, and learned that it is a hallowed place for Somerset youth. It can be the humblest place like a bench or a street corner, anywhere to hang around with mates and dream about a time they can get into pubs and clubs; either when they are not too young or too skint.

Roddi was full of admiration for Watchet's Esplanade shelters with their view over the new marina where expensive yachts got stuck in the mud. Despite it being very draughty kids hooked up there, depending on the time of day, to swear a lot and knock back what Roddi assured me were soft fizzy drinks. That was until the late night canoodlers came to chivvy the kids away, or 'lairy' drunks at closing time unnerved them.

"What about strange smelling substances?" I asked in good humour to Tom's snort.

"Er, sometimes", said Roddi looking at his feet, as if on some truth drug. "But I've heard there's covert police about ever since the burning."

Arsonists in Somerset seemed to be a roving bunch. One of the Esplanade shelters suffered a similar fate to Bridgwater's Willow Man and was rebuilt as a peculiarly modernist affair totally out of keeping with the rest of Watchet's architecture. On Roddi's recommendation, given with the prejudice of his youth, this shelter was now the best for being welcoming and friendly; any other had yobs and druggies hanging out, especially the shelter in the Memorial Ground. I knew that place. I had volunteered to umpire an Under 13s cricket match between Watchet and Wivey there. A keen home team lad had gamely chased a leg swoosh to in front of the shelter. Bending down twice, he returned towards the wicket with the ball in one hand and a charred stub of a roll-up in the other. He was quicker getting rid of the ball, so I was forced into making an unpopular decision.

"I like the Memorial Ground." said Tom playing with his cigarette lighter. Such is local knowledge.

"Chard's rubbish, really iffy. My Mum's new bloke's from Glasgow. He said he wouldn't go near her until we moved. We're in Taunton now, but it's still rubbish." Cloe was having her say. For those prepared to listen, Saturdays on the high street were really bad. A human void that even people from Bridgwater avoid. "Do you know anything about Bridgwater, Mr Wood?" she asked.

Well, just north of it between the A38 and the Parrett estuary was 'Turkeyland' to me, that small part of Somerset from where Mike Thorne, the Wivey butcher, ordered my Christmas dinner, together with three hundred others that grew up in the company of thousands. But that probably wasn't close enough for Cloe.

I wracked my brains. "The people the other side of the Poldens are very different," I said, "And that's strange, because they're only little hills."

Then I remembered 'NFB', and that allegedly certain doctors had made fun of patients from Bridgwater who appeared to be acting oddly. The doctors' concurred that the patients were 'all loopy and had flat heads'. By way of a chance chat with Chris Sidaway, the Arts Officer for Sedgemoor District Council I discovered a possible reason why. With the coming of the railways, families from Birmingham used to come to Bridgwater for their holidays. This was a remarkable enough fact in itself; but there was more. The Brummies would often bring their mad maiden aunts and other mazed relatives along with them. When the holidays were over, the potty ones would be left behind in Bridgwater to be looked after by the local authorities.

In 1999, Peter Bruntnell wrote a song called NFB. During an interview at the time he recalled: "A couple, who are friends of mine, ran a particularly rough pub in Bridgwater, and the landlady was telling me one day that the doctors in Bridgwater use the abbreviation NFB meaning 'Normal For Bridgwater' when describing their test results for slightly disturbed local patients." Like the Somerset fast bowler Andrew Caddick, Bruntnell was born in New Zealand, yet adopted the West Country. Both have been overlooked and underpromoted. If Caddick has possibly been England's best bowler for many a cricket season, then Peter Bruntnell is probably the country's finest singer-songwriter. He is a phenomenal talent. Bridgwater should feel privileged. But I wondered if he had ever heard of the Manchip, the jam-filled rolled pastry, almost unique to

Bridgwater, that's the town's only culinary claim to fame.

Then, of course, there was September's St Matthew's Fair. Of this I had no idea whether Bridgwater was privileged or not. Farmers used to take off their wellies, leave their sheep, and come down from the Quantocks and Mendips for the nude shows held in a tent, where for a shilling the men of Somerset could watch girls taking their clothes off. But now, of course, the farmers have got the internet, and the fair restricts itself to a big wheel and fluffy pink candyfloss.

However, during Victorian times a local curate, H.J.Prince, did more than enjoy nudity under the cover of canvas. He had a penchant to enjoy it on his altar. Not only did his oratory have a remarkable effect on women, he also decided that he was the Messiah.

An alter ego, so to speak. It was rumoured that he was from Charlesworth, although the villagers there are still in vigorous denial.

In 1846 he set up 'Agapemone' or the 'Abode of Love' in Spaxton that amounted to a love nest of himself, a few chums, and a whole harem of ladies. These ladies brought substantial endowments with them that resulted in Prince battling life-long law suits from their relatives, outraged that the curate should benefit from such a large amount of wealth, to which he had no title. The relatives wanted the money returned, even if their daughters and wives did not come with it.

To the horror of prudish society, Prince deflowered a sixteen-year-old, called Zoe, on the chapel altar in front of his devoted congregation of acolytes, who called the event the 'Great Manifestation'. Unfortunately, the ethereal atmosphere rather evaporated when Zoe embarrassingly became pregnant. Prince said it was the Devil's work and the 'Final Dispensation'. There was little surprise when Zoe soon fell from favour.

If this was not enough for locals to get their heads around, Prince continued to do his shopping in Bridgwater, with an acolyte walking ahead intoning "Blessed is he who Cometh in the Name of the Lord." Much to the disbelief of his followers, Prince was not immortal and he died before the nineteenth century saw itself out. However, the naughty man's community lingered on without him, and the last follower died as late as 1950.

What else was there? Oh yes, the Guy Fawkes Carnival, but everybody knows about that.

After paraphrasing all this to the students, Cloe just shrugged and returned to her monologue about Taunton high street on a Saturday. It was full of biffas and honey monsters pushing prams, stuffing themselves with Maccy Ds' then putting their greasy fingers on the clothing in 'Primani' before going down to Poundland; whereas she and her mates chilled out in Starbucks. Cloe seldom went into town after dark, because it was 'too heavy', apart from sometimes getting 'trashed' at Deller's Night Club.

Lisa piped up that she had once twisted her ankle falling down the stairs at Deller's.

Somebody had spilt rum and coke; and she knew that is what it was, because she had tasted it on her fingers after picking herself up. But really, the ankle was the fault of Lisa's bloke. If he had not gone and stuck a fiver in the pole dancer's knickers, Lisa would not have been in such a rush to leave.

Then bang; into the room came Shane grinning from inside his hoodie, walking the walk in spotless white trainers and cuddling an empty plastic bottle that had contained white cider. Shane had just passed his driving test, and according to Cloe was a 'jammy chav'. Chav is an unendearing acronym that translates as 'council housed and violent'. Cloe then laughed that Shane would now be attempting to gain meaning to his small, boring, boring life by doing handbrake turns in Tesco's car park.

This appealed to Toby who was a prep and an obvious candidate for a public school wanabee. Millfield or Wellington, King's or Queen's; it would not have mattered which. Slouching back in his chair, sweat pants hanging below the hem line of his Abercrombie and Fitch underpants, Toby pushed his hands through big hair, after he finished fiddling with his ipod. He had views on chavs that prompted an altercation with a now grinless Shane, who ended it with the words 'snob yob'. Toby also had a few views about Yeovil, because his dad was a budding future contender for a contemporary ancient mariner. He was in the Royal Navy and had a desk job at Yeovilton.

"Yeovil town centre, how crap is that," said Toby turning whingy and going on to qualify the reason. There were loads of weirdos about so you see what happens when cousins marry; and there were too many people with limited horizons. Chewing gum was everywhere sticking to the bottom of your shoes. Shitty pigeons spoil Glovers Walk and tramps hang around in the bus station. There is warm beer drunk by thugs who after ten pints and unable to wait for Friday's night clubs smash the place up, and fight any poor sod who happens to walk past. A & E was full to popping with cuts and bruises at weekends. The style of girls is from years' back; shellsuits and knot top haircuts. And to cap it all, Toby's dad had told him that Yeovil was swimming underneath drug crime with the help of a snorkel.

"But the smack heads are surprisingly happy for junkies. You should go there, Tom," quipped Toby perking up with a smug conclusion to his eulogy.

"Shut up, Muppet." said Tom.

And Toby did, only to fiddle with his iPod again.

What was so important, I asked him, that it couldn't wait.

'Pineapple Thief', he told me with kindled enthusiasm. Apparently it was a really cool band whose vocalist-cum-guitarist Bruce Soord was absolutely brilliant and would soon be Yeovil's best known resident. Brucie was better than the Bruntnell bloke he had never heard of.

"Way to go." I sighed, bereft of all humour. "Let's do some work now, shall we?"

On my way home that afternoon to find solace in a mug of Earl Grey, a fat man with a baseball cap turned back-to-front on his head, and knuckle dusters on gloved hands that gripped the steering wheel, shot passed me in a battered red Megane. The car weaved through busy Taunton traffic pursued by four shrieking police cars. Soon, beyond bland housing estates, I saw the Megane again. It was in a hedge scaring the sparrows with a big dent in the side, and beside it was a worse for wear police car. The fat man was belly-down on the roadside verge, hands handcuffed behind his back and mouthing obscenities as blue lights flashed. By the description I gave, my kids agreed the fat man was dressed as a 'Gangsta'.

I went into mourning. My Somerset had changed. Gone was the genial smock dressed yokel chewing on his bit of straw in a Thelwellian countryside. Progress gnaws away at memory. Tarmac turns orchards into empty park-and-rides, and blackbirds chak-a-chack loudly at ten o'clock on an October's night, kept awake by the bright lights of Taunton train station invading the shadows. But there was still another Somerset with corners where the birds could sleep and sing without raising their voices. And I knew where those corners were. All would be well after a mug of Earl Grey tea and dreams of Nempnett Thrubwell.

LESSON EIGHT
PIPS AND PARSONS

"In each plum gourd the cidery bite
of boys' teeth tears the skin;
the waltzing wasp consumes his share,
the bent worm enters in."

Laurie Lee.

Somerset has a self-help economy. To get a job one either has to get off one's backside and go and call upon a friend or failing that, text them. In Somerset it's all about 'who you know', and, with penury ever present, I was lucky enough to know Becky. A school teacher in apple country, an hour away from Wiveliscombe, if driving towards Yeovil at a steady sixty along the A303, she asked someone nicely. I began part-time teaching at a secondary school beyond the sign for rocking horses in the pretty village of Stoke-sub-Hamdon, and got to play with lumps of plasticine and video cameras.

The village sits comfortably on the northern rim of Ham Hill. Full of sculpted hollows hiding picnickers and truants, the hill has been well quarried over the centuries to provide stones of devotion and stones of despair. Although the stone for abbeys, churches, manor houses, and farms 'grew' here, so did the flagstones of the notorious Ilchester gaol and the stone for Ham Hill's amphitheatre. Wild beasts imported from far distant jungles would have fought unfortunate souls to provide entertainment for a Roman holiday. Anyway, that's what I told my students to spice up their days. And just to add depth to my stories, I said that they should check out the molehills for any unearthed scraps of pottery.

The honey-coloured sandstone, imaginatively called 'hamstone', makes almost everything else built from it look warm and safe. And despite the inevitable student-in-a-lather about some clot having thrown his or her shoe, or bag, or worse onto a roof and 'could-I-help-but-not-tell-the-headmaster', I felt a sense of being cocooned from the real world. From the top of Ham Hill you can see as far as the Blackdowns, Mendips, and Quantocks, as well as the foreign Dorset Downs.

Also towards the top is the 'Prince of Wales', a very good pub selling a wonderfully refreshing cider that became temptation's lure. From memory it was heavenly. Trying not to let it become a lunchtime habit, I would wobble-balance myself before returning to school for short after-noons.

Sometimes, when school pressures made it necessary to nestle even closer to God, the desire was there to share sandwiches with the magpies. Being nice to them perhaps ensured they were individually nice to me. Yet there are so many on Ham Hill that the world becomes black and white, and if two bring joy, then joy is multiplied a hundredfold and becomes infectious.

It must have infected Llewellyn Powys who lived a literary life eighty years ago, a feather's spin away at Montacute vicarage. He knew that to take an autumn walk at the end of Ham Hill furthest away from the school was to enjoy the spirit of the ancient hill at its least disturbed. What was dear to him was surely dear to the whole of Somerset. In a prose style sadly now lost in today's scribbled English essays and never tapped into a school laptop, Powys wrote:

'It is easy to understand how the finer spirits of the neighbourhood have taken to the civilised and honourable employment of apple growing, tending their Tom Puts, Horners, Leather Jackets, and Pippins under clouds as grey as the feathers of a wood pigeon's breast, clouds scarcely distinguishable from the blue mists that from morning to evening in the autumnal haze obscure the course of the River Parrett as it idly meanders through one fat meadow after another of the most fertile valley in the West of England'.

Powys wrote at a time when pigeons had beauty and apple trees were commonplace. In the same year as Coleridge penned his Ancient Mariner, John Billingsley recorded *A General View of the Agriculture of the County of Somerset*, a long-winded title that basically meant 'Pissed on the Job':

'Men's daily labour in winter
is 1s per day with cider.
Men's daily labour in summer
is 1s 4d with cider.
Woman's daily labour in winter
Is 6d per day with cider.
Woman's daily labour in summer
is 8d with cider.
Mowing grass 1s 4d per acre, and one
Gallon of cider.'

The hobnail-booted could not function without being fuelled by cider, a tipple made in Somerset for at least seven centuries. Ten per cent of farms were planted with cider apples to provide the daily ration for the field workers. Cider was a country drink not popular in the cities. This had the one big benefit of it being exempt from the tax levied on beer, wines and spirits after the First World War, when the government needed to refill its coffers. With no tax to pay, cider making became profligate and Somerset's farm labourers were kept rosy cheeked.

There was a time when almost every farm had a cider press and every village a cider-house. Apple-picking was the last harvest of the year. Long ashen poles were used to 'rattle' the fruit down from the top most branches. The crop was then plonked in baskets, piled in heaps, and carried away by cart for cider.

In the old days, after the picking was done, village folk used to go gleaning for the apples that remained. Calling it 'pixy-wording', they used to say the fairies held the last fruit on the trees to make a hoard. Although they looked so sparse and few, when put together those stragglers made up 'a tidy vew.' Sadly the fairies are gone, and the pixyworders too. But stories involving varieties of apples abound. It is usually accepted that one apple tree grows one variety of apple. However, I am curious if the old apple tree at Keeper's Cottage in Nunney supports this belief. Certainly, the fourteenth century castle was not the only thing of wonder.

Walt, who lived at Keeper's Cottage, gave Alice a large apple from the tree, when she visited his wife in 1941. What happened afterwards, Alice's daughter Maisie retells:

"The walk home wasn't a short one, so Mum negotiated the fields and stiles and feeling peckish, started to eat the apple. The colour was so inviting, lemon merging with speckled burnished orange. Mum reached home where Dad was due so hurried to prepare tea, dropping the core in the geranium pot outside the kitchen window and forgetting it.

Next spring Dad noticed some tiny plants appearing in the pot. He moved them into the garden and they grew to sizeable trees that produced varying apples; one a codling, one a small sweet red one, the most prolific was orange and lemon shaded, tasting somewhat of Cox's orange.

Mum always used to send apples from those trees to friends at Christmas who knew them as 'Alice's Apples', and all said they were delicious. The apple trees are still there where Dad planted them. What the apples are really called is still a mystery."

In the county as a whole, bringing the apple harvest from orchard to factory each year was eagerly awaited. The owner of the cider factory in Wivey recorded for posterity that "big farmers would send in a team of four, matched, heavy horses. Small farmers, only one. Every equipage was at its smartest, horses well groomed, harness and brasses shone …

The atmosphere was one of pride and rivalry, the air full of the sound of men calling their horses, iron shod feet on the road of men and beast, and wheel, the creaks of leather and wood, the rattle of chains, the smell of apples, horse and healthy outdoor unwashed male." Once the apples were unloaded, the scratting and pressing could begin. Today, the spectacle has been reduced to the Dulverton bus being unable to pass a car on 'double yellows', when its driver has popped into the Wivey Spar for a bottle of cider made from Slovakian concentrate.

Yet with cider once so abundant and with the need to uphold Sunday values, a country parish must have seemed attractive to an open-minded clergyman. The verger of a well used Somerset church, that shall go unnamed so as not to embarrass sensibilities, spoke not of the bells or the rood screen but of the vicar's wife who drank 'fair turrible". Marriages are not the contracts cider helps.

In his parish on the Brendon Hills, the flushed-faced Reverend John lit his pipe, puffed some puffs, and sat back on a sofa that was not his. A bit like my cat, John went wherever the mood took him. And he was never short of invitations. Never have I come across a vicar more affectionately cared for by his church-going parishioners. These folk could have queued to say that John had either brought God into their lives or brought God back. On his good days, if faith had basis in laughter, John would become a saint. When singing 'The Lord is My Shepherd' he was a match for the best of Exmoor voices. His oratory would fill a church whether it was beside the pub in Brompton Regis, behind farmyard ploughs and in the company of chickens in Withiel Florey, or in Skilgate where a woman fed him and on whose sofa he sat.

John, however, was a man with a weakness that, he admitted, was nobody's fault but his own. Cider. And in turn this frailty had given him some problems. Bills went forgotten and unpaid, so to try and telephone him was futile. Driving the roads of his parish carried an element of danger. The non-churchgoers had taken the moral high ground. Letters were written to the Bishop. Sadly, the Church of England did not hold John's view that what goes on behind closed doors is a private life. This was politics, and as Harold Bale, the farmer with the Withiel Florey chickens, told John, "All politicians are as bent as a dog's hind leg". Then, after looking John up and down, Harold added: "You still got permission to wear that collar?"

"Just for a while." John replied with dew filled eyes.

From the safety of the sofa John told me a story set in a town, any town, about a man scattering sand from a bag that he carried.

"'Why are you scattering that sand?' a passer-by asked.

'It's magic sand.' the man replied. 'It keeps dragons away'.

'But there are no dragons here.' observed the passer-by.

'You see,' said the man, 'it works'."

I went on to tell a story of my own by making a television documentary called 'Dragons – A Portrait of a Country Parson' that was broadcast on HTV. It was a story of how the Church had taken away the life of a man of kindness and humanity. Shown at a time when feelings were still raw, Alan and Betty, both churchgoers at Brompton Regis, cried as they shook my hand. 'Thank you' they said.

My story had a footnote. John was given a job behind the counter of a hardware shop in Minehead, until it shut down, unable to compete with the DIY superstores. A 'snitch' recently told me that John used to search for whatever it was customers wanted, screws, curtain hooks, whatever, by first looking underneath his counter. This gave him the opportunity to suck on a plastic tube that led into a box where he had stashed a demi-john of scrumpy. It was practiced skullduggery, before sobriety was forced upon John by his checkout job at Tesco.

How did I know John? Well, he is my son's godfather. Cider should be drunk with caution.

'The Stag' in Dunster also used to keep scrumpy underneath its counter. It was not supposed to be there. If the brewery had found out, it would have been cross. The scrumpy was made by a local man called Bill Liversidge, and sold because it was cheap. The pub was owned by Barbara; a straggle-haired, sunken-cheeked Mancunian in old slippers. She smoked a lot and complained about her customers, 'the Evening Bohemians'. A scruffbag crowd of the unshaven who wore woolly hats, large coats, made rollups and cluttered the place up. Just the look of them, she moaned, made it impossible to succeed in her dream of having an art gallery in the skittle alley.

Also behind the bar was Barbara's son, the bright-eyed ever keen Barnaby; a gangling 'innocent abroad', always wearing the same brightly coloured tank top, and who never spent any money unnecessarily. Occasionally Ken, Barbara's ex–husband, would come down from Manchester 'to make himself useful' and muddle-by willingly. His catch-phrase was 'Ohhh Barnaby!'. I liked that eccentric pub with its random Edwardian sewing machine by the fireplace, the mix-match of comfy time-worn chairs and the gentle banter.

One lunchtime with business its usual slow self, a family of dad and mum and two children on holiday walked in. They were just passing through on their way to Cornwall where they hoped to be by supper. Big and grey-bearded Bill Liversidge sat in blue dungaree overalls on a barstool. Richard, a friend of mine from Libya days, and me were the only other customers.

The dad asked Barnaby what he recommended. The scrumpy under the counter was really good, Barnaby advised. At only a £1 a pint it appealed to his frugality. Obviously driving, the dad looked appealingly at the mum. "'Tis only apple juice" reassured Bill.

By the time Barbara had made the family their order of sandwiches, the dad had finished his pint of 'apple juice'. He was lying on the carpet, holding his tummy, giggling hysterically that his legs had gone 'all funny'. I remember the mum throwing car keys at him. Bill left muttering that there was "little danger of the cidered up running riot once they're wiggling on the floor like upturned beetles. 'Twas dif'runt wi' lager louts, whisky rogues and the ale laries; they're a right pain in the arse." Barbara, bless her heart, offered the family a room for the afternoon. They did not depart until the following morning, but Richard and I had enjoyed the floorshow.

Barbara eventually had to sell up, and she and Barnaby moved to Nether Stowey, possibly to discover their Gormenghast. Sadly 'The Stag' was never the same, becoming a run-of-the-mill eating pub and all very above board. Even the 'Evening Bohemians' went elsewhere.

A little talk to Bill about his 'apple juice' would be good, I thought. So with summer's passing I paid an autumn visit. What would his secret be? "Long grass," he told me. "When the scrumps fall, they won't bruise and turn nasty. Once they wrinkle a bit, they'll be just right." So I asked Bill to put that by me again, and I got it second time round.

Grass around apple trees should never be mown because the long grass protects the ripe windfalls. A windfall apple was the scrump. Those that remained on the tree, failing to mature into anything worthwhile, were the crumplings. These even left a parson disinterested.

A parson, Bill said, used to come there every day and stalk about under his trees. "Fond of apples it was and really loved the pips. Probably shot for the pot now." A few moments of alarm passed before I realised Bill was talking about a cock pheasant. It was the bird's white neck feathers looking like a vicar's dog-collar that made him call it a 'parson'. Rather fitting, I thought.

In Bill's opinion Kingston Black or Stoke Red were best for cider. But for his scrumpy he used whatever fell his way. Scrumpy making was a way to fill his retirement. It was an art, but 'bloody hard work', especially the scratting, which reduced the apples to a pulp called pomace by grinding them with a stone in a stone trough. It was the old way he had learned during his working life spent on the Dunster Castle Estate. Poignantly, he was the last employee to be laid off when the Luttrell family sold to the National Trust.

In a tin-roofed shed shared with the scrap iron from an agricultural past stood a twin-screw cider press. There was a sadness to Bill when he described how the cider 'cheese' was made. In the good days, even just a few years ago, he used straw, but drifting chemical sprays now mean that straw can bestow unwanted nasties into the scrumpy. At this point he got quite heated about 'nouveaux barons' with helicopters and wished that 'Jesus nuts', holding chopper blades to fusilages detached themselves. Anyway, Bill has switched from straw to hessian.

Making the 'cheese' seemed a convoluted process. Bill used a square wooden frame about two and a half feet square centred over a dish that sloped slightly towards a collecting tub. He would then place his hessian over the frame. The pummy of crushed apples was squished into the hessian that he folded over like an envelope. Bill said this apple parcel was called a 'lisson', and I said I was; and imagined a 'Lisson with Mother' all about cider making. I received a good natured grunt whilst noticing his lisson was probably six inches thick. Once done, Bill's hands removed the outer frame and picking up some light ash laths, they made a grid on top of the lisson. Then he did the process over and over again, until he had six lisson layers three feet high. Blowing out his cheeks, he strained to lower the top of the press. Low and behold his 'apple juice' began to flow. If he pressed quickly, he explained, the juice would be light coloured. What he preferred was to do it slowly, so that the juice would be much darker.

The tub below collected the squeezings. Using a plastic funnel and a long plastic tube similar to the Reverend John's, Bill 'racked' or transferred the juice into a steel fermenting barrel. Telling me to pay proper attention instead of admiring his sheep, he insisted that the tube must reach the bottom of the barrel, so that air bubbles did not get into the juice. And apart from sheep that was all there was to see. However, after a period of fermentation Bill would siphon the young scrumpy into a clean barrel and leave it for several weeks. The longer it stayed, the stronger it became. When Bill took a glug and smacked his lips, it would have been time for a barrel to go to 'The Stag'.

As I was about to be on my way, Bill asked me to come back the following March. Thinking that kids needed educating about country matters, he wanted to make a short video about 'How to Skin A Lamb'. He was sure it was something that could be shown in schools. "They have to know about the things that matter" Bill said, nodding in the direction of his grandchildren who were coming towards him holding hands with their dad Russell, Bill's son. Russell was the modern sort of labourer not liking the hard work that brings on a sweat. Instead of a spade he owns a JCB. Apparently it helps his bad back, as he spends his days tearing 'gurt sods' out of West Somerset.

I told Bill I would be back. At least the apple blossom would be nice to look at. Around where I lived, it was sadly becoming scarcer.

A couple of years ago while in Moldova, I met a Serbian called Nebojsa Pjevic. As he could speak English, Nebojsa and I got talking about life's rich tapestry and what not. "If the Serbs came to England, they would eat your dogs," he smiled. I replied they could make a starter out of next door's poodles. "That would probably be enough," Nebojsa said wryly. Serbia was getting smaller. They had lost Montenegro and were in danger of losing Kosovo. "We have a saying that soon all Serbs will be meeting under one tree". It occurred to me that if things went on as they were at home, there would only be one tree for all the cider drinkers of Somerset to meet under.

The old apple orchards with duvets of mistletoe are vanishing under new housing estates. And with the EU taking the view that apple trees are chattels and not part of rural heritage, grant money was given to the unscrupulous, so that continental fruit mountains could be reduced to hills. Apple and pear orchards were rooted up and Somerset roads filled with shiny new four-by-fours; Christmas mistletoe has become really quite expensive.

To be fair, Somerset still has quite a few businesses making cider. Some like Bill are one man bands. Between Walford Cross and Burrowbridge, in a barn on the left hand side of the road, a variety of homemade ciders can be tried by the less squeamish whilst sitting in an old dentist's chair.

However, I think the time has come to dust down the Taunton Stop Line. Sneakily, the county of dwile flonking, tittermatorter housing and windmills has already slipped by. Norfolk is here and its man on the ground, Keith Skipper of Cromer, should be written to and given a right telling off.

Not only has The Gaymer Cider Company ensconced itself in Shepton Mallet, but by a secret recipe of industrial process it is making the clear and clean waters of Somerset have the distinctive taste of Norfolk's River Yare. And whose idea was it? The Yanks.

Gaymer's is owned by Constellation Brands Inc., whose base of operations is in Fairport, New York. American investment has ensured that Gaymer's is the second largest cider maker in the world. A hydraulic ram squeezes cheeses in a Swiss-made Bucher-Guyer press. Just to keep things going, Gaymer's has planted three quarters of a million characterless trees at a mind boggling cost of over three million pounds. From now on in, more than thirty thousand tonnes of apples will be squished every season to bring you the taste of America, with the help of Slovakian apple concentrate by the tanker load.

Blackthorn Cider, that used to be made in Norton Fitzwarren outside Taunton, succumbed to the pressure and that, too, is now made in Shepton Mallet under a watchful Norfolk eye to ensure American profits. But at least Somerset has a first class county cricket team. Norfolk does not.

The Norton Fitzwarren factory was bulldozed to rubble, carried away by lorries, and unceremoniously dumped. Six hundred new homes are being built on the site with an address to delight the few that can afford them: 'The Old Cider Works'. Industrial history is chic. The days of coopers, barrels and drays are gone, so indeed is an output that annually exceeded thirty million gallons.

I am glad to say that west of Bratislava, Sheppy's and Thatcher's ciders, as well as several others, are still hanging on in there as pure Somerset alternatives, true to the high blown verse:

'Where'er the British spread
Triumphant Banners, or their fame has reached
Diffusive, to the utmost bounds of this
Wide Universe, Silurian Cyder borne
Shall please all Tastes, and triumph o'er the Vine.'

Back in Bill Liversidge's stomping ground there remains a winter tradition designed to ensure local apple trees serve up a good harvest in the coming year. Wassailing.

For all intents and purposes it's a fertility rite and a wholly night time affair. The word 'wassail' comes from the Anglo-Saxon words Waes Heil, meaning 'be whole or healthy'. Traditionally people drank to each other's health from a large wassail bowl, filled with a drink such as 'lamb's wool' made of hot cider, nutmeg, and sugar with roasted crab apples. Having drunk the tree's health, people gathered together and fired shotguns into the branches to drive out the evil spirits or the ghosts of thieving birds.

I did not know quite what to expect one January 17th, when I set off to the Butcher's Arms in Carhampton for the first time, but I was sure children of today would rather be shown a video about liquid lamb's wool, rather than about actual lamb's wool and bloody skin.

Both an owl and I arrived at the same time. Either the owl was new to the area, or it had forgotten to look at its calendar. Passing over my head without a hoot or screech, it disappeared into the blackness to hiss and snore somewhere.

I mingled with the crowd as a large bonfire was lit that was soon crackling and spitting sparks. Soon a bunch of men rolled up with shotguns and drinks of hot cider. Then from among them a chap in a waistcoat stepped forward and soaked a piece of toast in a tankard. He then placed the soggy toast in the boughs of what must have been the most venerable apple tree as an offering. As a wreath of bonfire smoke blew over, the rest of the tankard's contents were poured on the roots. 'Oh apple tree, Oh apple tree, we wassail thee!' bellowed the bunch with guns, whilst raising their tankards.

Then the chap in the waistcoat burst into song:
Old apple tree, we wassail thee,
And hoping thou wilt bear
For the Lord doth know where we shall be
Till apples come another year.
For to bear well, and to bear well
So merry let us be,
Let every man take off his hat,
And shout to the old apple tree!
Old apple tree, we wassail thee,
And hoping thou wilt bear
Hatfuls, capfuls and three bushel bagfuls
And a little heap under the stairs,
Hip, Hip, Hooray!

Bang, bang, bang, BANG! The bunch with guns blasted a volley into the top boughs of the tree.

"Oi!" someone shouted from the crowd. "You've shot a pissing owl". Sods' law it was my bird the bunch had made ghost, despite it being innocent of thieving.

I had to wait for a Wurzels gig in Minehead to try hot cider for myself. It went through me like a dose of salts. Cartons of supermarket apple juice mixed with soda were perhaps a better idea for a while.

LESSON NINE
A SOMERSET PATCH

"Youth is the first victim of war, the first fruit of peace.
It takes 20 years or more of peace to make a man; it takes
only 20 seconds of war to destroy him."
(Boudouin)

"Somerset people are not warlike – it is not something in our make-up."
(Harry Patch)

At the end of 2004 the Gaymer Cider Company produced a limited edition premium quality sweet cider. A spokesman for the company said at the time, "It was a fun project for the cider makers." The cider with its quaffable and not too destructive 6.8% volume had been produced to celebrate the life of a special cider-loving pensioner.

It was whilst I was on a tram in Dresden knowing that my eldest son, Lawrence, was in training for his posting to the war in Afghanistan that I remembered Harry Patch. "A sparrow of a man, wheelchair bound but with an astonishingly alert face and self-composed manner" was how the Poet Laureate, Andrew Motion, described him.

When I first heard about the celebration cider, I had been bashed out of the queue for homemade fruitcake at the village fête. Focused octogenarian men had used walking sticks like offensive weapons as they battled for sustenance during the duck races. Whoever the bloke was, deserving to be celebrated by a special cider had to be very special, I grumbled.

The story of Henry John "Harry" Patch begins in the village of Combe Down, which perches on a ridge above and about one and a half miles to the south of Bath city centre. When Arthur Mee penned some lines in 1940, the village was sitting in a sea of buttercups. The only thing to catch his attention was inside the 19th century gothic looking church. It was a window to the men of Combe Down, who passed over in the Great War showing "Christ in a white robe with four roundels of little scenes: Ezra's tomb, Cape Helles with a ship, St Omer with a wooden cross, and Cambrai with an aeroplane flying round its church tower."

He failed to mention the two things that Combe Down was famous for at the time. One was the Jewish burial ground that is now one of only fifteen in the country to survive from the Georgian period. Dating from 1812, the last recorded burial was six years after Mee's visit. The other is a local woodland wild flower. Although he mentioned the buttercups, he perhaps failed to come across Bath Asparagus, also known as the Spiked Star of Bethlehem. The flowers appear on a three-foot high spike in June. At the unopened stage the flowers used to be gathered in small quantities as a fresh vegetable by local people; and occasionally sold in local markets. As the Star of Bethlehem flowered back in 1898, Harry was born in the village on 17th June.

At the time of tapping these words, it had been proposed by Somerset councillors that the thin triangular column of Wellington Monument should be allowed to fall down. It was front page stuff in the 'Welly Weekly', the local rag.

Some say the monument was built as a suck to the 'Iron Duke' who owned a nearby manor, and that it symbolised the bayonets used at the famous battle during the century in which Harry was born. On the other hand, the local historian and television 'Time Team' personality Robin Bush insists that only having three sides saved on concrete. The monument is less about being a suck to a Duke and more about Somerset folk not being over effusive about war. I am sure Harry would agree.

Around the time of the newspaper article Harry has just had his 110th birthday party at the Fletcher House nursing home in Wells, where he lives these days. He remembers war only too well and still poignantly recalls the church window being installed as clearly as recalling his local market selling Bath Asparagus. Harry had become the second oldest living man in Britain, and the last surviving Tommy having faced combat in the First World War. As an extra birthday present he has been made an honorary member of the Royal British Legion.

Before he was called up, Harry was an apprentice plumber. When a private in the Duke of Cornwall's Light Infantry he was a Lewis gunner who fought at the Battle of Passchendaele wearing khaki wool puttees labelled "Fox Wellington Summerset F.P.I. Patent 4214-1909." A more practical manufacture than its monument, Wellington puttees were made 'simple stupid'. Each puttee was marked as left or right by the addition of a small brass plate to the corner of the puttee bearing either an 'L' or 'R.'

The battle claimed the lives of more than 70,000 soldiers in just three months. Heavy rain coincided with the opening assault on 31 July, which produced thick, clinging mud, caking uniforms and clogging up rifles. Sharing his experience of the battle, Harry described it as "mud, mud and more mud mixed together with blood." During the fighting he was badly wounded from shrapnel and three of his best friends were killed when a shell exploded just yards from where he was standing. His war had come to an end.

For others it continued and they are remembered in the Thankful Villages. All the men from Tellisford, Aisholt, Chelwood, Rodney Stoke,

Stocklinch, Stanton Prior and Woolley who went out to the Great War came home again. Seven villages. No other county has so many. There are only another thirty-one lucky villages in all of England that didn't have their beloved lions die because of donkeys.

Harry was rewarded for his military service. He is the proud possessor of the British War Medal and Victory Medal, the National Service Medal and the Hors de combat. In 1999 he was awarded the Légion d'Honneur by the French government together with some three hundred and fifty surviving Great War veterans who fought in the trenches of the Western Front.

In the summer of 2007 Harry revisited the site of the battle in Flanders to pay his respects to the fallen on both sides of the conflict. Beside the war graves, he described war as the "calculated and condoned slaughter of human beings" and said "war isn't worth one life. Any one of them could have been me." Millions of men came to fight in that war and it felt incredible to him that he was now the last survivor in the world.

Recent night time memory flashes, triggered by lights in his nursing home, show the war continuing in his head ninety years after the Armistice. However, in August 2007, his autobiography *The Last Fighting Tommy* was published, making him one of the oldest ever authors. Everything in the book was shadowed by the war, even when the subject had nothing to do with fighting. Harry's early memories of nibbling the apples and pears from a farmer's fruit trees that he reached by crawling along the potato furrows, are couched in language that anticipates his time in Flanders.

Featured in the 2003 television series 'World War I in Colour', he was quoted saying "...if any man tells you he went over the top and he wasn't scared, he's a damn liar."

In the same series, he reflected upon his lost friends and the moment when he came face to face with a German soldier. He recalled Moses descending from Mount Sinai with God's commandment 'thou shalt not kill' and couldn't kill the German. He shot him above the knee and in the ankle. Harry recalled he had about five seconds to make the decision. "I brought him down, but I didn't kill him".

In November 2004, he had met Charles Kuentz, a 108-year-old veteran who had fought on the German side at the battlefield of Passchendaele and who oddly enough was on the French side in World War II. Before they shook hands, Harry was a bit doubtful about meeting a German soldier. However, afterwards he said, "Herr Kuentz is a very nice gentleman. He is all for a united Europe and peace, and so am I". They exchanged gifts, Charles bringing along a tin of Alsatian biscuits and Harry giving him a bottle of Somerset cider in return.

A month after giving away that one bottle, he and his friends were given the present of 106 bottles of 'Patch's Pride Cider' by Gaymers who had been alerted to both his story and the fact that he enjoyed cider. Bottles were also sent to the Bodmin museum of Harry's old regiment. The cider company is happy to admit that Harry helped with the development of the cider, tasting several versions before the final bottles rolled off the production line. It was not designed as a commercial venture, but as a tribute to Harry.

Attributing his long life to clean living, Harry avoids what he describes as the "three sins," smoking, drinking and gambling. "Fresh air, no petrol fumes and no cars," that was his secret of how to survive in Somerset.

The BBC asked him on his recent birthday what the most important thing was to him that had come about during his lifetime. After all, so many changes had happened, so many new inventions.

He was quick to point out that as far as he was concerned most inventions were either by the military or the navy. His personal favourite is the lifeboat as folk risk their lives to help others. It's poignant to point out that perhaps the most astounding feat of West Country lifeboat-men happened in Harry's lifetime, a story that's shared between Devon and Somerset. *Forest Hall*, a three–masted full-rigged ship, floundered in the Bristol Channel on 12th January 1899 during the worst of storms, prompting C. Walter Hodges to write an account of lifeboat heroics in his book *The Overland Launch*. The lifeboat-men were unable to put to sea at Lynmouth. Their only chance to save the *Forest Hall's* crew was to tow the lifeboat by horses overland in the dead of night to Porlock, thirteen miles away, but not before they had ascended steep Countisbury Hill and descended the infamous Porlock Hill. Harry was then barely six months old.

Andrew Motion was commissioned by the BBC's Inside Out programme to compose a work for the veteran. He called it 'The Five Acts of Harry Patch - The Last Fighting Tommy'. The poem was first read at a special event at the Bishop's Palace in Wells where it was introduced by the Prince of Wales saying, "Mr Patch epitomises the courage, long-sufferingness and tenacity of his generation."

After the reading, Harry was quick to say, "It's a great honour to have a poem written for me. That's all I can say."

Harry Patch's life so far is perfectly summed by Andrew Motion. He described the veteran as one of nature's gentlemen, and justifiably proud of his celebrity and his story.

Proud, but bashful. "Most people who become eminent," the Laureate said, "do so as the result of a definite effort of some kind; Harry has achieved his fame by accident. He never meant to be the last survivor of the trenches."

On the 17th June 2008 a message was posted on the 'Army Rumour Service' website:

"Never was the term 'Old Contemptible' more inappropriate but, ironically, more deserving. Happy Birthday Harry."

LESSON TEN
CONCRETE UNDERSTANDING

*"As dawn broke over Taunton to a clear, calm day on Saturday, 2nd April
2005 and after 20 years in the waiting, a bridge over the railway crossing
on the Silk Mills road was lowered into position at approximately 11.00am.
The 1,200-tonne crane took the full weight of the bridge at 8.00am
and the bridge was then gently guided into position to rest on temporary
support stools before being finally fixed into position on its bearings."*
(Somerset County Council.)

It was nothing more than a trip to Taunton Tesco, when Ez and I got stuck
in the jam of goggle eyed traffic. What timing. We watched the large
crane lower the spanning section of the Silk Mills road bridge into place. It
was like putting a lid on the past. By this I don't mean an end to finger-
tapping at the main line level crossing waiting for the 'da-da-da-dum' of
the Penzance to Paddington. Instead, the neatly restored Second World
War concrete shell of a pillbox, squatting beside the railway line was, as we
looked on, being hidden from view. In retirement it's now out of the rain,
boasting a trim of new bricks laid by careful trowels. A shot had never been
fired in anger through any slit embrasure. It had been a story repeated
across the breadth of Somerset. And it's a story worth a mention.

In retrospect, things turned out rather spiffingly. Those magnificent men
in their flying machines did the trick. God bless the Spitfire. However, back
in 1940, like the rest of the nervous nation, Somerset was on the back foot.
The news was out that the British Army had taken a beating at Dunkirk. Any
further decisions affecting the war effort had to be based on the 'what if'
scenario. What if the RAF got a thrashing by the Luftwaffe? What if the
Royal Navy got clobbered? What if Jerry landed in Cornwall and Devon and
fancied its chances of advancing heavy armour on Bristol and beyond into
the English heartlands? Opining that all things Cornish and Devonian
would be rubbish in having any stalling effect, precautions had to be taken
should Somerset become the sleepy front line.

Long before their hardbacks, paperbacks and latest bestsellers
seduced bookworms with the memoirs of war heroes, Waterstones in
Taunton had formerly been the County Hotel. A refinement of pressed
linen tablecloths slightly stained with tea. In June 1940 the hotel hosted
a meeting hastily convened by the Army. Various local building contrac-

tors got invited. There was gloomy acceptance that out of season, the scrum-capped Wivey front row could not be expected to stop a full-on German push into Somerset, nor indeed could any of the best Somerset packs, not even Bath's. It would also have been unreasonable to ask either Harold Gimblett to stand at the wicket at the County Ground and thump grenades high and handsome; or suggest to W.H.R. 'The Hand That Bowled Bradman' Andrews, that he bowl Jerry some bouncers. So the Army turned to that instinctive mix of survival, concrete.

The Army had a plan and it was called 'The Taunton Stop Line', a continuous anti-tank obstacle that would follow the lie of the land and stretch across the county. It was to be one of over fifty similar defensive lines that were constructed around England.

Work got under way with some urgency in Somerset. The local contractors set to and busied themselves building structures of defence and irritation. Men inspired by the Somerset Wyvern implanted heavy sets of concrete molars, aptly nicknamed 'dragons' teeth', alongside riverbanks. They were bad for tanks and good for morale. So all was good and dandy. Almost. There was a problem with the pillboxes.

Although the concrete for the walls was hand made on site, embrasures were available precast and factory produced to standard designs. As these were in short supply, the true spirit of local improvisation prevailed. Embrasures often ended up being made from 'borrowed' bricks or of ripped up concrete paving, causing many a muddied shoe and sprained ankle.

A few months before work got under way, Arthur Mee had written that the best thing of all about Knowle St Giles "is the peace and serenity, a great view, and a bank by the church gate where roses and sweet honeysuckle grow." He probably wished he had kept the secret of the 'great view' to himself, because very soon a large gun emplacement was built to enjoy it.

The whole object of the exercise was to delay Jerry tanks long enough, so that mobile Army units could get theirs acts together and give the unwanted bullies a bloody nose. Well, that was the theory. What they would do it with was another question, as the Army had abandoned most of its equipment in France after the Dunkirk evacuation. The answer was to mobilise the Home Guard, the glorious Dad's Army, and provide some revamped naval guns from World War One.

A state of war was bad for business and especially so if you happened to be master and collector at Somerset's last toll bridge. Freddie Dyer, the last man on the Burrowbridge toll, was ignored. First by the rumbling lorries carrying sand and cement, then by everything else on wheels that followed by example. Poor Freddie must have taken Neville Chamberlain's pre-war joke 'peace in our time' seriously. As the sand of auction ran through the wooden-framed glass, he bid £1,725 in 1939.

The toll was a bad investment. But what could he do? Spitting vitriol at the nest of rifles, or privates with pitchforks, hidden in the pillbox hastily plonked beside his bridge, must just have seemed foolish.

It was not long before the pillboxes became a source of artistic entertainment. At Creech St Michael, the remains of wooden brackets inserted into the concrete can still be seen. They held the camouflage designed to break up the pillbox's outline. And indeed, pillboxes were provided with ingenious disguises. Things even went as far as employing the services of Britain's most celebrated theatrical props designer. Somerset should feel privileged that he found the time. Throughout the 1930s and 1940s, Oliver Messel was the creator of lavish costumes and sets for ballet and stage productions in the country's most prestigious venues. As such, he was the envied rival of Cecil Beaton; not only in professional endeavours, but in private life as well. However, it's best not to dwell on this, save to say that Society tittle-tattle had it that Messel socialised among the most glamorous and extraordinary celebrities of his day. His friends included Noël Coward and Lord Berners. Berners based a character on Messel in his novella *The Girls of Radcliff Hall* (1937). The 'girls' were all based on gay men and Messel was one of them.

Under Messel's guidance, in those odd times of 'lovies' and tomfoolery, it was all about blending in. Pillboxes posed as railway signal boxes, water towers, newsagents, and on the Cad Road, west of Cad Green, one was disguised as a bus shelter with fake timetables on the outer wall facing the road. But if Jerry would ever have thought it possible to catch a bus, our double-agents must really have done a brilliant job. However, Messel's pièce de résistance could arguably have been 'the haystack'. A potential shock awaited courting couples and rambling Germans alike. Messel finally pulled a veil over his state of confusion by later designing HRH Princess Margaret's Mustique island home. How so? Well, Messel was the uncle of her husband, Lord Snowden, erstwhile Anthony Amstrong-Jones. It's nice to think that someone related to the royal family could turn concrete into straw. With today's modern world the way it is, perhaps the time has come for another to step forward and have another go.

However, standing at the junction of the Bridgwater and Taunton canal and the old Taunton Chard canal, and taking a lead from Messel, was the White Lion Inn. A pillbox was built inside on the off chance Jerry fancied a 'swift one' or wished to partake of 'a round'. In his book *Somerset at War,* Mac Hawkins described it as "entirely constructed within a house without disturbing the structure". Some time after the war the pub reverted back to a cottage that's now demolished. The concrete of the pillbox though was too tough to get rid of and is still there.

On its completion the Taunton Stop Line from north to south ran down from the Pawlett Hams, then meandered with the River Parrett before taking off along the Bridgwater and Taunton canal that was full of water, and the Taunton and Chard canal that was not. It met up with and followed the Great Western Railway near Ilton down to Chard, where it took the Southern Railway a spur, until it met the River Axe. After briefly crossing over into Dorset in a couple of places, the Stop Line finally ended at the seaside, on Seaton beach. A phenomenal amount of concrete had been used in constructing over three hundred pillboxes plus machine gun and anti-tank gun emplacements, anti-tank ditches, infantry trenches and of course, dastardly dragons teeth. It was a case of no holes barred.

The Taunton Stop Line was one of over fifty similar defensive lines that were constructed around England, all designed to compartmentalise the country to contain any breakthrough, until reinforcements could arrive. Stop Lines used a combination of geography and construction to make continuous defences. The innermost and longest was the GHQ Line.

And as the Stop Line wended its way south, the General Headquarters Line went east from Highbridge, making the town feel self-important. Then off it went along the River Brue, the Kennet and Avon Canal to Reading, around the south of London, south of Guildford and Aldershot, to Canvey Island and Great Chesterford in Essex, before heading north to end in Yorkshire. The Second World War was a strange time. As tramps knapped stones in exchange for a bed for the night, contractors mixed a concrete heritage. In the end, both were total wastes of time. Hitler invaded Russia instead.

However, the threat of Swastikas on Dunster Yarn Market and flapping from the Bishop's Palace in Wells had been very real for the people of Somerset.

As an epilogue, farmers after the war were paid five quid for each pillbox on their land they could demolish. Despite the cash incentive the pillboxes won. Beaten but unbowed, one farmer near Burrowbridge with an eye to diversification, turned his pillbox into a high security henhouse. At Godney a pillbox stands in a field of spring buttercups and contains a jumble of old farm tools including, just in case it might ever be needed again, a pitch-fork. And not far from Creech St. Michael, concrete road-blocks were hauled a short distance, presumably by tractor power, to become useful milk churn stands. These though are the minority of cases. For the rest of the Taunton Stop Line there is only decay and spray canned graffiti, or, in Nature's attempt to make Oliver Messel clap his fingertips lightly together in happiness, an enveloping cloak of brambles.

I'm glad the pillbox at Silk Mills is safe. A memory with a lid put on it, passed daily by the Penzance to Paddington.

LESSON ELEVEN
THE BECKET CUP

"Treasure your relationships, not your possessions."
(Anthony J. D'Angelo)

The Becket Cup is treasured. It's not something won by an athletic nag at a Point-to-Point, or for thumping a cricket ball, or something sipped from whilst 'waiting for Godot'. But it's apparently a collectors' piece that is hundreds of years old and therefore is worthy of description.

If you are content in Somerset and want to live a long and happy life, it is best you don't toddle off and slay the Archbishop of Canterbury. Such advice went unheeded by Reginald Fitzurse and Richard Brito, who had spent their childhoods together splashing about in the Swilly, the river that gave Williton its name a long, long time ago. Give some folk a nudge and they will gladly call Williton, 'Swillybobs', even today.

Back in 1170 when King Henry II said, "Who will rid me of this turbulent priest?" referring to his friend Thomas Becket, he didn't really mean it. He was pissed, stuck in France, and feeling frustrated that Becket was obstructing his kingly ways. However, Reginald and Richard were among the four men who took Henry at his royal word and travelled on a knights' errand. The other two, William de Tracy and Hugh de Moreville came from Devon and Yorkshire. As Hugh kept back a swelling crowd by poking with his sword, Reginald, Richard and William used theirs to make a mess of Becket's head and brains on the flagstones of Canterbury Cathedral. Unnoticed by the four of them, somebody, it's said, slipped away to find anything useful to scoop the archbishop's lifeblood into.

A broken wooden cup, stained with blood, is a religious relic now kept in Taunton Museum. Long before the days of DNA testing it was found hidden in Kewstoke church behind a sculpted figure built into the wall. Originally, folk say, it had been sold to nearby Woodspring Priory by the monks of Canterbury claiming that it was the cup that had caught the life-blood of Thomas a Becket at the time of his murder.

Historians have thought this story to be plausible. They assume that a priory monk had the bright idea to protect the treasured cup by stashing it away in Kewstoke when the priory was dissolved. Evidence supports the theory because the priory, founded by a grandson of one of Becket's murderers, had a cup as its seal. Also the priory itself was built where the ringleader to the murder, Reginald Fitzurse had earlier made a chapel so that prayers might be offered for his victim's soul.

Then again, if the legends of Glastonbury are anything to go by, monks had a habit of making money for themselves through human gullibility. If someone had thought of bottling 'Becket's Last Breath', saintly air would have been sold far and wide. So chances are that the blood on the cup is that of a luckless bunny, before it was popped into the pot.

Bibblers across Somerset are never slow to agree that 'drink' addles sense. Things can be said that are never meant, and a 'rush of blood' can have unforeseen consequences. This was no different in the case of Henry. When he heard about Thomas's demise, he was really rather cross. As punishment for Reginald's and Richard's ill-judged, impulsive deed, Henry denied Williton its ecclesiastical status to hold a range of church services. This is the reason why there is not an old graveyard in the town.

Legend has it that Reginald and William are buried on Brean Down, which up until the medieval period, when the surrounding land was drained for agricultural purposes, was essentially an island in a swamp. They lie in unhallowed ground facing north, with rare Chalkhill Blue butterflies fluttering around. But when one considers the Becket Cup, the question to be asked is: where lies the fool?

In modern times Brean Down has become famous for radio and film. One of Brean's oldest inhabitants recalls that her parents often spoke to Guglielmo Marconi, when he was experimenting with wireless and said he transmitted the first message across water from Brean Down to Flat Holm. This was before he claimed to have made "the world's first radio transmission" from Brean Down to Lavernock Point near Penarth in 1896.

Over a century later, in June 2006, the cast and crew of the film *The Golden Age*, a film about Elizabeth the First, descended on Brean. Huge tents and props were craned into position and the Down became a huge set for star Cate Blanchett to be centre stage. Dressed in gleaming armour and sat on horseback, she gave her rousing speech of defending England from the Spanish Armada surrounded by mock cannon and two hundred extras running around wielding pikes, and other weaponry. Perhaps the ghosts of Reginald and William would not have looked too much out of place, just a little retro.

LESSON TWELVE
POLES APART

"Which is better: to have fun with fungi or to have idiocy with ideology?"
(Aldous Huxley, writer)

After the Norman invasion, give or take several centuries, came the Poles. And now Tesco's in Taunton provides food shelves sagging with heavy brown East European bread. One Polish man was twenty years ahead of the plumbers and decorators, pig slaughterers and turnip-tuggers, hand-scythers and those beckoned by the call to work at Butlins. He listens to long-term forecasts and waits for the turning of the tide.

Somerset is home to Tad Manziej, that's 'Man-jay', a bango, bodhran, and Northumbrian bag-pipe playing sculptor and woodcarver. Indeed, the Canadians once crowned him 'Woodcarving Champion of the World' and he is the man who carved the palace gates for the Shah of Iran. Imagine former Pope John Paul II and you will have a physical likeness of Tad in your head. They were related. Tad, however, chuckles that he is Asian despite his Polishness and being a British subject. And instead of being a good Catholic, he describes himself as an 'aesthetic recyclist', saying that after departing this life his atoms will be of some organic benefit to Somerset, if not to the cosmos. Should that be the case, the barley in Porlock Vale will undoubtedly grow a tad more golden.

But it's another of nature's harvests that Tad looks forward to most. When the year feels neither half in, nor half out, he will yearn for "a little bit of dry and a little bit of wet," and utter wistfully, "Oooh, autumn in the woods," and rub his hands happily together. It's the season for fungi and collecting them is in his blood. Holding a wicker basket by a handle that has the patina of years, he will wander West Somerset seeking out morning delights upon moss bank and amongst leaf mould. The Boletus cep, or 'penny bun' is his passion, and the sound of sizzling ceps fills the breakfast kitchen in early autumn. The table, spread with sheets of news-paper, is annually covered with an assortment of chanterelles and hedge-hogs, parasols and shaggy ink caps, stink horns and fly agarics. Many will be for eating, others will be carefully chosen as models for his wood whit-tled carvings of beauty.

The worry for him is that he now has competition from the Polish influx. Scarcity, caused by congestion, is not something he likes to dwell on. He remembers the last time Poles were here in any great numbers. They had formed a large part of workforce that built the vast Wimbleball reservoir and dam at the time he first arrived in Somerset. The peaceful corners around Upton and Brompton Regis were full of big men in plastic bright yellow raincoats carrying small baskets, tip-toeing about the woods. After the construction ended Tad had the pick of things more or less to himself by using nature's clock. But no longer can a cockcrow be relied upon. As people set their alarms earlier and earlier to beat the rush hour, in the quiet of West Somerset Tad will need to do the same.

The autumn's all very well, but what about the rest of the year? What does Tad do then?

Well, if the truth be told he designs things in his head. A collapsible canoe, he thinks, would be great to take on the bus. And then there's his Dimples Theory. Why does a golf ball have dimples? To make it aerodynamic, of course. Dimples reduce drag.

So what if you put dimples on a boat hull? Now there was a question. Tad had been playing mind games with dimples of differing shapes: squares, rectangles, and hexagons. And hexagons, he thought, would be best. Asking why he kept the Dimple Theory to himself, Tad was quick to reply. If the Poles got to hear of it, they would set sail from Swininoujscie and Gdansk and be here quicker than a flight on Easy Jet.

What hope of finding a cep then?

He was born in Kurdkurdistan into a Polish refuge convoy that left Siberia, trying to escape the 1939-1945 war by tugboat, train and lorry. One of his earliest memories was aboard a ship under the cover of darkness. Nearly everyone else was below deck and Tad was with his mother, leaning against the ship's rail watching a twinkle of lights across the sea. "That's Mauritius," his mother told him. The Poles were arriving in Africa.

What has this story got to do with Somerset, you may ask? Well, one of the places Tad's convoy stopped was the mud hut village of Bwana Ma Kubwa, near the Zambian city of Ndola. Many years later, when Tad was living in West Somerset, he strayed into the 'Notley Arms' in Monksilver, to wet his whistle. At the time the pub was owned by Jim Mellors, a larger than life South African fellow who had formerly been a hangman. Above the bar hung a beautifully carved wooden spoon. Tad complimented Jim on the workmanship. Giving the broadest of smiles, Jim agreed that it was very good. Adding that he had given the carver a three-day reprieve to finish the spoon before he hanged him. When Tad mentioned that he had passed through Africa as a child, Jim asked:

"You weren't in the convoy of Poles in that mud hut village of Bwana Ma Kubwa I saw whilst waiting for the spoon?"

Not long after the bar room episode Tad went to look at a fallen lime tree in a garden, on the outskirts of Wivey, as a possible source of wood. The garden belonged to Baden Powell's daughter, who was then well advanced in her years. She and Tad got talking and discovered that they both had spent childhoods in Africa. After Tad spoke of the convoy, she queried whether he had been one of the Polish refugees in the mud hut village of Bwana Ma Kubwa. She had been a volunteer there at the time, helping the nuns. Bless.

After his world adventures, Tad had arrived in England accompanied by his cousin, Waldemar Januszczak. Waldemar was later to become Head of Arts at Channel 4 television and art critic for *The Sunday Times.* After Tad moved to West Somerset in the late 1980s the pair would take walks in the countryside around Tad's Williton home. One day they were ambling close to a house called 'Bardon' owned by Tad's friend Roy Heard, a man who loves telling tales about the house being haunted.

Across the fields and behind Waldemar's back, Tad saw a black Labrador being taken for a walk. So a little mischief crossed Tad's mind, and he being a rascal-roodle, it stuck there. Keeping his eyes on the Labrador, he tickled Waldemar's imagination with a story.

Among Bardon's ghosts is a black dog seen on the lawn by Thomas Joyce, a former partner in the Williton solicitors firm of Risdon and Co. Thinking the dog newsworthy, Joyce told Clement Kille, a journalist at the *West Somerset Free Press,* all about it. In true reporting style, Kille dug deeper and found an aged local with a tale about an exorcism. There had been more than a phantom pooch at Bardon. The early 1800s had seen seven parsons with bell book and candle cause the house spirits to take on the solid form of a black dog possessed by a rage of snarls. The parsons were clever in their shrinkage because the ghosts included a coach and horses, a man carrying another's head under his arm, a lady harpsicord player in a silk dress and a white dove. A brave servant grabbed the dog, shoved a halter over its neck, dragged it to the nearest pond and chucked it in. Despite the parson's warning him not to look when splash followed yelp, the servant could not help himself. He had to peep and saw a pillar of flame shooting upwards from the pond. The job done by the parsons was rubbish, Thomas Joyce could vouch for that. However, the pond had felt its last touch of warmth and has remained an eerie and chill place ever since.

As Tad saw the black Labrador heading towards a gate he managed to manoeuvre Waldemar around just before the tail and hind legs vanished from sight. As white as fine flour, Waldemar, pointed a trembling finger and exclaimed "Did you see that? It's the Black Dog!"

"What dog?" said Tad, knowing full well that his friend Roy would relish hearing about it.

And he did.

However, Tad has a serious side. This showed itself as we were prattling on at his kitchen table about swearing-cap-wearing-kids yanking at studded collars on nasty dogs and telling older generations to 'get-a-loife'. The phone rang. "Ace Abortions. No foetus can beat us" he said, answering it as jocular as ever. Tad plays with words like other men of his age compulsively play with trains. But that call was not the time for mirth. Someone, a Polish speaker, needed Tad's help and it was needed urgently.

Polish people had gained a reputation in Somerset for working hard and well, both on the farm and in the building trades. There are companies that have exploited this ruthlessly. Scurrilous Polish speaking 'gangmasters' recruit Polish labour.

They did this for a local property developer 'doing up' Williton's old workhouse. The company's reputation had already seen them banned from trading in other parts of Europe. But through a network that spread back to Warsaw, young Polish men were told that they could have a guaranteed job in Somerset, if they first parted with £300. About £1000 to an English wallet. Promises of earning £7 or more an hour were given in return.

Mental arithmetic did the sums that this was sound investment. Sadly, so many were taken in.

The newcomers, who live in fear of losing what little work they've found, are beyond the reach of the well-integrated first-generation Polish community that includes Tad. Once on the Williton site £7 quickly became £3 following company 'deductions' for bedding, rudimentary cooking and washing facilities and the 'usage' of non-existent cars. None of the workers had the safety of National Insurance stamps and they had become little better than slave labourers.

It was a whistle-blower who was contacting Tad for help. The workers needed an interpreter so they could expose the rookery-nook. Unsurprisingly, the company's response was predictable. Loaded minibuses were driven to Norton Fitzwarren and even to Cornwall. The Polish problem simply melted away, before television and radio could gain any interviews. Quite literally, the Poles had been taken for a ride. And those that went were soon replaced. Since the autumn of 2007 it became a criminal offence for a business to use 'an unlicensed labour provider'.

Gangmasters found guilty face a prison sentence of up to 10 years or a £10,000 fine, or both. But, as yet, no one has been prosecuted. Tad's anger is absorbed by his worldly wise eyes. As a sculptor he knows the two sides of the human face are never the same.

Such wisdom is respected and recently prompted Watchet Town Council to ask if he would help choose a statue. Somebody had had the bright idea to have a statue cast of Coleridge's Ancient Mariner, for no other reason than the poet having had the germ of an idea in a Bell Inn bedroom. Despite feeling miffed that he hadn't been invited to submit a design of his own, Tad's good nature prevailed. He was soon surveying a range of waxes produced by hopeful artists and being scrutinised by a room full of eyes. The chairman of the AMSC, the Ancient Mariner Selection Committee had a personal favourite and, such is the power of a personality, this was undisputedly the one to go for. But what did Tad think?

"The mariner appears to have a deceased herring gull at his feet," observed Tad, "I thought the bugger killed an albatross. An albatross has a wingspan of eleven feet.

"You're going to pay £12,000 for a herring gull, when you should be getting more bird for your money." A few bums shifted uneasily on seats.

There was a clearing of a throat and a whispered voice asked whether Tad would like to submit something of his own. This was met by a brave nod of heads and a scowl from the Chairman. Tad, however, was happy to oblige and a month later produced a manikin of wax of his own interpretation, complete with crossbow and proportional albatross. Rumours soon filtered through that the majority of the AMSC liked his effort best. Sadly though, there was no happy ending to the story. The herring gull just became bigger. When Tad rang the Town Council asking to have his model returned to him, there was hesitation at the other end of the line, before a voice said "I'm very sorry, but it's broken. The Chairman accidentally sat on it."

The Ancient Mariner, sculpted by Alan Herriot, a Scottish laddie, now stands on Watchet's Esplanade and is proof of the fact that there are some stubborn folk in Somerset.

A few yards away from the mariner, a statue of John Short cast by the same Scot appeared in spring 2008. Nicknamed 'Yankee Jack', Short was a true son of Watchet, who was both a sailor and a famous shantyman. He consigned words and tunes of dozens of shanties to memory and never wrote anything down. The common belief that what he memorised was actually correct probably came from the power of persuasion and sheer weight of personality. Needless to say, when the statue was being commissioned, Tad didn't get a look in.

The usual Watchet youths in caps and hoodies were hanging out in the Espalanade shelters the last time I strolled passed 'Yanky Jack'. On cue, a herring gull flew from his cap having done what comes naturally.

As the white splotch dripped from peek onto nose, the thought came to me that Tad is poles apart.

At Sunday Folk Night opposite the 'Bearin' Up' the sash-windows of the 'White Hart' were half-opened to the street on a damp May evening. Joe, his beard and shoulder length hair damp with effort, sang lustily that there was "a rattling flea, on the rattling feather, on the rattling wing, on a rattling bird, on the rattling nest, on the rattling leaf, on the rattling twig, on the rattling branch, on the rattling tree that grows in the bog in the valley." Burning off a supper of Thorne's lamb and mint sausages, rake-thin Kitt from Rotton Row further bruised his acoustic guitar in accompaniment. Helped by the breeze from the window, Tad on the cider worked up a sweat beating away at the bohran, the Irish drum. Taut pigskin played by an untaught pig, he claimed. The usual load of nonsense full of shrewd half-truths.

LESSON THIRTEEN
INDIANS ON HORSEBACK

"Remember that the most valuable antiques are dear old friends."
(H. Jackson Brown, Jr., American writer)

Somerset is full of old stuff and some makes its way into antique and bric-a-brac shops, where woodworms make their kingdoms of dust and metal becomes tarnished.

Pat McHale used to have just such a shop in Roadwater, just around the corner from Cleeve Abbey. Called 'Junk and Disorderly', the shop was a pun at his own expense because, if the truth be told, Pat was a bit of a biddler. He used to drive around in a cast-off undertaker's hearse and be tickled with amusement when pedestrians doffed their hats and caps, paying reverence to a passing wardrobe with death-watch beetle.

Whenever he was asked what his speciality was, Pat would reply that he dealt in the 'carcass trade'. And he always had a keen interest in the antique world around him. There was a wealth of good stories, but the one about his friend Chris Giddings and the Remmington was perhaps his favourite.

Chris, a Wivey-based antiques trader, who had a corner shop in the town square where a café is today, was a familiar character to locals. His Wivey storeroom, a disused Methodist chapel, was featured in local news-papers when it was invaded by a massive flock of starlings that 'darkened the sky'. When the birds finally departed they left a heap of guano, esti-mated to weigh a couple of tonnes, against the back wall of the chapel. Chris, however, claimed the estimation was "a load of old crap".

Under a battered cloth cap, his grey bearded face, with glasses on the end of his nose, became unmistakable after he was the subject of an HTV television documentary made by the resident filmmaker Ronnie Maasz. Ronnie had had the responsibility of being the cameraman in the back of the Minis in the original 1969 version of 'The Italian Job', because he was so tiny. The experience of having fifteen minutes of TV fame made Chris chuckle, especially when he recalled the time Ronnie did a whole day's filming without putting a tape in the camera. Had he not been so absent-minded, the story of the Remmington could have been captured on film for posterity.

Remmington bronzes are figurines, each one unique, that embody the spirit of the American West. Cowboys and Indians, stallions and ponies, are all very, very collectable by the wealthy wallets with thousands of pounds to spare. Whenever the President of the United States made a speech to the camera, there was invariably a Remmington standing symbolically behind him.

Tad was walking down a street in Minehead, without the asset of money. His surprise can be imagined when he chanced upon a bronze labelled 'An Indian on Horseback', with Remmington stamped on its base, standing prominently in a shop window. And he could have been knocked over by a fezzie feather when he saw the price ticket. The shop was only asking £300, but this was still a couple of hundred more than Tad had to his name.

All he could do was try and borrow. It was the opportunity of a lifetime. He off hurried to find his friend Chris Giddings.

When Tad told him the story of the Minehead Remmington, Chris was equally excited and readily lent Tad the money that he needed. The sale was made and, with thoughts of happy retirement, Tad and Chris rushed to take the bronze to the local auction rooms to get the Remmington valued. The valuer gave it one look and said "Not another Indian on Horseback, people have been bringing them in every day for the past week. Value? £20 tops." The bronze was counterfeit, a forgery; and Tad had lost £100 of his own money and now owed Chris £200.

"Oh well, not to worry" said Chris, "Let me take it back to my shop. Perhaps we can get £480 for it." As good as his word, Chris placed the bronze, with a small attached label that read 'Indian on Horseback', in his Wivey shop window. Not right at the front, but discreetly behind some other objects, with just enough of a view to generate interest from a knowledgeable eye.

After a short while a local rival cast a quick glance at Chris's window and took a second take. Seeing him outside, Chris went and hid in the back of the shop. There was a mutual loathing between the two of them. With a ding the door opened, and after counting to ten, Chris re-emerged from his hiding place.

"What have you got there then?" asked the rival, pointing at the bronze.

"Oh, just an Indian on horseback."

"How much do you want for it?"

"What it says on the ticket."

"Seems a bit steep. Perhaps I'll come back, but I don't know if I will."

With that, the rival went out the door. By craning his neck, Chris watched him scuttle across to the bank at a rate of knots. A couple of minutes later Chris's shop door bell dinged the familiar ding.

"£480, you said?"

"Yep." And the deal was done.

"You're a bloody fool, Giddings," said Chris's rival, with a largest of grins as he left, clutching the bronze to what was undoubtedly his fast beating heart.

The following day the rival was back. He was holding the bronze and was absolutely fuming.

"This isn't a Remmington!"

"I never said it was," said Chris. So Tad got his money back with more than a fair amount of interest.

LESSON FOURTEEN
CARAVANS AND CABBAGES

"The song that we sang could be heard for miles around
the air was full of harmony you should have heard the sound
as we gathered up our differences and threw them in the air
and gave them to the wind that shakes the barley."
('Harvest of the Moon', Steeleye Span)

Felix was staring out the car window at a gypsy caravan at rest on a wide roadside verge. Washing, draped over a spoked wheel, dried in the wind. A white horse grazed while tethered to a mallet banged peg, as a waist-coated man tinkered with a primus stove. Close by a young girl was repeatedly throwing a cabbage in the air and catching it again.

"Would you like to live like that, Dad?" Felix asked.

As I rubber-necked, a 'Wind in the Willows' image drifted into my mind of Mr Toad riding a canary coloured cart along the open road. My leaky roof, I thought, was no better than one made of canvas over a frame of sticks. Like a goldfish, I opened my mouth, then shut it again. The romantic me was gagged by the practical one. The home washing machine was churning away at my children's spoon to mouth food disasters, and at the blood and mud of the sports field. Then I remembered my snuggly duvet and that I was allergic to horses.

"Dad?"

"No," I said, "I don't want a life like that." But I knew there were people who did, and they lived at Tinker's Bubble, close by the school where I taught in Stoke-sub-Hamdon. The evocative name stems from the time when hippies and travellers took it upon their fancy to camp by the bubbling hill spring. A few put down roots and now it's muddled into an organic farming commune. Like most other people I first heard of 'The Bubble' by word of mouth.

"A bunch of nutters in baggy jumpers picking peas at midnight," was how a fellow member of staff described the rural affair to me in an apparent need to let off steam. I was all ears, welcoming the distraction from scraping plasticine away from behind my fingernails. To call anybody 'a bunch of nutters' seemed a bit harsh when born out of a somewhat biased opinion. Singular irritation can become collective. A scruffy mum had lost her rag in a school corridor when told that her tousled-haired darling of a son needed to 'smarten up', because he looked like 'Stig of the Dump'. He was one of four children who lived with twelve grown-ups under trees, in a cluster of self-built houses on top of the hill. They overlooked the house and garden of Lord Paddy Ashdown, the former leader of the Liberal Democrats. This recollection made me inwardly cringe.

Once, when researching a lightweight film about celebrities and their cats, and knowing that Paddy had one that used to sit on his House of Commons questions, I telephoned his secretary. Paddy's, not the cat's. I explained what I was doing and asked "Would Mr Ashdown be prepared to get involved?" Without hesitation, the reply was negative.

"Sorry, but Mr Ashdown is too busy at the moment. And we would want to avoid headlines like 'Paddy Likes his Pussy', wouldn't we really?" On reflection, I had been a little insensitive. At the time the tabloids were chocker with allegations of a secretarial affair. Far better than that, he is remembered fondly by his constituents. One in particular had cause to thank him. Karl Schmidt, now a man in his nineties who clicks his heels together when he greets you, was once a conscripted soldier in the Nazi SS. After the war he became a psychiatrist. Caught up in Sarawak jungle fighting during the Borneo and Malaysia confrontation in the mid 1960's, a British SAS officer personally pulled Karl to safety. That officer was Paddy Ashdown.

Paddy was happy to be distracted by his first constituency communards. When they initially clubbed together to buy the land at Tinker's Bubble, South Somerset district council turned down their planning application to build something called 'low-impact housing'. With Paddy's help the appeal was won. I had read about this in an article by Robert Nurden appearing in the *Independent on Sunday*. Although I learned that ragwort could poison cows called Milly, Fern and Bracken, and that one man had a penchant for picking up a hand scythe at five in the morning, Mr Nurden didn't say what low-impact housing was.

I got it into my head that it was to do with navigational troubles and wasting fossil fuels. Hilltop skimming antique aircraft escaping Yeovilton's Fleet Air Arm Museum and tree hopping naval helicopters armed to the teeth often have Tinker's Bubble on their roaring and 'der-der-derring' flight paths. There was a frightening possibility, to coin the phrase bandied about by folk of alternative persuasions, of 'becoming grounded'. But surely I was being silly. So who to ask?

I went to find Neil West, who would be dressed in a tricorn hat, frock coat, and silver buckled shoes, hammering a dulcimer with a pair of wooden spoons outside Taunton's pig market. He had featured in an article in the *Exmoor* magazine about his 'Baggins Wood' dulcimer making business and would know about all things low-impact.

"Benders and hobbit homes," he laughed. He has lost it, I thought.

I knew that a few guddlers in the Bearin' Up were prone to the odd bender and that Neil was a Tolkien obsessive.

"Elucidate," I said.

Apparently a bender was a home made from a frame of hazel branches lashed together with string and covered with tarpaulin. A Hobbit home was more interesting. What you need is a rubbish pile or a skip and access to woodland. Anything you can possibly want is in a skip somewhere, Neil insisted. Windows, floorboards, plumbing, wiring, stove can all be rummaged out in a manner more Borrower than Baggins.

"And, you'll often find a hobbit home covered in mud," he advised.

No kidding! Hardly surprising in fields awash with puddles and feet tied into black bin liners, splish-sploshing around.

Neil though ploughed on. The house frame and roof rafters are made of spare oak wood.

Together with sheep fleeces, straw bales straight from neighbouring farmers make great insulation and are like big 'Duplo' to build with. They are good for the floor, roof and walls. And the walls can even be coated with lime plaster, which is breathable and low energy. Spread plastic sheets over the rafters and cover the lot with turf, or mud. And there you have it, a home worthy of The Shire.

"You don't know Tinker's Bubble, do you?" I ventured cautiously.

"Know it? I've stayed there as a Wwoof (World Wide Opportunities on Organic Farms) volunteer."

I was intrigued. "Can you introduce me?"

"Even to Samson."

"Samson?"

The forty-two acres at 'the top of the hill' is laid to woodland, meadow, garden and orchard. Munching on grass amongst the apple trees was fittingly a large Shire horse. This was Samson, who seemed only too content to be idle rather than do the farm work and heavy moving that was his chore when summoned. Edging forwards to say hello got me stung by an abundance of nettles. Having reached for one of a large choice of dock leaves, I asked if the problem was ever attended to. "Of course. Nettles are Wwoof work" said Neil. I couldn't disagree, as I rubbed vigorously with a dock, that Bubble corner had gone to the dogs. Samson gave a snort, flicked his tail, and ignored me.

Mostly though, everything seemed very pretty and functioned reasonably well. The longer folk stay, the more hobbit homes have replaced benders. And the main communal building offered Hobbitdom at its most beautiful with kitchen, sitting area and loft, safe under a thatch of recycled reeds. Pots, dishes and sink, however, were relegated to the outside world of sparrow and midge to save space.

Energy at the Bubble comes from solar panels and a rusty windmill, which together provide electricity for lighting, a fridge and electric fences. Pumped spring water is abundant. When things first began back in 1994, the aim was to provide a place for people earning their living from the land 'sustainably and collectively'. It sounded like a grand idea, but conditions were tough. According to modern legend, rain fell consecutively for eighty-seven days. There was very little money, poor sanitation and comparatively little knowledge and skill. But they have been a hardy bunch and many have hung on being gluttons for punishment, if not for food. Veggie stewpots get added rather than run out. And 'healthy' brown rice and bean curry, dolloped with homemade yogurt from the communal kitchen is eaten sitting on logs, hunched around a fire like in the olden days.

Any sense of the medieval though evaporates when the telephone rings. This magic communicator is the sop to modernity. The line had been put in by the BBC for Libby Purves and her Midweek team for a programme they had broadcast from the Bubble. After the departure of Broken Biscuit Company, as it is fondly known by former ITV colleagues of mine, the communards thought the phone might as well be kept. This was despite sullen protests from a few hardcore traditionalists. But it struck me that the place was getting known, attracting radio and newspaper journalists, grafters like Neil and the merely curious like visiting eco-warriors from the USA. One writer on Somerset, Selena Merrett, lives in a yurt, a copy of the traditional Mongolian nomadic tent, and has this to say about new-age dwellings:

"I feel more dignified, more real, more alive, more creative, and more intuitive when I am in that kind of space. It's very hard to focus on the sacred in everything when you're living in a flat, in a tower block, made with unnatural materials that exude toxic fumes. I really believe that everyone has their part to play in restoring the Earth and if we all followed what inspired us we could discover our unique part in that jigsaw."

A more locally based eco-warrior is Simon Fairlie, the early morning scyther, who lives within the commune. Others grow cabbages and stuff, make herbal medicines or 'bodge' chair legs to sell at the weekly Farmer's Market in Glastonbury, or outside a local primary school. Simon sells scythes from the Potato Store at Flaxdrayton Farm, a small exhaust plume away up the A303. He swears by the hand-forged Austrian scythe called a Schröckenfux. But if the truth be told, so do those that help him scythe a four-acre field by hand before the sun is up, to ensure they make a full day of it. Certainly, if I was ever forced from under my duvet, I'd be saying more than "Stuff this for a bunch of monkeys."

Simon is proud of his Schröckenfuxes and imports them directly from the factory where they have been made since 1540. They are lighter, nimbler, more elegantly formed and easier for the novice to sharpen than traditional English scythes. Yet I couldn't help that snippet of Wurzel wisdom "I've got a brand new combine harvester, and I'll give you the key," from sticking in my brain.

There are still people around who remember the days before combine harvesters and mowing the first strip of wheat around the outside of the field to make room for the binder. It was jaw dropping for me to hear that scything with a good tool relaxes the mind and attunes the body. As Levin says to his brother after a day's mowing, in Tolstoy's *Anna Karenina*: "You can't imagine what an effectual remedy it is for every sort of foolishness." That told me.

Simon, I learned, subscribed to Ivan Illich's aim of retooling society with convivial tools that "allow men to achieve purposes with energy fully under their own control". The man is a scythe anorak. Whole kits can be bought off him including sharpening stones, peening equipment used for reshaping blades buckled on bolders and snaths. A snath is just another name for a scythe's handle. But I quote:

"The word snath can be spelt about as many ways as the name Shakespeare: 'snaith', 'snathe' and 'snead' are the most common variants. The Oxford English Dictionary gives ten different spellings which it says are "irregular and difficult to account for". The word comes from the word 'snead' or 'sned', meaning a lopped pole or branch from a tree, and a snedding axe is still the term for the tool used for limbing felled trees. It is related to the German 'schneiden', to cut. The US pronunciation rhymes with their pronunciation of the word "bath" or the English word "hath". Heigh ho.

Simon uses the 'hath' way of saying it. He is keen to point out that in the UK, as well as the US, he has heard 'snathe' rhyme with bathe, 'snaith' rhyme with bathos, 'sned' rhyme with bed, 'sneed' rhyme with bead, and 'snuth' rhyme with the Geordie bath, but never 'snarth' to rhyme with the upper-class bath. I prefer to still call a handle 'a handle'.

When I asked whether he knew the Somerset word for a scythe was 'Zyve', he told me it was irrelevant.

The long-term aim of Simon and his gallant supporters is to revive the activity of scything in the UK. "Scything summer growth by hand is usually quicker than using a strimmer, and there is no noise, vibration or pollution. Scything an acre of grass is probably less hassle than maintaining and using a motor scythe. Once you have learnt how to sharpen and use an Austrian scythe properly, mowing a meadow by hand becomes a joy, rather than a struggle." Way to go, Simon. The joy of a meadow is in flowers like the lady's smock and in butterflies, and not in hay-fevered eyes and sneezes.

In Muchelney church ladies' smocks could be put to pious use. The barrel-vaulted ceiling is decorated with Tudor angels with naked breasts. Less stuffy souls annually brave the pollen at Muchelney's annual West Country Scything Championships that are organised of course by Simon. In 2007 over a thousand people watched folk hacking as quickly as possible at five metre square patches of long grass. English took on Austrian and lost. The overall competition winner was another Simon, this time from Cambridgeshire, who learned to mow in Romania. After a rapid swish and swash he finished in a couple of minutes.

Potato Store Simon told the Polish website 'Polski portal o Anglii': "Eastern Europeans have maintained the traditions of mowing by hand, whereas in the UK it very nearly died out. We hope that migrant workers over here who are a dab hand will enter." He even had flyers printed in Polish and Slovak ahead of the Muchelney event. Very thoughtful.

Among the also-rans was a seven months pregnant Somerset lass who completed her plot in under eight and a half minutes with her Schröckenfux. Then there was the chap who despite a recent kidney transplant, scythed steadily to finish a close forty seven minutes after the newly crowned champion. He blamed his performance on short interruptions for cider, philosophical reflections and using an old fashioned English scythe.

Back at Tinkers Bubble, decisions are taken at monthly meetings. Up to now none has decided to invest in strimmers to attack the nettles, when folk become sick of the sight of a scythe. Such an ailment seems remote as Simon has the moral support of Mike, a former tea-planter in Sri Lanka, "green Christian" and fellow communard, who adamantly agrees that the Austrian scythe is superior to the English model. "Look at the way this blade curves just the right amount at just the right point. Ruthlessly efficient."

Unfortunately it still rains a lot and even Austrian blades rust if left out too long. Yet even if rain falls in stair-rods, gardens, if not nettle patches, continue to be weeded and planted. There are more than one or two grumbles, some come from folk who have moths attacking their fleece-lined roofs, but more particularly from kids who are actively encouraged to grow their own vegetables. They probably dream of fish fingers or a 'Maccy D' when they paddle about in mud, searching for free range teatime eggs laid by damp sulky hens.

Picking peas at midnight wasn't so daft, if you believe the local lore.

Sow seeds under a waxing moon if they are above ground plants like cabbage, peas and beans. Sow under a waning moon, if they are underground plants like carrots, leeks and swedes. If the moon's good for sowing seeds, why not for picking the peas?

Seen from over the rim of a grande Starbucks mug, the white vergeside horse was pulling the caravan down Taunton High Street, slowly led by the waist-coated man who had probably peened many a scythe. Perhaps he was on his way to buy a part for his primus stove or another cabbage. The large queue of motorised traffic stretching out behind honked its collective irritation. From around the corner came the tune 'Harvest of the Moon' played on a dulcimer by a pair of wooden spoons.

LESSON FIFTEEN
LONG STRIDES AND DINING FORKS

"Manners are a sensitive awareness of the feelings of others. If you have that awareness, you have good manners, no matter what fork you use."
(Emily Post, 'Etiquette')

Despite being only a small village in the meadows below Ham Hill, Odcombe was worth praising for its wholesome and pleasant air, its wool, its sweet springs of water, and most importantly, the love and unity of its inhabitants. A place so endeared to the heart of a chap called Tom Coryate that he felt compelled to mention his thoughts. He considered the village church 'being erected upon so loftie a place that it overprieth and overtoppeth the whole countrie round about ... we all from the verie highest to the lowest are most firmly knit together in an indissoluble knot of friendship." They were words written just before the start of a great adventure.

I was in Venice where that adventure led him, sitting on my cold backside, my camera on my lap, in the middle of St Mark's Square. It was early December in 2006 and I felt a little self-conscious, although I was fortified by mulled wine from a Christmas market. An odd couple in black capes and floppy, wide-brimmed, black felt hats photographed each other, as I filmed them in close up being perches for large numbers of Venetian pigeons.

Yes, they may have been an odd couple, but I didn't think they were the Odcombe couple that should have arrived by now. The pair in the viewfinder looked too arty and showed none of the wear and tear of having walked and cycled from that praiseworthy village that is down the way from Tinker's Bubble.

For my part, I was making a documentary about a Moldovan in Thailand. Do not ask why, as the reason was very complicated. On the other hand, Chris Worledge and Michele Roberts, both thirty-somethings, had set off for Venice for a clear reason. They were following Tom for charity. It was their hope to raise money to help fund the construction of wells and dams in the Eastern Province of Kenya, supporting the Akamba Tribe and for Breakthrough Breast Cancer, the UK's leading breast cancer charity. With a bicycle each they had left Odcombe five months earlier.

If Chris and Michele were following Tom, then Tom must have arrived at an earlier date. He did, by nearly four hundred years, and became an inspiration. Thomas was born the vicar's son in 1579. After setting out from Odcombe in 1608, he not only walked east of Frome, but all the way to Venice. In five months he travelled one thousand nine hundred and seventy five miles with only one pair of shoes to his name.

To have achieved what he did gave a hint that Tom was an educated man, and he was. Oxford scholared, he became part of the household of Henry Prince of Wales, the oldest son of James I, where he was a sort of unofficial court jester. This probably had something to do with his appearance. He was a strange looking, freakish, dwarf-like man, with a heart large enough to take on the world. "The shape of his head was like a sugar loaf inverted, with the little end before, as composed of fancy and memory, without any common sense," Fuller wrote rather unflatteringly about him when Tom was still around to read it. It's always good to know who your friends are.

And Tom had some special ones. They all went to the same London pub, the Mermaid Tavern in Bread Street, Tom calling them the "Right Generous, Joviall, and Mercuriall Sirenaickes." Their names were John Donne, Ben Jonson, and William Shakespeare. However, even they couldn't dissuade their friend who called himself 'The Legge-stretcher' and 'The Peregrine of Odcombe', setting off on his first epic journey to walk to Venice and back with his 'sugar-loaf inverted' on his broad shoulders, having understandably tired of court life.

Tom wrote down the story of his European adventure on his return to Somerset. Before he did so, he hung his shoes up on a hook in the nave of Odcombe church, where they remained until 1702, when they seem to have vanished. Perhaps the soles went to heaven.

The book itself was a strange mixture of travel observations and poetry. Not for him a simple title to arouse local curiosity like 'From Odcombe to Frome and Beyond', instead Tom called it something much more descriptive. The title to trip off the tongue was "Coryats Crudities, Hastilie gobled up in five moneths travells in France, Savoy, Italy, Rhetia, commonly called the Grisons country, Helvetia alias Switzerland, some parts of high Germany and the Netherlands; newly digested in the hungrie aire of Odcombe in the County of Somerset, 1611."

Getting the work out proved difficult, because in those days the king had to give his permission for any book to be published, and James I did not like Tom's. Only after pressure from the Prince of Wales did James finally consent. Perhaps it had something to do with a petition Tom wrote to his princely patron, to "cherish and maintaine the scintillant embers of my diminutive lampe by infusing into them the quickening oyle of your gracious indulgence." The king is addressed as "Most scintillant Phosphorus of our British Trinacria," and the queen as "Most resplendant Gem and radiant Aurora of Great Brittaines spacious Hemisphere." Flattery can get you anywhere, even into print.

Overnight Tom was a big success. London's elite was interested in all things Italian, and his accounts of life in Italy were avidly read, especially his descriptions of the use of table forks and parasols, unknown in Britain at the time. Somerset can be proud that one of its own gets the credit for introducing civilised meal times and possibly elegant picnics.

To all intents and purposes 'Crudities' was the first guidebook, centuries ahead of ' The Rough Guide' and 'Lonely Planet', and showed the way for hundreds of wealthy young men who took what became known as the 'Grand Tour'. However, only one reference to Tom still remains on his actual route. Near the top of Passo St Marco, in the Italian Alpi Orbie, is a plaque on a mountain refuge, thanking Tom for copying down the original Latin inscription on the last building in the Venetian Empire. It's a long walk from Odcombe.

When I got home to Somerset from my trip to Venice, I discovered that Chris and Michele were feeding the pigeons in St Mark's Square a month before the arty couple. It would take them a further seven months to get back to Odcombe to discover they had raised a thousand pounds. Perhaps it wasn't much, but like Tom, they had made a contribution. One is reminded of how rapid a long strider he was by the final paragraph of his book:

"The Cities that I saw in the space of these five Moneths, are five and forty. Whereof in France five. In Savoy one. In Helvetia three. In some parts of high Germanie fifteene. In the Netherlands seven. FINIS."

In 1612, the leg-stretching son of Somerset was off again, travelling through Asia Minor and Egypt, then back to Palestine and eastwards to Persia and India, where he passed on five years later to await his soles joining him in heaven.

A Hamstone replica of Tom's shoes was commissioned in the year 2000 to celebrate the Millennium and can be found in Odcombe Church. However, a more convenient reminder of Tom can be found in the fork tray of the cutlery drawer.

MUD-HORSE IN HOT WATER

"Privately owned Hinkley 'B' with its massive outpouring of isotopes contributes to making the Bristol Channel the most tritium-contaminated sea in the world. We believe radioactive pollution has increased cancer deaths from Minehead to Burnham. Nuclear power is not cheap and it is not safe."

('Stop Hinkley', March 2008.)

I had known Mark Hirst since we had been teenage undergraduates. He was understandably nervous of all things nuclear, as 'things nuclear' could potentially go wrong. Even the best intentions had that habit. Now a senior manager in one of London's NHS Trusts, early discovery of the next year's budget had already put him near the edge. Stress was never his strong point. Now with designer grey stubble and grey coordinated T-shirt with 'Nineteen Sixty Nine' printed across the chest, I was clueless to the significance of such words under a grey rain cloud sky. He shifted uneasily when I stopped to take a photograph of 'Burnt Cottage', a small house actually called that, sitting under intersecting electricity lines. They were lines attached to competing sets of giant pylons brazenly marching out from Hinkley Point nuclear power station. And we both felt the buzz.

"We don't have to go," I said.

But that September morning, Mark wanted to carry on and meet Brendon Sellick. I had told Mark so much about the mud-horse fisherman of Stolford. And after I'd pointed him in the direction of a website exhibiting the black and white work of photographer Scott Ramsey, Mark had deserted his job for a whole twenty-four hours. Best of friends at university, its end had seen us go very different ways. Or was it that girl, Virginia? The memory, it fades.

For Mark and me the university daze was a half-life ago, which is nothing compared to the millions of years half-life of nuclear waste. A nightmare inheritance. As we drove around the corner one culprit loomed at us, a problem with a heart of uranium filled tubes. Looking like oversized rectangular boxes, the Advanced Gas-cooled Reactor of Hinkley B - the 'B', locals feel sure, stands for 'beast' - feeds beside the intertidal mudflats of Bridgwater Bay.

Close by, where the River Parrett flows into the bay from 'Turkeyland', is a world of saltmarsh, shingle ridges, and sandflats that offer happiness to waterfowl and wintering waders wanting a diet of ragworms and lugworms, if not glow-worms.

The 'beast', however, craves only a liquid diet, sucking greedily at soft water from the Brendon Hills. This is then demineralised and made artificial by a treatment process that's the first of its kind in Britain. A meddling with nature that becomes the ultra-pure stuff, scientists say, essential for reactor cooling, or for heating into steam, so that generating turbines, capable of supplying electricity to over a million homes, can be turned. Either way, the wet stuff of nuclear soothing ends up being released into the sea, and fish find themselves in hot water. Something they can enjoy for several years to come.

Standing on the mudflats at Stolford with the horror vision of the 'beast' less than a mile away, Mark and I were in the realm not so much of the Wimbrel and Bar-Tailed Godwit but of the guinea-pig. I took a moment to reflect, that once after police had escorted trundling lorries containing guessed secrets through the streets of Bridgwater in the dead of night, I had seen the 'beast's' insides through my camera eye. Having taken the nuclear shilling for a day, I had peered out at the indescribable through a visor, a feature of the full-on encasing silver coloured headgear, coming with matching suit, gloves and boots. Collectively, it was a drag of heavy sweat and protective lead. But having signed some papers, thrust under my nose by an official shirt and tie at the time, I can't say more than that. However, Paddy Ashdown, the saviour of 'Tinker's Bubble' and now a sponsor of the 'Stop Hinkley' campaign, has no such qualms:

"Hinkley 'B' managers have admitted there are several cracks in the graphite moderator bricks which make up its reactor core. These could delay or make impossible the insertion of control rods that shut down the reactor in an emergency. Moreover the cracks could create that emergency through localised overheating. Hinkley 'B' is due to close in 2011, but British Energy has amazingly indicated they would like to extend the life of the cracked, polluting reactor for another ten years."

It's all a bit of a worry and Paddy has been joined by some famous voices including Julie Christie, star the film 'Don't Look Now' and Raymond Briggs, writer and illustrator of the nuclear age book *When the Wind Blows*, a work the *Guardian* thought was "meant to break your heart to some purpose." These are heavy times in Somerset.

"So does Brendon really sell radioactive fish to the Dutch?" Mark felt compelled to ask, having heard the rumour.

How does one answer a direct question like that? With a fudge, I suppose. What Brendon had told me, more than ten years before, was that fish, and particularly eels, liked the warm waters around the power station's outflow pipe. To safeguard its own reputation, the Ministry of Food and Fisheries wasn't too keen to give a clean bill of health to what Brendon caught there, but in Holland people didn't seem to give a damn.

However, with an attitude of 'better the Devil you know', local folk continued to troll up to 'Mud-Horse Cottage' and see what Brendon had to offer. Now he is semi-retired and has passed the mantle of 'The Last Mud-Horse Fisherman' to his son, Adrian. It's a title that attracts the weekend broadsheets. Journos and paparazzi regularly appear up to their waists in mud, looking for new angles that tell commuters stuck in static M25 jams either how easy city life is, or what a romantic world they're missing. Despite my daily commute being from study desk to kitchen kettle via the carpeted stairs of home, I've formed my own opinion of the goings-on in that place of gales, bleakness and crying gulls.

If the Sellicks weren't pushing their part-driftwood contraption, nailed and lashed into a Neolithic design, of something half-sledge and half-hostess trolley carrying one or two wicker baskets at a time, then what? The only other jobs realistically available to Adrian are local yoghurt making, or across the mud in the bowels of the 'beast'. So of the three choices, it's mud-horsing that retains a certain cachet; although things aren't as they used to be. Adrian feels the urge for yoghurt. For Brendon there was only retirement. Back in the 1930s, Brendon's dad caught a 100-lb sturgeon that was offered to Buckingham Palace. Perhaps from some foresight, it was politely refused.

Both Brendon and Adrian have been described as relics working the mudflats considered by many as fathomless. The pair are the legacy of the communities that have worked here before King Alfred had to worry about Danes. A local historian has claimed that up to fourteen families once earned their living from mud-horse fishing. Even fifty years ago there would still have been about eight men.

Now with just the one mud-horse remaining, father and son still feel the need to slip and slide a hazardous navigation over the treacherous surface to the fishing grounds. Work is year round, and tide dependent. And it's dangerous toil. Once the tide turns, it can come in fast and the Sellicks have to move quickly, yet carefully. Not wanting to be alarmist, the slurping, oozing mud has the potential to swallow a man whole.

Eight to nine days will often be fished in a row until the neap tide enforces a break of a day or so to rest tired limbs. Rather than put his feet up in front of the telly on Christmas Day, Adrian has been known to don his waterproofs and go in search of the glory of Cod, conveniently missing out on the Queen's speech and miserable deaths on 'Eastenders'.

He is obviously a man who loves his work.

"Look at it. You can do a 360° turn here and it's beautiful. You can't do that in an office, all you get is the bare walls. No sound pollution either - just the wind and the gulls," he was quoted as saying in the *Daily Telegraph*.

The methods of catch are primitive, but effective. At the tide's edge, the Sellicks have battered stakes into the soft banks of mud a mile from the shore. Between the stakes they have strung thin, long funnel-shaped nets. The tide comes in and then, as the waters withdraw, the fish appear: cod and whiting in the winter; skate, sea bass and ling in the summer. August to October hopefully brings in a shellfish bonus.

Not long ago Brendon, in resigned acceptance, told a national newspaper that there used to be far more fish and shrimp. In truth there's not enough for the Sellicks to even eke out a living in what's become an economic Somerset sideshow.

'I blame the power station,' he said. 'They use so much water that it pulls in the shrimps, diluting the stock. They say that the amount of water going through Hinkley Point over four years is equal to the whole of the Bristol Channel.' This shows no sign of improving, as the government is considering building a new generation of nuclear stations with Hinkley Point a favourite site, despite all the indications that renewables can fill the energy gap.

Adrian, on the other hand, pointed the finger at overfishing by trawlers with drift nets and felt like a matchstick in an Olympic pool. Perhaps both Sellicks are right and that only makes matters worse.

On our arrival the Sellick chalkboard boasted 'Shrimps, live eels, flat fish, Dover Sole, Cod, Skate, Bass, Whiting, Conger, Bait.' But only shrimp, bait, and the non-committal 'flat fish' were 'on' at a price. The door was open to the outhouse of sinks, fish tanks and gutting knives that doubles-up as a shop. But it was deserted, and the small wood-fired stove used for boiling shellfish was cold. The weather had become chilly, too, with the wind beginning to whistle in imitation of a kettle. I suddenly felt isolated and a long way from home.

Far out on the horizon I had to squint to see one lonely figure sledging in the company of what looked like two dogs. The Sellick was on his knees pushing with the feet, whilst supporting both waist and forearms on the mud-horse. Beyond was Cardiff, invisible in the sea-fret. Either Brendon or Adrian was having a day off. But whichever Sellick was out there, with it being September, I wondered if there was a sieve of shrimp to be had, should Mark and I have the patience to wait an hour or two. Mark suggested we light the stove just in case. I reminded him the four-legged things halfway to Wales only 'looked' like dogs. Nuclear paranoia has a strange effect, and Mark's forced joke about shrimp becoming lobsters really wasn't funny.

Ten minutes later we decided to wend our way. Mark made his excuses that he wasn't too keen to carry a parcel of wet fish home on the train. And me? Safe to say, I had a packet of fish fingers waiting in the freezer cabinet of the Wivey Co-op.

Although environmentalists and rose-tinted spectacled journos make a habit of seeing mud-horsing as sound, sustainable fishing, they needed to pull their fingers out about 'things nuclear'. As the '125' pulled out of Taunton station, I realised Mark never did meet Brendon Sellick, and more than likely never would. The Hinkley Beast could well see to that, and no bird with a lugworm would care.

LESSON SEVENTEEN
FEZZIES AND GUZZLERS

"Gilded with leaf-thick paint, a steady
Eye fixed like a ruby rock;
Across the cidrous banks of autumn
Swaggers the stamping pheasant cock."
Lauries Lee

It was the season of nuts. The chimney was swept and the jackdaw evicted. Piled up behind my blue front gate and sawdust sprinkled, was the annual delivery of logs awaiting cold night burning. As mice became moon bandits, blinking, neck-swivelling, owls hooted nearer and louder. My crosspatch son, Lawrence, found himself compelled to open his bedroom window at two in the morning and shout at the neighbour's roof, "Shut up, you bloody owl!" The owl got off lightly.

With morning chill came the real autumn tingles. Snails, daddygranfers, biddles and yes, emerged from goodness knows where to make an uninterrupted trek to the log pile. The spiders who wove their dew drenched wonders of the world, were ignored. As was the blackbird and thrush breakfasting on manky windfalls and the last squidgy blackberry. Lawrence, then still in his teens, was too focused to notice.

The giant copper beech in Wivey churchyard got naked, its leaf spin settling upon the grave of William Bale, a Battle of Waterloo veteran, who had survived the guns in 1815. On the higher ground close by, a modern army was gathering. Lawrence enlisted and armed with a stout stick, went off to bash bushes with his cousin Lizzie. A new campaign was afoot against a feathered foe and survival was not an option. Rag oiled and ritually cleaned, shotguns were slipped into canvas bags and slung into four by fours. Labradors and Spaniels wagged tails, panting with wet-tongued excitement. October was here and business was brisk at the Wivey gun shop in the town square, where local business is tied up 'belt and braces' and delivered by Chelsea tractor, that sport utility vehicle, or SUV for short, like the Range Rover.

Polly Toynbee writing in the *Guardian* said that 'Land Rover rage is not a particularly pleasant trait'. However, Jeremy Clarkson's sod-you-all, I-hope-you-fry-in-global-warming face seems to be imprinted on the bonnet of every gas-guzzler in Wivey.

And this is a worry to me, as my hero worshipping sons are impressionable.

In vogue monster Japanese off-roaders' park hugger-mugger on the pavement outside the gun shop alongside mud-splattered Range Rovers, as those of the sporting life rush to buy the tweeds and the Barbours, Brasher sticks and gaiters essential for autumn country living. Traffic wardens kept their distance or were vilified. The wisp-bearded builder from 'Woodlouse Conservation' was seen out and about wearing a hat with a bird's long tail feather stuck in it, making promises he would be unable to keep, because he had the fever. Whilst far away in the lands east of Frome, young suited executives 'pow-pow-powed' with their fingers ahead of a shooting party weekend. Even Clint Eastwood and Ronald Reagan added celebrity to the Wivey blast. And all because of that Asian bird, Phasianus colchicus, locally known as 'the fezzie', or more properly as the pheasant.

The fezzie has become a feature of the countryside and of the Somerset psyche. Folk call them 'long-tail rabbits' and my children grew up with the Wurzel tongue twister:
  "I'm not a pheasant plucker,
  I'm a pheasant plucker's son;
  And I'll keep on plucking pheasants
  'Til the pheasant plucker comes."

My sons enjoyed shouting this around the house, accidentally on purpose ensuring the 'PL' became 'F'; so much so, that I was forever thinking my soft spot for them was a bog in the middle of Exmoor. And with my daughters, they were encouraged to look out for red lorries and yellow lorries while on the bus to Taunton. But like it or not, fezzies were everywhere.

The famous Wright brothers, thatchers of Compton Dundon, made a thatched pheasant their trademark on roofs throughout the county. They were a 'must have' rural accessory, much more subtle than a girt great SUV.

I told my sons that I accepted that people in rural areas should be entitled to drive whatever they find necessary to do their business; even, Lord help us, SUVs. But the sight of the smug sitting high up above the rest of us in their great tanks, a danger to all around, got my gander. These were my thoughts when Tony ran over my foot. I told him his Range Rover was a hazard to pedestrians like me, who had to negotiate a maze of bumpers to get to the Co-op. And judging by the numbers of local road kills, it was more a danger to pheasants than his gun was. If his tyres failed to kill them, then the carbon dioxide that his vehicle spewed out would. With that I went wheezing on my way. A week later Tony and I were having a drink in the 'Bearin' Up' and it gave me the opportunity to take off my slipper and sock and show him my bruised toes. "Sorry," he said. Which is all I wanted him to say in the first place.

What was the point of having something as big or even bigger than a Range Rover, I asked him. Looking smug all over again, he replied, that if it happened to hit something, anything, there was more of a chance of getting home afterwards. I thought about this before deciding that the Volkswagen Beetle, the people's car, must have been the poor man's SUV. By having had its engine up its backside, there was always a better chance of getting home, I could vouch for that. Take Maud for example. She was the lovely white Beetle I once owned that died with a loud fart on Porlock Hill. Before that she had survived, by tractor rescue, rolling nose downwards into the River Barle at Dulverton's Marsh Bridge, when I went for a walk leaving the handbrake off. And she survived a meandering forward descent down a Hawkridge hill scaring a Devon border control of weasels half to death amongst the pink campion. Again I had repeated the handbrake mistake. That latter incident had knackered me to jelly legs and nausea in my compulsion to chase her. And so I learned my lesson.

Tony listened sympathetically above the noise of the guddlers, then disagreed that a Beetle, even Maud, could ever have been a poor man's SUV. His Range Rover, he said, would never die with a fart.

During the lazy summer days clans of young fezzie striplings, called poults, were let go to soak up the rays. But the time soon came when they inadvisably dithered about.

One morning, with the crackle of guns not far distant, and Tony's in amongst them, the season to 'bite the pullet' and of the 'Pulletizer Prize' was underway. Three cock fezzies took it upon themselves to become absent for a while. Unfortunately, with pea brains rattling, and a beating of wings, they landed in Wivey's town square, a few yards from the gun shop door. For a few minutes they sat on the bench beside the iconic 'Elephant Dick'. For those not in the know, this is a modern work of sculpture that cost the Parish Council thousands of pounds to commission from a local artist; in recognition of the surrounding hills of the Blackdowns, Brendons, and Exmoor. The elected men and women of Wivey take it very seriously and the Somerset County Archaeologist calls it 'fantastic'. Although made of wood capped with silver metal, it's tall, black, and with the appearance of having wrinkles, so looking like the larger variety of hunting trophy the unelected locals of the 'Bearin' Up' describe it as.

Anyway, the arrival of a shiny black Isuzu Warrior, probably the most impressively immense of Wivey's regular SUVs, caused the three fezzies to stir themselves. Watching the driver suddenly hurry into the gun shop, possibly to make a fast and impulsive firearms purchase, motivated the birds into an act of bravado. They mooched over and admired their reflections in the vehicle's wheel hubs that shone mirror bright. Maybe they had to look their dignified best if their time was up, or had become aware that their numbers had magically doubled and had gone to say 'hello'. Whatever the reason, as the gun shop door reopened, the birds' heads turned as one with expressions that seemed to say: "Go on then, we dare you. There are witnesses."

One witness, an elderly lady, was on hand to waggle her walking stick and shoo the three birds away. Two took to the air and glided downhill towards the churchyard; but the third ran into the road and under a car driven by the traditionally built woman who was a home help from 'Somerset Care'. The wisp-bearded builder was on hand to add another feather to his hat as he carried away his supper.

However, it is not just SUVs that are a hazard to fezzies. My car currently is as well. As the woods wore the colour of autumn's meld, I drove in dappled sunshine, with the driver's window down, alone in my thoughts and enjoying the moment. A good distance ahead were two brown-boring hen pheasants looking to cross the road from right to left.

Being cautious of clots, I slowed down. You can never be too sure about fezzies. A fraction before I reached them, Clot One decided to play chicken and take off across the road in a rapid flurry of feathers. Her friend, not wanting to be abandoned, frantically followed suit. Clot One made it to the other side of the road. Clot Two did not. Making a serious miscalculation of judgment, she thudded against the underside of my doorframe. And like the ball during an unlucky Saturday at Yeovil Town FC, she 'hit the bar and bounced in'.

So I had a fezzie on my lap. A frantic kerfuffle of feathers and whirring wings beat at my face and arms. I went into incoming wasp mode, wide eyed and hand flicking. Neither of us was particularly happy about that state of affairs. Only in grabbing her by the neck, did I manage to get the car door open with a free hand and bundle the traumatised bird out. I am sure both of us lost several soul parts, but Clot Two had also lost her continence. To top it all she lost a considerable number of those small downy, floaty feathers, you can blow in the air as easily as a dandelion clock. These had attached themselves to her splodges of poo that made the inside of the car look like it had suffered a paint-ball attack.

I pulled a grubby tissue from my pocket, and smear-wiped the dripping steering wheel, before doing a three-point turn in the road and heading home to change my trousers and jacket and have a bath.

Looking back in my rear view mirror I saw Clot One and Clot Two tiptoe back across the road to where they had started. Was it just a game after all, I thought? By applying this principle to the shooting season, if a gun was to miss first time around, what was needed was the patience to have another go. What goes around comes around. There was always plenty of opportunity in the busy shoots round about. Although some of the busier ones can be a cause of local chuntering.

Take the very big and very private fezzie shoot outside Dulverton, for example. I came across it by ear, when a small peroxide blonde of a woman was spitting venom from her stalled beige Volvo estate stalled mid stream in Bury ford. Two dogs, that would not recognise a fezzie if they bumped into one, lay in the back with paws over their ears sharing space with a saddle and tack. I did not know whether it was the voice of their mistress or the very weird noises that blared from the woods that had this effect. The electronic sounds, like hawk screams, were a deterrent for foxes and weasels who thought fezzie tasty.

I do not think the alarms were doing the blonde any favours either. She had worked herself up into a fair old state. Her car's engine had become flooded. A misadventure caused by a lack of 'voompf' whilst driving through had allowed the waters of the River Barle to be sucked up the car's exhaust pipe. With water lapping at door-sills, help was on hand from opposite directions in the form of Gareth, a neighbourly homeopathic doctor and me. With the accompaniment of a gun symphony, Gareth approached with caution; wading to the rescue, to give advice about feet on accelerator pedals, 'giving it welly' and the benefits of the river weed impatiens controlling a temper. This seemed to prompt madam to begin thumping her mobile phone on the car dashboard and explode into a tirade about her pet plan insurance only covering her horse, we having no right to have smiles on our faces, and all men being useless. After a chivalrous push to shore and a point disproved, several minutes of raised bonnet delay while the plugs dried out, the cantankerous blonde was on her way.

As two pairs of doggy eyes vanished in a smoky bunny hop around the bend, I followed Gareth, as he went to put the kettle on with guns still going pop-pop-pop-pop-pop. The parties were in full swing.

Over a brew of camomile Gareth had a moan about finding pellets in his pants as they dried on his washing line, before complaining about the mallards. Both pants and mallards were in the same arc of fire. Shot pellets were landing in the Barle in such numbers as to cause lead poisoning to feeding wildfowl. "It's been a bit of a duck up," he said.

Eric Smith, an Exmoor forest ranger, calculated that a commercial shoot in the Luxborough valley, based on an equation of ounces per shot x number of guns fired x period of time, exceeds several tonnes in a single hillside. Adding weight to the rumour that a blind Japanese businessman shot six brace of fezzies in a day a few autumns ago. Not wanting to detract from his achievement, but by all accounts his 'bag' was a particularly scraggy one. It was not fit for the pot and gave rise to the local phrase 'Bite the Pullet'. Somerset's target of choice is now mass-produced by the million. Should quality suffer too much, there are mumbles in the 'Bearin' Up' of awarding a 'Pulletizer Prize' for the most novel method of dispatch.

The smaller shoots tend to be more genial, plumper affairs. Some farmer or other is always good enough to set aside some land as a pheasant wood, so that a bunch of friends can gather around a primus stove leant against the hedge. Then it is just a case of waiting for the whistling kettle and instant coffees topped up by the contents of hip flasks, before the trudge to the poles to fire at flying feathers. The grown ups tend to do the shooting and the kids do the bush beating to flush the fezzies out. As the guns go off, dogs sniff out the casualties to be hung out on a washing line between trees. It's a very simple pastime making for many a pockmarked tree and patted doggy head.

During a question and answer session at Wivey's Kingsmead Community School, the teacher asked Lawrence if he had ever been beaten in his life. "Yes," said Lawrence, "nearly every Saturday in the pheasant season." Later, I got a letter inviting me to his parents' evening.

However, no self-respecting porch feels dressed without a brace of hanging fezzies to tickle the postman's nose. Sadly, we did not have a porch. So when Lawrence returned with his first day's payment for 'beatin', there was nowhere for them to go but behind the door of the downstairs loo. This caused a sudden fit of screams from my daughter Maddy, when nature called. I thought it best if Lawrence's fezzies were removed forthwith and found a recipe that was a really nourishing means of disposal. But I have two pieces of advice. First, chew carefully, because lead is painful to the teeth and, with the proof of ducks, indigestible; and secondly, have a blow-torch handy. The latter advice is nothing to do with the actual cooking process, but everything to do with preparation. Plucking a fezzie's big feathers is fairly straightforward, however the little ones are a pain in the bum. Gently scorching the fezzie with the blow-torch will get rid of them.

Pot Roasted Fezzie
Serves 4. Prep time: 20 minutes. Cooking time: 1 hour 20 minutes.
One brace of fezzies, cleaned
50g of butter

1tbsp vegetable oil
12 shallots, peeled
2 bay leaves
4 sprigs thyme
3 glugs apple brandy
50ml red wine
2tbsp tomato puree
300ml light chicken stock
4 rashers of Somerset streaky bacon

Method:
Melt the butter and oil together in a heavy based deep pan, then season the fezzies. Place the fezzies into the pan and seal on all sides. Add the shallots and brown. Then add the bacon and fry for two minutes. Pour over the brandy and flame. Add the red wine and stock and bring up to a simmer. Add the bay leaf, tomato puree and the sprigs of thyme. Cover with a lid and place into the oven, cook gently for an hour or so, until tender.

When cooked, remove the fezzies and keep them warm. Strain the liquid into a saucepan and reduce by half. To thicken add a teaspoon of cornflour mixed with a little water and stir it in. Bring back to the boil, reduce the heat to a simmer and cook for five minutes.

To serve, pour the sauce over the fezzies on a platter and portion them up at the table under peoples' noses. Sumshus.

LESSON EIGHTEEN
A THORNE IN THE FLESH

"If we're not supposed to eat animals,
how come they're made out of meat?"
(Tom Snyder, Amerivan TV personality).

If you are standing second in queue, in the half light of Christmas Eve morning outside the door of one of the top one hundred shops in the world, the decision in which direction to turn your bum is important. We're not talking about a queue outside Selfridge's, London, here, or even Jayalakshmi in Cochin, Southern India, but Thorne's the Butcher in Wivey.

Point your bottom one way, and the queue behind will head back along the white walled 'London House', towards the sound of the Santa hatted brass band playing carols conducted by Charlie Donald. Point it the other, and folk can look at the public gardens, desultory blackbirds and the littered excesses of the previous night's revellers. It all depends on your degree of humbug. For the majority, getting to see Mike Thorne in the flesh is a high-light of Christmas, that is if next day's dinner is to be a local turkey or a goose, or even a duck or a free-range chicken.

Mike and his family will have been at work into the early hours getting things prepared. Checking the hand scribbled order book against a final computer list of three hundred Levels-reared turkeys, twenty-five geese, fifty ducks and eighty or so chickens, falls upon his wife, Rosemary. Then there's the finickity job of labelling what bird belongs to whom, and ensuring there are enough marrow-bones for a ribbon-tied present under the tree in homes with a wag-tail pooch.

But even having taken such care to get the orders right, modern relation-ships can chuck googlies of delay. The unmarrieds with partners are the problem. A turkey may have been ordered by 'Brown' and pencilled into the order book as "Brown 12 lb turkey", but will be eagerly asked for from the front of the queue by 'Green'. Of course such a problem will solve itself after much crosschecking and deduction, but secrets will out. The Chinese whisper will make its way back with the festive greetings through the queue. "Oh, did you know that 'so-and-so' and 'so-and-so' are living in sin." By the time the whisper gets to the end of the line the named couple have more than likely been happily married for years. Such is the way with gossip. The joys of shopping locally can have its problems.

Mike talked over a boiling kettle in the back 'snug' during his tea break, as I wondered why there was an old £1 note in a plastic bag pinned above the doorframe. Adjusting the spectacles on the end of his nose, he advised me that the process of Christmas ordering should be a mutual decision, wherever possible.

Very occasionally somebody, he had observed, would want something for nothing. One year, not too long ago, a lady was insistent that she had to have a tenpound turkey. Mike apologised that the closest he could provide was ten and a half pounds. After a pause she again insisted on getting the round ten. Much to Mike's amusement, those in the queue behind the lady's back began to aim silently mouthed insults. He and they were no fools and knew that the lady was haggling for the larger bird with the cost of half a pound knocked off. The saying 'every little helps' didn't cut any Yuletide ice with Wivey folk.

As the microwave pinged, Mike's twin grown up sons, Jason and Jonathan, known as 'J' and "J", adding constant confusion to customers who only 'think' they know who is who, began to clatter around us, handling steaming tin pans of cooked pie mixture and the beef, pork and sausage meat mix of faggots.

"Useful things, faggots," nodded Mike, "An easy supper warmed up in onion gravy, or sliced cold into a salad."

This was traditional fare to sit beside the newly tempting. Meatballs and spareribs in sauces, and fancy cuts of meat are time-consumingly prepared these days to catch a customer's eye. Sadly, the half-legs of lamb or pork, so much a part of my own family's Sunday roasts, have become unfashionable.

Sausages, however, are as popular as they were even before Mike and Rosemary bought the place back in 1979. When a chap called Dick Hawkins owned it, the distinguished actor Sir Michael Hordern, that long-faced character player of the rumpled establishment, came again and again just to buy bangers. He was as impressive playing 'King Lear' as he was 'Badger' in *Wind in the Willows*. And as police inspector Bashford in the film 'Passport to Pimlico', he was the very epitome of the English constabulary, a meld of dignity and bafflement.

On me telling him this, Mike believed he had recently met such a copper. It was after a gang of thieves broke into his shop a night not long ago. Having made a mess of drawers and shelves, and leaving the door to the cold store wide open, all managed to get away scot-free with nothing more than a bad temper, despite leaving their faces on the new CCTV outside the 'Bearin' Up'. Mike is careful with his cash these days. Kids after drug money, he thinks. Or, as was the sage-like agreement in the 'Bearin' Up', 'three fast-food knuckleheads who had heard mention of joints'. Whatever the reason, the need to have a solid metal door and an iron bar security gate installed within a rural shop is enough to make one weep.

Having seen their shop change with the times, the Thorne family has discovered the hard way that not all publicity has a positive result. However, I had to ask the obvious question. How does a shop in Wivey come to be in the world's top one hundred?

"You never know who's going to walk through the door next," was Mike's answer.

It so happened that an influential neighbour, with a hand in retailing magazine editorials, had bought a local farm out beyond the Wivey rugby pitch. A visit to Thorne's was enough to charm him. Obviously price, quality and service mattered as much on a small scale as on the larger, but there had to be something more. Whatever it was, the right seeds were sown in the right place and soon Mike was talking to television cameras and journalists. The local MP sponsored the shop as his personal choice for 'South West Retailer of the Year' and invited Mike and his family up to London for a photocall at the Houses of Parliament, where Thorne's won the collective vote. It was all heady stuff that's remembered in newspaper clippings sellotaped to the shop wall behind the time-worn rocking horse.

And there was the answer. The rocking horse is the little bit extra. Well, perhaps not only that. Being able to sell customers your own home-raised beef and lamb helps hugely. Mike's third son Rodney runs the family farm. It's just out of range of balls walloped high over the boundary nets and of the sound of raucous singing emerging from the 'Three Ferrets' pavilion, of Brompton Ralph Cricket Club, on nearby Pittsford Hill.

The family's lambs are sensibly born between seasons. In the butchering trade one has to look ahead. The two hundred lambs that bleat before Christmas will meet the demand for Easter. A time when local farmers, too sentimentally attached to eat their own animals, join the shop queue. Still in their working wellies they chance it, leaving muddy Landrovers ticking over on double yellows. At other times a farmer might pop in with a couple of rabbits 'stripped of their jackets' or a gamekeeper will bring in a box of prepared fezzies. People still have the stomachs for this sort of fare. Venison is harder to come by. A way of denying income to a poacher is to insist the meat officially stamped.

In the past, Mike got his venison from Eric Smith, the calculating forest ranger before he retired out Roadwater way, who kept his own deer larder in the woods. It was tough, calulating, chisel-jawed Eric who gave me my first television news feature for BBC Points West, back in the early 1990s. There had been a spate of fun-seekers out and about at Christmas time firing at Bambi with crossbow bolts. My task was to film a dead hind among some Christmas trees and interview Eric.

"They either shoot and kill 'em or leave 'em to linger," said Eric to camera. There was something about Eric's gruff "kill 'em or leave 'em," that made the news editor think it was great pre-watershed evening entertainment. If I remember right, he was later transferred to Birmingham's Pebble Mill for 'beat 'em up stories' in the Bull Market.

But in Wivey folk tend not to move on. And mid-morning gossipers always seem to stop for a chat outside Thorne's shop window, where the pavement's at its widest. One day as I was passing, a woman was hanging onto an extendable lead clipped to a Jack Russell terrier. She was deep into shouting gossip at a lady holding a bag of meat, as road menders used a flat plated jack-hammer to smooth over a filled and newly tarmacked hole, almost in front of the shop doorway. A strangled yelp made me turn round. "Excuse me," I said, tapping the dog-lady on her arm and receiving a glare, " sorry to disturb, but your dog's choking. They've just jack-hammered its lead." Her head did the owl thing.

"Jack!" she screamed. Well, that's original, I thought. Jack, the Jack Russell, had been jack-hammered. The lad on the job was holding his tummy, convulsing with mirth. He didn't mean to embed the lead in tarmac. Jack, though, seemed to make a quick recovery from his trauma; going from gasping to bottom wiggling when given a morsel of raw mince from the lady with the meat, and comforting pats from close-at-handers.

Mike, however, preferred to be of help to people rather than to dogs in the street and spent four years as a first response paramedic. Trained in the skills of basic life support, he was on duty six or seven days a month. When there was a problem, he confided, people did feel comforted by having someone arrive whom they knew. My understanding was that Paul Barrington, the local undertaker, had also been approached for paramedic training. Granted, both a butcher and an undertaker are probably able to find their way around anatomy, but to have both arrive in the event of someone being poorly, may not have enhanced psychological powers of recovery.

Having retired himself from the green and yellow, Mike's future is with the shop. Taking all the publicity to one side, could he sum up why Thorne's was such a success with locals? "People praise us up, and the proof's in the eating," he smiled. I had to agree. Folk survive where there's community. And so indeed do dogs fed marrow-bones or mince.

As I left with a tenderloin of pork, I felt that I wanted to be a child again and ride on the rocking horse. I had to tell my friends about it. And the £1 note? Well, I could always ask about that tomorrow, when I come to buy one of Mike Thorne's 'happy hens'. His words, not mine for the meaty, feathered bundles that have the run of expansive barns with access to fox and gale, if the mood takes to follow their beaks outside.

Needless to say the ones on the shop tray are cold and plucked.

LESSON NINETEEN
A BIT OF A DRAG

"The eyes of a stag are peculiarly beautiful, soft, and sparkling.
Surely the laughing girls who every August gather at Cloutsham
Farm to kill so god-like an animal, as it were for a game, must have
hidden their hearts at the breaking of the cold summer's dawn
in the grey water of Watchet or Bridgwater Bay!"
(Llewelyn Powys 1926)

Sometimes you just get lucky. The four red deer stags were walking in a line on a ridge between Joaney How Cairns and where Dunkery falls away down towards Selworthy. That early mizzly wind gusting Exmoor morning in February 2005 I framed the camera just ahead of them and waited for them to stroll into shot and out again one after the other. As four deer ran the branches of Yggdrasil, the Norse 'World Tree', to represent the four winds, so those winds then caught my breath with beauty. A beauty conjuring spirit.

By lunchtime the bibblers were chuntering in the 'Bearin' Up' about the bunny lovers. Life had gone from riches to rags and was nothing to do with the Minehead Hobby-Horse. I borrowed Clive's newspaper that he had gloomily folded in two and used as an outsized beer mat. A long-term friend, Clive always wore a spotless cravat to keep up standards even in the grubbiest clothes. As a square-peg in the round hole of stockbroking, he had been a casualty of the Black Monday market crash. Instinct had made him flee west to a new life of odd jobbing for the nouveau rich and the gentry, specialising in climbing ladders and garden maintenance. They were ideal things for a rake. Clive adored the countryside and what had given him a spring to his step were thoughts of staghunting.

As Clive fiddled with his cravat, I saw that the headline news was bad. The Countryside Alliance had lost its appeal and hunting with dogs was banned. That meant staghunting was now outlawed. Those people having the opinion of Llewelyn Powys had held sway. It was news to make men like Jim Sanders, who used to sing traditional hunting songs in Exmoor pubs, turn in their graves.

"Hark to the tufters' challenge true,
'Tis a note that the red-deer knows!
His courage awakes; his covert he breaks,

112

And up for the moor he goes!
He's all his rights and seven on top,
His eye's the eye o a king,
And he'll beggar the pride of some that ride
Before he leaves the ling!
So hurry along, the stag's afoot,
The Master's up and away!
Halloo! Halloo! we'll follow it through
From Bratton to Porlock Bay!"

Such immortal lyrics now come from the voices of ghosts.

In recent times a hunted stag was considered to have earned his freedom, if he reached the sea; and was left alone. Not so in the old days. Then the hunt took to boats and headed with splashing oars towards Wales in his wake. Indeed, several instances were recorded in the nineteenth century, when such a beast was pulled out of the water by a passing coaster. The crew would thumb their noses at the Somerset gentry impotent with rage.

Scanning the letters columns, I found somebody called Bill Harris in Tasmania who had obviously distanced himself from the hunting issue when he decided to write.

"It is beyond my comprehension as to why certain people seem to get pleasure from dressing up in silly clothes and chasing one animal from their precarious position on top of another. Then again I fail to understand why people spend hours and hours queuing up to join another forty or fifty thousand extremely noisy individuals in a packed arena, often in the rain, to watch 22 men chasing a ball. I guess it's a matter of taste and one would have thought a modern democracy would take this into account."

Perhaps he thought hunting was an eccentric condition, but I had to agree that it could be very precarious sitting on a horse. I've got it into my head that even getting too close to one can mean getting hurt. Probably something to do with being dumped by an evil-eyed pony into a Tarr Steps nettle patch, after being persuaded to ride as a whippersnapper. Do not get me wrong, I have tried to like horses from the moment of my first testosterone surge. Then 'Sixpence', the pony ridden by the doctor's pretty daughter went and trod heavily on my foot before trotting amuck in my parents' vegetable garden. An adventure that left mashed potatoes, crushed cabbages and splintered canes of runner beans, and me with a paternal clip around the head and much allergic itching and sneezing. Not good. My last attempt at friendliness ended in getting reins caught around my wrist and getting dragged on my tummy through horse dung and molehills in a frosty field. The closest I get now is behind a slow moving horsebox heading a traffic queue. But each to their own, I say. Let those who wish to ride do so.

Although to ever suggest that a taste for drag hunting could prove as popular as supporting Yeovil Town might have been pushing it. "Hell's bells," said Clive, who had tried to temper his language since becoming a father of three, "What will old Maurice do now?"

I had known Maurice Scott, the joint master of the Devon and Somerset Staghounds for a good many years. I had filmed lambing in his sheds, drunk his tea and rattled around across his fields in a Land Rover; and I knew that he loved Exmoor's red deer with a passion and that he was potty about staghunting. Although foxhunting is the most notable activity banned under the Hunting Act, staghunters were a doughty and resolute lot and for the likes of Maurice staghunting was more of a way of life. On the doorstep was the largest herd of red deer in England, all within a ten-mile radius of Dunkery Beacon, and maybe the country's oldest inhabitants of unbroken ancestry.

Living just down the road from new Gupworthy neighbours Simon McCorkindale and Susan George, who incidentally was chosen by 'Empire' magazine as one of the '100 Sexiest Stars' in film history, Maurice runs his Brendon Hill farm with his wife Diana. Rather than title-tattle about their celebrity neighbours, the Scotts still dine out on the story of their horse 'Priceless' winning an Olympic bronze medal and the World Championship. Deer and horses make a rather good combination for them both.

I knew the news about hunting would be a stab to the heart. With a single deer nibbling three times as much grass as a sheep, and having several dozen deer at a time on his land competing with sheep and cattle for every blade, Maurice had every right to see them as a pest. Yet in the past he had been tolerant. He knew he only had to ask Diana to tie his stock for him before he put on his red hunting jacket hanging from a set of antlers in the porch. And after hauling himself up into the saddle and wetting his whistle from the stirrup, he'd be off in pursuit of happiness. With old habits dying hard, I hoped he could avoid getting himself into trouble.

I couldn't see him being particularly enamored with Henry S. Salt, a contemporary of Powys, who felt the need to offer a few castigatory thoughts on men like Maurice. "We do not compare the drag-hunt with the stag-hunt, in the sense of saying that it yields equal excitement; it lacks, no doubt, the thrill of the life-and-death struggle that is going on in front of the hounds. But for those who are aware that such excitement is cruel and morbid, the drag-hunt may be made to provide an excellent substitute for blood sports, with plenty of exercise; and sportsmen who refuse such substitute merely give proof that their addiction to a barbarous practice is very strong."

Was such a telling off enough to think the idea of chasing a rag smelling of aniseed and blood a sensible one? I thought not.

Maurice is as much a countryman as Jeff White, a farmer I once worked for as a teenager, until digging sheep out of snowdrifts at the time Kate Bush sang 'Wuthering Heights' made me look toward pastures new.

Apart from hunting and guddling there was nothing Jeff liked better than a game of cards. 'Black Maria' or 'Find the Lady' was his favourite. Invariably this was played by candlelight on the frequent occasions he couldn't be bothered to go out the back and bang his generator with a lump hammer. Every so often he would stamp his right foot loudly on the floorboards. "Rats," he'd say. He never stamped with his left because it was wooden, as was the rest of the leg.

Jeff never saw his wooden leg as a hunt handicap, but unfortunately his horse was. It was a boggler, prone to stumbling, but not falling. As a pair they were made for one another. Hardly a season would go by without Jeff several times having to dust himself down, rotate his leg a hundred-and-eighty degrees and remount for the chase. He retired from riding to meets when he retired his horse, but this was not until he had achieved the enviable feat of making a lady faint. He appeared at her feet with a sickening thud after having flown over a hedge. Cursing and cussing, he adjusted a horribly contorted leg, dusted himself down, patted his horse and then remounted again for the chase. It was all too much for woman. Years ago when drag hunting was only an idea for the pony clubs, Jeff said, "Bugger that for a lark," and played another card.

Why was it, I asked Clive, hunting had been banned, but shooting wasn't? For heavens sake, I said, both use dogs.

Clive gave a tut. "The antis say with shooting there are clear steps that people can take to minimise suffering. Being a better shot is the only one I can think of, and I've been trying to no avail for thirty odd years."

Thinking about it, even in the 1960s John Hillaby recognised that if hunting was stopped, farmers would have no compunction in shooting the animals that stray on to their land, and they were entitled to do it. What else to do? They can't be driven away, for there is nowhere else they can go.

I had followed the staghounds for a few years as a television news cameraman and I never quite got the gist of why the antis were so anti. So much of their rhetoric seemed to come from mixed messaging, imagination and prejudice. They basically wound themselves up and so caused bad feelings. If you weren't pro or anti, sitting on the fence, or hedge, you could only hope against a pincer movement as both sides were suspicious of the other. Following the hunt with a rather large camera got my car damaged on more than one occasion by horseboxes and trailers, and by thugs in balaclavas with paint pots. I was grateful that Maurice took me on trust.

However, the footage I filmed was revealing and quintessentially

English. Similar to the watercolour pictures we had on the wall at home when 'Sixpence' went gardening. One day in particular was memorable. Starting the windy wet morning being licked silly and made extra wet by hounds excited about leaving their kennels, I caught up with Maurice's horsebox at the Boxing Day meet in what I call 'Jodphur City,' and others call Exford. It was a cheerful crowd, but I think I was the only one not wearing a necktie. "Is he all right?" I heard a farmer type ask.

"He thought you were an 'anti' here to hassle us," said Maurice before I followed the riders and the hounds out onto Exmoor in my battered car. It was only Maurice and Diana's horses that didn't seem to be wearing tinsel.

Tapes, now in the TSW archive in Plymouth, were a mixed bag. One shows a stag flanked by two hinds, trotting down a steep moorland pasture towards a wood. They are big animals. Two mounted hunters were behind them, and staghounds in between. The deer's trot was faster than the hunters' canter and as fast as the all-out run of the hounds. Maurice blew the horn.

They were off over a soaked, slippery sheep meadow, between the stone posts of a narrow gate, down a muddy track perilous with ruts, into a country lane barely an arm's length wide, and away. I managed a few wheel spins before arriving at a hilltop above the woods. On the crest of the far slope several dozen members of the hunt were sitting on their horses. They watched two dogs sniffing the underbrush below. Two men in scarlet coats were nearer to the dogs, watching them sniff.

I filmed Maurice bringing in his tufters, the older experienced hounds, to separate the stag from his two ladies. The singling out wasn't working perfectly. Chosen by the harbourer for its lack of Darwinian promise, the hinds still thought he was worth running away with. Across the valley the 'whipper-in' with the job of bringing up the full pack was holding off. The stag refused to go it alone.

Then my back wheels span themselves into the mud and I was stuck. There was a spate of elderly, excited driving as hunt followers hurried to find a better view. A grizzled man with bushy sideburns and tweed cap stopped to give me a push, saying the stag was solo at last.

I finally parked up, only to be told the stag either did or didn't go into a strip of woods. The hounds weren't sure. The followers weren't sure. The hunters went into the woods and came out. This sounds as interesting as cricket. And to me and the hunt followers, it was.

The usual outcome would be the stag, at last, turning 'to stand at bay' and face the hounds. These do not then rip the stag to shreds. They bark. What else can they do to a pissed off antler-waggler? But that day the stag vanished. Wind, rain, and temperature grew worse. The hunt descended into a precipitous dell where I'd have thought the riders would have to walk their mounts. They didn't. However, the stag and every trace of it had vanished. As the rain began to lash harder than whips and the cold began to numb, the hunters decided to "pack it in to spare the horses". I watched Maurice head back to his horsebox, stoic, but clearly disappointed. On the way he found Diana and they stopped to talk to their friend Tom Yandle, chairman of the stag hunt, and as doughty and resolute as they come.

In the 'Bearin' Up' Clive added more sog to his newspaper by spilling a splash from another pint. "The bloody ban has less to do with loving animals than with bullying people," he seethed. Thinking of the balaclavas and paint, I agreed. Although in a way, the bullies are understandable. They probably feel smug in taking something away from folk perceived as having been too self-confident for too long, folk they misjudge as having dominated society, but whose dominance is slipping away.

But this wasn't a class struggle. The Labour peer Baroness Mallalieu has vouched for that. Instead, a certain kind of urban elite "with shaved heads and five earrings and their husbands just as bad", as Tom Yandle recently put it, are getting back at what they misconceive as old fashioned elitism without any use. Such are the ways of perception.

How would it be now with just using two dogs, if the letter of law within the new Hunting Act was followed? This is the conundrum. Two hounds are not enough to break the stag away from the hinds. Two hounds are not enough to make the stag stand at bay. Two hounds were certainly not enough to make the music of a pack in full cry. Will a traditionally elegant crowd on horseback listen to a talk from the hunt secretary about strict adherence to the law, especially in the matter of using just two dogs? Of course they'll listen and their grey-cells will be ticking. How to beat the ban? Now that was the thing.

I thought of Maurice and the two tufters and the way they worked. Surely nobody having fully reflected on the matter would ever think that using the pair in the time-honoured fashion I had so admired out on wintry Exmoor was illegal under the wording of the act. Would they? After all it's just two dogs and a question of luck. However, experience brings a luck of its own. On another day the tufters might well be successful in separating a stag from his hinds. Having a pack of hounds out for a stroll nearby could be said to be purely coincidental. Should they then do the hound-doggy thing and give chase, like a spaniel taking after a bunny, they could be woofed away as just an unfortunate misadventure.

Clive though didn't say whether this was feasible or not. He just looked miserable. His life had just become a bit of a drag. Pessimism can destroy any man who lacks spirit, I thought, toying with the last drops of Grouse in my glass.

The following year Maurice was in trouble. In October 2006 the *Daily*

Telegraph reported, "The joint master of a hunt is due in court charged with breaching the hunting laws in the first prosecution of its kind brought by police in England." The report didn't mention the tufters.

Both Maurice and Jeff with his wooden leg might like to know that according to the Hunting Act, "The hunting of rats is exempt."

The Keeper
The keeper did a hunting go
And under his cloak he carried a bow
All for to shoot a merry little doe
Among the leaves so green, O.

(Chorus:)
Jackie boy! (Master!) Sing ye well! (Very well!)
Hey down (Ho down) Derry derry down
Among the leaves so green, O
To my hey down down (To my ho down down)
Hey down (Ho down) Derry derry down
Among the leaves so green, O

The first doe he shot at he missed;
The second doe he trimmed he kissed;
The third doe went where nobody wist
Among the leaves so green, O.

The fourth doe she did cross the plain,
The keeper fetched her back again.
Where she is now, she may remain,
Among the leaves so green, O.

The fifth doe she did cross the brook;
The keeper fetched her back with his crook;
Where she is now you may go and look
Among the leaves so green, O.

The sixth doe she ran over the plain;
But he with his hounds did turn her again,
And it's there he did hunt in a merry, merry vein
Among the leaves so green, O.

(From Cecil Sharp's Collection of English Folk Songs, vol.II, ed. Maud Karpeles, 1974.)

LESSON TWENTY
HAIRY JOHN AND DAISY BRANDY

"Moo may represent an idea, but only the cow knows."
(Mason Cooley, aphorist).

There are two hairies down Folly Lane. One can speak eloquently and cuts his hedges east to west following the sun; the other, much larger and shaggier, is an iconic, blind, sharp horned, beige Highland steer. I went to say "hi" to both hairies at Folly Farmyard. These were difficult times. East of Frome, Boris Johnson had been elected Mayor of London.

What young bloke these days wants to work long hours for bugger all? Well, Jonathan does. My greying bearded friend, Jonathan Farey, runs his farm as it would have been a hundred years ago. There are no fertilizers on his thirty acres, just farmyard manure. He's proud to be completely organic. A small mixed farm of this size would have made a living for a family, not particularly comfortably, but adequately years ago, but nowadays it's very difficult. So for Jonathan, Folly is more of a way of life and a labour of love.

And Hairy John, his Highland steer, embodies it.

On a day of sunshine and showers in early May, I dropped down off the Blackdown ridge beyond Castle Neroche, in a car making horrid grinding noises, and crossed the margin line where the lime soil and beech trees end and the clay soiled ash and oak begin.

At the foot of an oak pollard grew an inspiration of English bluebells. Pale yellow primroses mingled with the blazing yellow sunrise of celandines. And without pesticides and sprays, purple spotted orchids flourished. Both sides of the little lane burgeoned with bright colour, apart from where it becomes narrowest. Here was a muddy scar, bare roots of blackthorn and dying trees. It was the latest bug-bear for Jonathan. So much so, that he had been writing letters to the council. In its wisdom, a whopping great dustbin lorry was sent fortnightly down the lane to play merry hell. The vehicle had scraped away at least two feet of the hedge bank. To its credit, the council said "sorry," but the damage was done.

As a farmer, Jonathan is used to life and death, but death only with a good reason. The hedge bank in the lane could recover. It would just need care and the time of future years. But time was not something that was on the side of Hairy John. And as reasons for life and death go, the question of Hairy John had made Jonathan's mind do somersaults. Robert, the local vet, wanted to test Hairy John for TB, but was afraid of the long sharp horns making for a short-term stay of the inevitable. How would Jonathan, his wife and four daughters cope if the Ministry ordered their family pet to be slaughtered?

When I arrived, Jonathan was standing in his Folly Farmyard, putting the world to rights with the local GP Andrew Tresidder, while a limping lurcher, a terrier and a black bog-brush tailed cat, vied for attention. But it was Hairy John that held the magnetism. "Hello, Charles," said Andrew, "We heard you coming."

A GP for over twenty years, Andrew is a gentle crusader carrying not the Cross of St George but tiny, dropper-capped, labelled brown bottles. They contain the healing power of flowers, known to the ancient Egyptians and Aborigines. I first met Andrew at a dinner party in a house where the infamous hanging Judge Jeffries had had a courtroom. The stuffed cat-killed, twig perching kingfisher that I had coincidentally passed up Wivey High Street a few years earlier and was now sitting on a windowsill behind the dining table, got Andrew chatting. It was the sort of talk to make a Medical Board frown. For them the jury is still out. Yet the flower essences he makes, be they of Impatiens or Daisy, Rock Rose or Gorse, or indeed anything floral, wow Somerset folk, including Jonathan. Medicine cures the body, but people aren't just bodies, they are minds, emotions, thoughts and feelings as well. And for that matter, they are complex beings.

Trace dilutions from flower heads he floats in bowls of the freshest water are vibes from nature that he captures in apple brandy. It's complementary sort of stuff that tastes good. Essences are tools, he once told me, that help people feel better, and if they feel better, they heal better. "Some of the central values may seem rather way out, when actually the real problem is that society is centred way wrong," he had told me over the landline.

A mobile fries his brain.

It would be fantastic, I thought, if Andrew's tools could help my car. Leaving it with a silent prayer, I gate-crashed topics on the calming effects of flowers and whether Jonathan and his family could eat Hairy John.

Back in the mid 1970s, Jonathan had been a member of a Forestry Commission gang working out of Smoky Bottom below Neroche, with men having names like Grabham and Vile. Bliss was in their self-containment. They had their own deerstalker and venison larder for the roe deer shot by a queue of wealthy folk willing to pay the price. He often spent winter nights at Smoky Bottom, sleeping off cider whilst his lurcher at the time, Wellie, a great wolf of dog, curled up and slept in the snow. Gang colleagues were always surprised when he seemed to be the first to work. Then, after lay-offs and cut-backs, Jonathan became almost the only one left. With a lack of conversation forced upon him, he needed something else to occupy his mind.

He had first found Folly Farmyard thirty years ago when he chanced to drive past. If the truth be told, Jonathan hadn't come very far. The distance between Smoky Bottom and Folly Farmyard is a short one, but it was love at first sight. The building that was to become his farm cottage was then just a tin roofed open-ended barn taken over by a Rambling Rector. Not an itinerant vicar, but a prolific variety of rose. The barn became Jonathan's folly at auction and is now home for himself, his wife Maria and their four young daughters Jemima, Otterly, Polly and Lily.

Now I looked beyond the old Smoky Bottom Land Rover that had finally given up the ghost. Behind some breeze-blocks, a few scaffolding tubes and a cement mixer was the electric fence Jonathan assured me wasn't on. There was no need for it to be. Highland cattle are docile creatures. Blind Hairy John with a green field all to himself wasn't going anywhere. Why should he, when looked after by a friend? And that was where the problem lay. Jonathan had bought him ten years ago, having felt sorry for him. At the time the steer was eighteen months old and scraggy. No good for meat slaughter at all. He had survived the threat of BSE and Foot and Mouth to become a family pet and a photo opportunity for ramblers and for myself. He was beautiful.

A sudden downpour made the three of us leave Hairy John to his own company and head for the kitchen. Unanimously deciding on a brew of tea, Jonathan put the kettle on the soot-webbed Rayburn to boil and we arranged ourselves around the table. I remember a tree surgeon in Chard once saying "The bigger the house, or the closer to London, the more the kettle is knackered. You never get offered a cup of tea." Jonathan, however, lived humbly and seldom had cause to visit Frome, least of all go east of it. The small terrier skittle-scattled around the tiled floor in repeated pursuit of a yellow tennis ball, before settling down to moult hair on my lap. The black, bog-brushed tailed cat did the same to Andrew's trousers. And Jonathan felt the need to speak what was on his mind. Hairy John's is a story that encompasses an unprecedented episode in beef farming. Rules and regulations have changed over the past twenty years to now mean that any cattle born before 1996 cannot enter the food chain full stop.

"Recently they've lifted the thirty months scheme, because BSE has gone over and Hairy John is just young enough for eating. Even dairy cows of his age get minced. In the meantime, over the past ten years, he has become a family pet. He's something of a local landmark and he's a friend.

"I've come out every day through the winter and fed him hay. Last year he came into the yard and got stuck in the feeder – I've got a big round feeder where the silage goes in – he got stuck with one horn in one horn out. I came out in the morning and he was stood there, as good as gold. He couldn't move so I had to hacksaw quietly one of the bars away and I thought, 'Right, you're not coming into the yard again, mate.'

"As I started hack-sawing through the bar he started throwing his head around and the whole of the feeder was rocking this way and that way. I started telling my wife about it and she said, 'You must be mad. You could have had your finger cut off, or crushed.' So now he stays out in the field all year round.

"He's blind and it would be unfair and inhumane to move him, to put him onto a lorry and haul him off to a slaughterhouse, which is what would normally happen to an animal. He would have been slaughtered here, bled and taken off to the slaughterhouse to be dealt with, then we would get him back to eat him. As he is fairly old, we would probably have most of him minced up for stews, cottage pies and that sort of thing."

"Something like 'Pie Minister Moos' would be good," I suggested, thinking of the posh steak and ale pies that were made in Bristol. Then the look from Jonathan and Andrew made me wish that I hadn't said anything. Back in his field I could feel Hairy John's ears burning.

The whistling kettle came as a welcome distraction. Andrew collected his thoughts and asked whether it would be emotionally difficult to eat a family pet. Jonathan thought about this. "No," he said. "We've had pigs, steers, heifers and poultry which we've eaten. It's not difficult. You rear animals with love and respect. You treat them well. You kill them humanely and eat them in the same way, with love and respect.

"I know farmers who sell their animals off to be slaughtered and go down to the local butcher, because they won't eat their own. I'm not like that. My family realises we're involved in an age old process. It's not a problem for us at all.

"One week we were struggling to find something for our Sunday lunch, having forgotten to get a joint out of the freezer. One of my little girls piped up 'We've got a lot of piglets running around, why don't you kill one of those Daddy, we can eat that.' I thought how fantastic that was for a child of five. She's picked up on what we do and has no qualms, she understood from the start that we rear animals and that they are killed to be eaten. We love having them and whilst they are alive, we cherish them. I would rather Hairy John was killed and eaten, rather than wasted."

But had they ever lifted his fringe and looked into his non-seeing eyes? Had they?

"A cow's eyes can make you vegetarian for life," Carla Lane, the comic writer of the hit TV shows 'The Liver Birds' and 'Bread', had said to my camera more than a decade ago, on route to the abattoirs and cattle trucks of Liverpool. I thought she was talking sense, but then she went and eradicated the rat population on her island off the coast of North Wales, once inhabited by Augustinian monks with black habits. With ratty missing, the black rabbits introduced by the colour coordinating, carnivorous monks had no predator, so they burrowed away at leisure. In a bunny lover's eyes rabbits are cute and unable to do wrong. Rubbish. The eco-balance of centuries was gone in a few weeks, and erosion triumphed. Carla followed this by pouring two hundred tonnes of concrete on top of the sacristy to make a bunk-house for herself and her two grown up sons. I carried on eating cow just to be bloody-minded, and because it tastes good. But eat Hairy John? No, I didn't think so. Sensibility can be a very emotive thing.

The story of the island rats made Jonathan bristle, and mutter something about silliness and lady dogs, death having to have a reason, and a mere personal distaste not being reason enough. Then the sun came out. We all needed some fresh air and Andrew's idea of a stroll up the lane seemed like a good one. So good, that the limping lurcher, the terrier and black, bog-brush tailed cat came, too.

We entered through a gate into a pasture, where a rusting carcass wreck of a Morris Minor van was home to nettles and a family of stoats. Further across the field was a small herd of brown and white Hereford crosses. Bull, cows and calves were all catching some rays. Seeing them brought a tender smile to Jonathan's face.

"Look at those cows, they're peaceful, aren't they?" he said. This was not pointing out of the obvious, but a voicing of thoughts. "They're content in what they're doing. They fill their tummies up with feed. They chew their cud. As long as they've got feed, clean water to drink and their family around them, they're at peace. Take their calves away, they turn into wild animals. The cow thinks, where's my calf, the calf thinks, where's my mother. Leave it later, nine or ten months, and a cow thinks, 'Hang on a minute, I'm fed up with this calf tugging at my teat all day, I'm happy for it to move away.' There's a nicer time for parting. These calves will have a great start. They'll go out onto lovely, luscious grass in a day or two. The cows will feed their calves and they'll live in harmony all through the summer. I see them every day, check them over and I can see that they're happy. And that makes me happy. It's a peaceful thing to do, to be a part of that. We can really learn something from them.

"They are relatively uncomplicated creatures with a simplicity about their way of life that is enviable. We've got much more going on. Our lives are so complicated and so hectic that we've forgotten about that business of survival. That's all they're interested in. We need a balance and to find some peace and tranquillity in our lives, so we can cope with all those stresses that are bombarding us right, left and centre."

Suppressing a smile, I asked Jonathan if he had heard of the black and white Fresian cow that thought it was a magpie. Both Jonathan's and Andrew eyes narrowed in frowns. "It thought it could fly," I said.

It was a truthful story. Standing proud on a ridge near Curry Rivel is Burton Pynsent steeple, a one hundred and forty foot high Tuscan column, in part designed by Capability Brown and paid for by William Pitt the Elder to the tune of a staggering £2000 in 1767.

The column inches were in memory of Sir William Pynsent, who bequeathed his estate to Pitt in, as he put it, veneration of a great character of exemplary virtue and unrivalled ability. In reality, the posthumous flattery was for Pitt fiercely opposing a tax on cider that had hit hard at Pynsent's purse. These days the steeple's bottom entrance is locked, although this was not always so. The magpie cow climbed the internal staircase and lingered to look at the unaccustomed view before discovering too late that it wasn't a magpie after all, before it could even flap a leg."

"One for sorrow," said Andrew.

"Oh dear, cows don't go backwards; the farmer should have kept the door shut in the first place."

A wise man, our Jonathan. And he told me something I never knew about buttercups.

He calls them poisonous gold and very bad on pasture land. Creeping roots render it difficult to eradicate. If cattle eat buttercups, they will blister their mouths, so they tend to avoid the plant. Happily it's fine in fodder, as the poisonous substance in the leaves is rendered harmless when dried.

I asked him if he'd ever rolled a cow over at night. Or was it a Wivey thing to creep up under the cover of darkness on a cow asleep on its feet and shove so hard that it falls over?

"Only in my misspent youth," admitted Jonathan with a guilty smile, as he clanged the gate shut. We were back in the lane.

As I stroked the black, bog-brushed tailed cat in preference to the limping lurcher, Jonathan and Andrew ambled passed the oak pollard. The bluebells caught Jonathan's eye. "These are so pretty," he said. "Walking through the carpets of bluebells in the woods at this time of year, where the light has filtered through the trees and has encouraged a lovely carpet of bluebells to grow, is absolutely wonderful. You walk through and you think, 'I don't really want to walk on the bluebells, because they're so beautiful.' Yet because nature has provided you with this rich and bounteous carpet, you end up walking on some of the flowers and crushing them. This wonderful smell comes up and gives this amazing feeling of springtime. It's filling our body with the essence. You can feel the energy coming and the sap rising."

Together, he and Andrew, have found a mutual sense of harmony and peace. It was because of people like Jonathan that flowers were there at all.

If land on the Blackdowns is neglected, brambles will grow. And over years the dominant tree will be the sycamore. Ending up with a wilderness will be Okay for nature, but there would not be the diversity. By farmers using the land the way it is, there are species-rich hay meadows and permanent pasture. The biodiversity that goes with the animals is crucial. There are orchids and wild flowers in the lanes and on the field margins, and in the fields there's a whole lot of species of grasses and herbage. These would disappear, if left to nature. It's through Jonathan's grazing cattle that the balance is maintained in Folly Lane.

As if to prove the point, Jonathan crouched down and took the flower head of a purple-spotted orchid between his index and middle finger. "They resemble a woman's private parts. But it's unnecessary to tell you that." More smiles.

Then he showed Andrew some 'Jack-by-the-Hedge', a tallish plant, with delicate white flowers and long pods, growing a couple of feet high. Pick the toothed, heart-shaped leaves and use them in your cooking or in a salad as you would garlic or wild garlic. It has a much more subtle flavour, but you still get a delicate garlicky hint and it is very nutritional, too. It is very prolific and could be seen up and down the lane.

"Don't worry if you've got this in your garden, Andrew. It's not a weed," said Jonathan before his eyes widened in delight at some wild strawberry flowers.

"Oh, to be able to stop with your daughters on the way home from school and pick a handful of wild strawberries is a wonderful thing. Daddy gets a few more brownie points for that. A very special old lane this," he concluded. And it was.

I left Jonathan and Andrew admiring the pink and purple flowers of an ivy-leaved toad flax that clung on for dear life, through a delicately threaded root system and a vestige of moisture, to the dry stone wall of a barn. It must have gasped with glee, as the rain poured again. But yes, Somerset life can be hard and needs to be coped with. Best to heed the advice in an old Romany poem:

"O, do not step upon a flower, but listen what she says..."

As my car ground her way back up the hill, I hoped that the administrations of 'Terry the Magician' at Bellamy's garage might provide her with a stay of execution. Yet it was sad and likely that neither my car, nor Hairy John would be surviving very long.

LESSON TWENTY-ONE
THUDDING CLOSE TO THE NORMAN

"The Mangold-Wurzel or Mangel-Wurzel (Beta vulgaris vulgaris) is a member of the family Chenopodiaceae. It was developed in the 18th century for cattle fodder, probably derived from sea beet which is indigenous to southern and western Europe. Identified by its large white or yellow swollen roots. The original name comes from the German for beet (mangel) and root (wurzel)."
(The Mangold Hurling Association)

I had accidently come across something really exciting on the web. Experience has taught my children that I'm a gullible old thing, so I was grateful to a dear friend at Musgrove Park hospital for giving me some insider information, before I made a pillock of myself both at home and in the 'Bearin' Up'.

The Doctors Mess at the Taunton hospital was in sombre mood. The government was trying to modernise medical careers, but the health minister Patricia Hewitt had made a hash of it. Many well-qualified and experienced doctors would be left without a job at the end of their existing contracts. And those jobs were ending in a couple of months. Not even a march of 12,000 doctors protesting through the streets of London could sway matters. Only two out of the nine young surgeons slumped tired in the uneasy chairs had something to look forward to. As for the majority, what to do other than emigrate to the Antipodes?

The problem was all of them rather liked Somerset. Then somebody came in with the news that one of their own was having fun and that Louise Gardiner, a specialist nurse practitioner, was feeling very pleased with herself. Through her own grit and determination she had become the first woman to do something that had previously been totally outlawed. It transpired she had broken a rule dreamt up by her husband, a local GP. Yet in these hard times Louise's happiness was like a ray of sunshine.

Dr Stephen Gardiner adores Somerset and felt that he wanted to make a difference. Possibly during a spare moment between patients at his Bridgwater consulting room he got a spark of interest in ballistic root vegetables. It may have have been something he'd heard on 'Gardeners' Question Time' or read in *Farmers Weekly* or just by keeping his ear to the ground, but it was certainly not anything published by the Royal College of General Practitioners. A junior doctor, whose father was a farmer, thought Stephen was inspired after having his car clamped in a Bridgwater sidestreet. A clamp, he was quick to point out, was also a Somerset term for a triangular heap of topless mangels stacked waist high, then covered in straw and earth to resemble a rather large tube of 'Toblerone' Swiss chocolate. The mangels were dug out and used when needed to feed hungry sheep. Let them eat cake, he thought.

What Somerset needed was a confection of entertainment from things traditionally readily to hand. Something to enhance Somerset's culture and silly enough to potentially be enjoyed in the county's arable acres without the need for expensive protective clothing, or causing any risk to hoof or claw. With welly-wanging passée and a sport for young farmers at summer fêtes, what happened next is becoming the stuff of sporting legend.

Browsing the internet for inspiration, it's said, got Stephen watching the 'SwanCam' of mute swans swimming in the moat of the Bishop's Palace in Wells. A fleeting idea for a game of hooning acorns or walnuts across the water to try to tinkle the famous bell flickered in his head, but was dismissed as possibly having repercussions of a professional nature. However, he kept the idea of hooning in mind. But what to hoon?

Norfolk gave ideas. Dwile flonking was a game of soaking a floor cloth in beer held in a chamber pot and then hurling it by use of broom handle at the opposing team. Being a sensible doctor Stephen realised this was a waste of good beer, so it had to be a spoof.

Inspiration finally came to him close to home in the small Levels village, halfway between Wells and Burnham-on-Sea, of Wedmore. The village has recently been described as a place where "old farmsteads sit amidst the rolling green hills and where tourism helps support the people in the area." Although Stephen didn't much like that word "tourism", he knew that 'withy' baskets were locally made as grockle fodder. Now that was a start.

A withy is a willow stem produced either by pollarding or the plant-ing of a sapling and the moors near Wedmore are the most important withy growing areas in Britain. Willows with colourful names like Champion Rod, Dicky Meadows and Black Spaniard live here.

Stephen, they say, chose not to discriminate despite Rod definitely sounding best.

The withies thrive in the soggy soil and withying has been a Somerset industry since before there were historians to record it. At its height in the 1890s, over 2500 acres were dedicated to withy growing and the industry, being labour intensive, directly employed well over fifteen hundred people.

Even with technology and the internet ruling our lives, there is still a need for withy growers, the basket weavers and their intricate art. Apart from making baskets ideal for mangold hurling and those for catching eels, the withy has braced corsets and the guardsman's bearskin. It was also in great demand for picnic hampers and for making the perfect container for delicate or explosive devices that had to be dropped by parachute.

History seemed to be important to Stephen. He became very taken by Wedmore, as it's one of England's most historic places. Alfred brought Guthrum here after having beaten him in battle and summoned the Witenagemot to make a peace treaty that our world leaders today should learn from. It was a peace made "as well for born as unborn, who reck of God's mercy, or of ours. "And it went on: "then there is this – if a man be slain we reckon all equally dear, English and Dane, at eight half marks of pure gold."

However, he must have realised the village not only inspired basket makers and kings. The name Wedmore derives from the Saxon term meaning 'hunting moor'. If the doctor had his way, folk should start hunting again, but only for something that they had personally hooned into the long grass. With the peace treaty in mind, he let battle commence on beet nibblers like rabbits, blackfly aphids, turnip gall weevils and mangold flies, as things became clear in his head. After many a false start over objectives and rules there was a coming together of local produce and the internet.

Stephen called this new game 'mangold hurling' and soon founded the Mangold Hurling Association with a bunch of willing cloth-capped friends. However, it has nothing whatsoever to do with the Irish sport of hurling, which is a game similar to hockey, that is played with a small ball and a curved wooden stick and is Europe's oldest field game. The only similarity it has to mangold hurling is that they both need a field.

Neither should mangold hurling be confused with cricket. Despite cricket being a game involving willow and played on a field, the season for mangold hurling is much shorter.

Perhaps at this point a little explanation is necessary. First and foremost Stephen knows his game is a minority sport like Eton Fives, Mud-wrestling or Tossing the Caber, the latter being the closest to the mangold hurling concept. Mangold hurling is the sport of hooning the mangold-wurzel whilst standing in a wicker basket that must be constructed solely through the art of weaving. The basket's base must be "circular and of sufficient size to accommodate both booted feet of the contestant at the same time, but with a diameter of no greater than one cubit." And the idea is to hurl one's mangold as close to a target called the 'Norman' as possible.

The Norman is just an ordinary mangold with its leafy top removed. Discussions still continue in both surgery and upon the ward whether the target got its name from a rather cantankerous medical consultant called Norman or from a government NHS policy adviser. Others say it may be that the topless mangold's shape was thought to resemble a helmet of a Norman soldier, but of course, this is pure conjecture. Doctors are sworn to secrecy.

However, the main point must not be lost. The Norman has to hooned, and hooning is described in the game's rules as 'hurling'. This requires "skill, strength and cunning". The mangold must be hurled with a straight arm, in one fluid movement, but as a word of warning the Association wants it known that a streamline mangold can be a deadly missile, particularly if it's "cultivated singularly in a clay pot." They recommend that the root must be removed from the pot before hurling. To be on the safe side, it is better to soil-grow mangolds in well tilled ground rich in nutrients and pig poo.

When the rules of the game were debated, it was said to have been mooted that a hurler should be disqualified if he carelessly landed his mangold in a river or rhyne and disturbed the eels. Stephen is rumoured to be a big fan of a pot of jellied Anguilla anguilla, and took umbrage at anything that might possibly curtail their chances of growth and numbers for culinary purposes.

Mangold hurlers are keen to point out that eels were caught by a clot, although this was not a hurler splashing his mangold into the water but the name given to a cluster of earthworms. Each worm had strong worsted thread drawn through its body. Being soft and tough, the thread could not be bitten through. When an eel bit greedily, it could be yanked into human hands before relaxing its hold.

In more modern times, as eels have become rare, the clot was replaced by the hully, a peculiarly shaped, long waisted basket trap made of woven withies that eels swim into, but cannot turn round in and swim out of. Such is the decrease in the eel population that local withy weavers are turning their attention to producing larger willow baskets suitable to meet the demands of mangold hurling instead. This surely put Stephen in a quandary. Either eels were caught for his tummy or more baskets were made available to stand in. The solution was simple: eels are not mentioned in the mangold hurling rulebook.

So, in summary of the game, each contestant on or around the first of October, which is the time of the mangold harvest, selects his mangold from a cart of mangolds which has been provided by the owner of the Field of Play and blessed by the local parson. The thrower must then stand with both feet in the withy pitching basket and on the command "Hurl!" must pitch his mangold at the target, which is a mangold called the Norman. The thrower whose mangold is closest to the Norman is the winner. In the event of two or more mangolds being approximately the same distance from the Norman, the umpire will give the call "Willow 'e!" to ask for the measuring willow to be produced. Distances are then measured and compared. The winner is crowned Mangold King and presented with a selection of village beauties or mangold maids from whom he will select his Mangold Queen. Any woman of the parish may apply to be a mangold maid, provided that she is an unmarried virgin aged sixteen years or more. There is no upper age limit.

Verbal abuse or attempts at distraction of the hurler by spectators are never permitted. It is especially unacceptable to mock a less than excellent attempt with cries of "Where's it to my boy?" Likewise, supporters whose favourite has been beaten are asked to refrain from cries of "buggerbiddle" and other such profanities. Spitting and discharging of firearms or inappropriate root vegetables are naturally frowned upon.

The Association does have an Equal Opportunities policy. Participants in Mangold Hurling may be of any age, religion, gender, sexual orientation and ethnic origin. There are exceptions. The main one is that "contestants must be adult males". Louise, Stephen's wife, desperately wanted to play but was told she could not, because it was against the rules. However, she took it upon herself to stand in a basket and hurl a mangold anyway. She claims she made a good account of herself.

Interviewed by a national newspaper, a spokesman for the Association also wanted it to be known that participants from the gay community were welcomed by the Association, but were urged to be aware of prevailing attitudes in the local population, particularly in the remoter parts of Somerset. The same advice was also offered to foreign participants, for instance those originating from Devon.

Back in the doctors' mess all eyes turned to the PC monitor perusing the mangold hurling website. Sadly, despite thudding close to the Norman being so convincing, it was a spoof for basket cases nevertheless. Yet there was so much to read, so many daft photographs of vegetables and chaps in peculiar hats exhibiting skills, so many game rules. So much wonderful idiocy. Both men and wishful women yearned to put aside their job woes over the forthcoming weekend for some fresh air activity around Wembdon. Hooning mangolds would do a lot to help pent up frustrations.

Stephen Gardiner really is having fun and his job is apparently absolutely safe. The uninitiated though should be cautious, if he prescribes them outdoor exercise to beat bugs. The junior doctors agree he is a rascal. They will miss Somerset, but wherever they might end up the tosh of mangold hurling will surely spread. Word has it though that the newspaper took the game seriously. Neither the earnest reporter, nor her editor picked up on Stephen's mischievous meddling with Keats' verse from 1820.

Season of mists and mellow fruitfulness,
Close bosom-friend of the maturing sun;
Conspiring with him how to load and bless
With fruit the vines that round the thatch-eves run;
To bend with apples the moss'd cottage-trees,
And fill all fruit with ripeness to the core;
To swell the gourd, and plump the mangold root
To a sweet wurzel; to set budding more,
And still more, later flowers for the bees,
Until they think warm days will never cease,
For Summer has o'er-brimm'd their clammy cells.

To have checked this against a reputable collection of poems would have clarified that everything the Mangold Hurling Association said was, to coin Stephen's phrase, just a load of old buggerbiddle.

LESSON TWENTY-TWO
HEAD FOR THE HIGH GROUND

"We must build dikes of courage to hold back the flood of fear."
(Martin Luther King, Jr.)

Americans, bless them, have the habit of saying the daftest things when expressing their observations. Like the time I was sweating in the tomb of one of the Ramases pharaohs in Egypt's 'Valley of the Kings'. I remember breathing out the sort of "phooar" noise many of us are prone to make when confronted by the wonder of hieroglyphs. An American lady tourist standing beside me turned and said in a stage whisper: "Yeah, it sure is hot in here; but ain't the graffiti awesome."

So on a summer's day in Burrowbridge, what would gush forth from the middle-aged American couple joining me on the top of a sun-scorched Burrow Mump to stare out across the Somerset Levels? Below the withies in their beds were green growing and the River Tone having flowed from Taunton, joined the River Parrett, a name that has nothing to do with talking birds and feathers, but means 'Barge River' from the Latin 'barse'. Sailors once went as far as Langport.

It was also the end of the eel season. During January through to May, the Parrett had provided a source of eels and many young elvers had been caught by hand netting. The elvers used to arrive on the spring tides in the River Parrett from their hatching place in the Sargasso Sea and travel across the Atlantic, up the Bristol Channel and then make their way into Somerset. Back in 1770 eels on the Levels were "taken in vast plenty out of holes near the banks of the river in frosty weather; for the people walking upon the edges of the banks observe some places not to be as white as the rest, but of a green colour, whereupon searching they are sure to find heaps of eels."

Eels don't create quite so much excitement these days and both the Parrett and Tone looked at ease. Beyond them was Tim Morgan's Athelney farm.

He was the last Somerset farmer to grow teazels commercially. I had heard about him as I probed into local life over a pint at lunchtime in the 'King Alfred' pub at the foot of the mump. In fact, I learnt all about the Levels folk I should meet whilst sipping that one pint, because I found myself chatting to Jim, one of Tim Morgan's labourers. Soon afterwards I was visiting Tim's barn full of spiky seedpods that had earned the teazel the name 'Fuller's Thistle'. Since pre-Roman times they had been used for scouring newly woven cloth. Back in early 1990s falling demand had reduced three harvestings a year to two. With the pods developing unevenly through the season, the picking of the kings came first. These were the big heads. The smaller twerts came later. I spoke again to Jim who had been harvesting prickly teazels all his working life. He conceded it was time to put his thick gloves at the back of a shelf for the spiders, however he didn't seem too gloomy. There was to be more time for ferreting.

The land on which the teazels grew had once been an island in the marshes where King Alfred ate a diet of eels, built a fort and later, after victories against the Danes, a celebratory abbey around about 888, now marked by a small obelisk enclosed by iron rails.

"This is all the pilgrim can find to help recall the memory of the great Saxon King, his hiding-place and wanderings, and the triumph that came to him at last. Nor today in spring or summer is it easy to picture this ancient Isle of Nobles. Only when the swollen river breaks its wall and winter floods arise all round – when west Sedgemoor is a swamp, Stanmore a sea, and Southlake 'drownèd' as they say, does the Island of Athelney, one-half the size of a small farm stand out alone, as it stood in the old fen, and justify for a week or so its claim to the title."

Walter Raymond wrote these words in the *New Liberal Review* at the beginning of the twentieth century, like seeds blossoming in a flowerpot and an exaggerated billet-doux to nature. Be patient, I thought to myself, as I edged into eavesdropping distance of the American 'pilgrims'. Just bide your time, Chazzer. Then true to form, out it came. It wasn't the pearls of wisdom I had expected. "Gee, ain't the sky big here."

"And it drops a lot of wet stuff," I said, offering my experience. When rain clouds opened there was always a likelihood of trouble. Pinching a Norfolk term, the Levels often became 'waterslain' during the dark soggy months of the year. Why? Well, the fall of the River Parrett, between Langport and Bridgwater Bay is only a foot per mile, so the river's prone to frequent flooding during winter and high tides. Such events were considered a spectacle across the Severn Sea in Wales. The Welsh once knew this bit of Somerset as the 'land of blood', because of the way red wintry sunsets reflected off the floods.

When the River Parrett broke banks in 1894, the floods brought some fashionable entertainment to Langport. An enterprising local boat owner running sightseeing boat trips through the town at 6d a head accepted the money of a rather snooty couple who lived on the high ground. The couple weren't particularly liked, as they tended to patronise the folk who lived "Down Under." Dressed respectively in top hat and feathered bonnet, they stepped into the boat only to sit aloof from their fellow passengers of ordinary town folk.

The story goes that indignant faces appeared at upper windows and voices exclaimed "Look 'ee here they be, the 'King' and 'Queen' of Langport!" However, fate had a smile.

A cross current of water capsized the boat, throwing boatman, 'King' and 'Queen', and all into the icy flood. The boat was quickly righted and turned back homewards, while the 'King's' topper floated away and the 'Queen's' bedraggled hat feathers drooped over her face. From behind twitching bedroom curtains came a spate of unsuppressed giggles.

Indeed, it was on a much more recent winter's day that two men in a van were taking bets of me getting through the water-covered roads, behind Tim's place. What the loser may not have considered when he thumped a fist on his dashboard was that I then drove a clever Citroen Pallas with 'up and downy' suspension. It was an over-engineered car that later died on an Exmoor hillside, from a blown head gasket, in a cloud of smoke that was mistaken for swaling. Admittedly, it could still go up and down, just not forward and back.

Not so very far away from the betting scene, Curload was also awash from a broken-banked Tone. Now in her eighties, Sue Nield had spent her childhood growing up there. And it never ceases to amaze me what Levels ladies of a certain age will divulge if you first say, "Morning. Lovely day, isn't it?"

For her childhood was a time of watery disaster memories. The event that loomed largest was the great flood of 1929. She told how swallows flew low, forecasting rain, before the new moon stood on end and emptied the water out.

"The River Tone burst its banks," she recalled, "and flooded Curload, Stanmore, Athelney and Burrowbridge to a depth of over ten feet. Some houses were completely submerged. Men rowed boats to the 'Black Smock' public house near Athelney Station that served drinks from the bedroom windows at the top of a ladder. There was no loss of life, but everyone who could filled sandbags and piled up valuable bundles of withies to try to stem the onrush of water. Children and old people were coach-loaded uphill to Stoke St Gregory."

I learnt that one farmer penned his cows in the only high ground available, the hump of the bridge over the flooded river. The cows lived there for several weeks while the farmer's wife rowed fifty pounds of butter every week to market. It was said to be the most fertile stretch of tarmac in Somerset, when the waters finally receded. Three months had passed before the water did subside and houses were habitable again.

Sue concluded that there was so much poverty. Many families had lost their work huts and also their valuable basket making tools. A relief fund was organised to help the village get back to normal and folk around gave more than they could afford.

But things could have been worse. A pamphlet doing the rounds in London in 1607 gave the appalling news of what had occurred at 9 o'clock in the morning on the 30th January that year along the shores of the Bristol Channel. "God's warning to the people of England by the great overflowing of the waters or floods," proclaimed the pamphlet.

History now shows it was the most destructive environmental disaster in British history. An estimated two thousand people or more drowned, houses and villages were swept away, over two hundred square miles of farmland was submerged and livestock was destroyed. Although the Welsh side was particularly badly hit from Laugharne in Carmarthenshire to above Chepstow on the English border, the seawater from Burnham lapped Glastonbury Tor, twenty-one miles inland. The Tor must have attracted more folk then, than those clambering it today to watch Michael Eavis' Glastonbury Festival firework display.

At the time, Rev. John Paul, the vicar of Almondsbury, wrote:

"From Mynhead to Slymbryge the lowe groundes alongst the ryver Severne were that tuornyng tyde overflowen, and many howses over-throwne, sundry Chrystyans drowned, hundreds of rudder cattell and horses peryshed, and thowsandes of sheep and lambs lost. Unspeakable was the spoyle and losse on both sydes the ryver."

Other accounts came from eyewitnesses who described" huge and mighty hilles of water, tumbling one ouer another, in such sort, as of the greatest mountains in the world had ouer-whelmed the lowe valeyes or marshy grounds."

Another said that the water advanced at a speed "faster than a grey-hound can run".

Survivors clung to the steeples of churches and to the roofs of the few buildings that remained standing. Corpses were washed out of grave-yards. To see 'Granfer', dead for a good few years, suddenly floating in the direction of the local pub must have been a little disconcerting. One woman saved her young children, gossip has it, by putting them into an empty trough and floating with them to safety. Historical records state that twenty-eight people were killed at Huntspill and a further twenty-six at Brean. Across the region there remain plaques up to eight feet above sea level, to show how high the waters rose up the sides of the surviving churches.

The cause of the flood remains disputed. 'Explanations' at the time blamed God. More recent scientific explanations ignored much of the written evidence and blamed bad weather, unusually high tidal peaks and a storm surge. Which in bog standard terms means there was a flood, albeit rather a nasty one. Now research suggests a tsunami.

This is the gist within a research paper published in the journal *Archaeology in the Severn Estuary,* in 2002. And it followed investigations by Professor Simon Haslett, from Bath Spa University, and the Australian geologist Ted Bryant, from the University of Wollongong. By looking at boulders, the shape of cliffs and silt along the Bristol Channel coast, they believe the flood was caused by a thirty-three foot high wave moving up the Bristol Channel at speeds of up to a hundred miles per hour, giving no warning to people caught in its path.

Ted Bryant went on record as saying: "You can't really imagine what it must have been like, other than the human tragedy of it. Quite catastrophic and how people dealt with it is amazing. A lot of commentators on the 1607 flood have put it down to a storm coming in, and as a child, you accept what you are being told by scientists and historicals and you don't really question it."

But he questions whether a storm really was to blame, looking back at recent large storms, such as the biggest one in living memory on the 13th December 1981, when low pressure in the Atlantic forced seawater up the Bristol Channel. This pressure combined with high tides and snow-melt brought crashing waves over the sea walls at Burnham and Weston. It was a heavy storm, but didn't match up to the force of the 1607 flood.

Dr Roger Musson, Head of Seismic Hazards at the British Geological Survey, added his 'ten-penny worth' by noting that the sea bed off the south west tip of Ireland is the location of an ancient and large fault line that could have caused a 1607 tsunami.

"This is exactly the sort of place where you could get a large earthquake happening," he said, just to tickle anxieties.

Indeed, on February 1980 an earthquake did occur there. Trembles measuring 4.5 on the Richter Scale were recorded. "The idea of putting a large hypothetical historical earthquake in this spot is not fanciful. The size, speed and strange sparkling of the waves all fitted the characteristics of a tsunami." said Dr Musson.

If the Somerset events of 1607 were repeated now, people along the Somerset coast would be likely to receive plenty of warning, but only if it was a predicted storm. However, if it ever should be a sudden tsunami, little or no warning could possibly be given. But be there flood or tsunami, the damage repair cost would be in excess of £13 billion, so the experts say.

Even in an ordinary winter heavy rains revert the wetlands to their old state despite modern drainage controls. Orchards are inundated, cottages flood and sandbags prove ineffectual, while South West Trains 125's rush by as if the embankment was a medieval causeway.

A good idea then to have a boat in your back garden and the Levels' pumping stations to be greased, oiled and have their sensors functioning. And for Tim Morgan to keep his rhyne 'wet fence' drainage channels well weeded and silt free. Failing this, head for the high ground, avoiding airs and graces. Or, one could always play 'King of the Castle' atop a ruckle and feel a twert.

Set against a tsunami, the two-foot Parrett bore, once so fascinating to the diarist Dr Johnson, is really quite a tranquil ripple.

LESSON TWENTY-THREE
COLD AND WINDY

"No ghost was every seen by two pair of eyes. "
(Thomas Carlyle, Victorian Satirist)

Down from Newcastle University, Jane Murgatroyd had the misfortune to be my PA that summer and had already taken the decision to stick to drinking water. It was a wise choice after I'd told her the job was way to get ahead. I was making a video documentary called 'Somerset, The Summer Land' and what happened while doing so could easily have tempted the weaker minded into intoxication.

We were both sitting in farmer Nobby Kerton's sitting room at Higher Farm in Chilton Cantelo. Out of the window we could see the Norman church on the other side of the little lane leading to nowhere. As Jane sipped tap water and I gulped tea with my camera at my feet, Nobby stood on a chair, reached into a little black oak cupboard above the sitting room door and took down a brown cardboard box. I knew what it contained.

During the English Civil War the people of Somerset and Dorset combined to form the 'Clubmen', an organisation devoted to keeping their counties safe from the attacks and plundering of either the Parliamentarian or the Royalist armies. They failed and the Royalists in Somerset had a bad time of it. The lobster helmeted roundheads took to heart the teaching of Bridgwater's Admiral Blake, who believed that none but an Englishman should chastise an Englishman. This was something I wanted to mention in the film.

In summer of 1645, Nunney's fourteenth century castle, built as much for show and comfort as defence, looks so pretty it must have been a pleasure to besiege. The stand it made against Fairfax and the Parliamentarian army did not last long. It is said a traitor informed of a weakness in the western curtain, which the roundheads bombarded. Once inside, Cromwell's men ripped out the floor joists and burned the timbers. When I turned up, there was nothing moving worth filming save pigeons.

Wells is the cathedral city of Somerset and its cathedral offered better visuals. Here Cromwell didn't exactly endear himself to local clergy. The dean, a nephew of Sir Walter Raleigh, was run through with a sword by the town gaoler. His crime was refusing to hand over a letter he had written to his wife. And the Roundhead cavalry stabled their horses in the cathedral nave before the Battle of Langport, whilst many of Cromwell's soldiers were billeted in Vicar's close, the only complete medieval street in Britain.

At the battle the Royalist army of Lord Goring met Fairfax and Cromwell at Wagg Bridge, then a ford on the Somerton road. Cromwell himself led the charge. Goring was defeated. His infantry was taken captive. The remnants of the Royalist force fled through Langport and made a huge nuisance by setting fire to the town. It was a futile gesture to what was virtually the end of resistance to the Commonwealth.

When the monarchy was eventually restored with Charles II, Theophilus Broome, a native of Warwickshire who supported Parliament during the Civil War, retired to Chilton Cantelo. He lived quietly with his sister. Yet he was afraid that when he died, the local monarchists, in wanting to get some of their own back, would decapitate his corpse and display his head on a pike. So he instructed his sister to keep it safe.

After he died in 1670 she did, and that's what was inside the cardboard box in Nobby's hands. Over the centuries, attempts have been made to re-capitate Theophilus, but each time his skull is moved, things tend to happen. Put on paper as long ago as 1791 by John Collinson in his *History and Antiquities of Somerset,* the haunting is well documented. A manuscript at the farm has written account from a number of people who attested to poltergeist activity happening after interment was attempted.

With the box lid removed and much to Jane's disgust and alarm I picked him up. He was a bit shiny through the handling of centuries and had lost his lower jaw. "It's just an old skull," I said to her and saw Nobby raise his eyebrows.

Theophilous's body was lying in the church opposite. So it was a good idea, I thought, to film the inside of the church, too. This required a set of two photographic lights. Lifting the latch, Jane and I entered through the large heavy oak door. The church was dark and cool despite the hot sun outside. Finding the burial slab in the nave was easy. I set up the lights, plugged them in and switched on. Both bulbs blew instantly. Shrugging this off as unfortunate, I decided I would film using what natural daylight there was. To have a grainy image was better than no image at all. I switched on the camera. Nothing. A dead battery perhaps? I asked Jane if she would get a spare one from the car. The church then went very cold. From the door, Jane sounded a bit panicky, that she couldn't go out. Nor, as it turned out, could I. No matter how hard I tried to pull up the latch, it wouldn't budge. Then, as suddenly as the chill inside the church had come on, it went, and Jane easily lifted the latch with her little finger. First thing we did once outside was to find Nobby.

"It's not just you," he said. "A strange thing happened to the last chap who came to film here." That 'chap' I learned was Clive Gunnell, the former HTV presenter, whom I had earmarked to narrate my Somerset film, before he decided to go on a long holiday to Barbados instead. He was a lovely bloke, who used to live at White Ball outside Wellington and was fond of a gin and tonic.

"To be fair, nothing strange happened here during the day of filming. But when Clive got home that evening an old framed map of Somerset with Chilton Cantelo on it fell off his hall wall and broke, as he was in the middle of a dinner party."

"And then," continued Nobby, "there was Dave Allen, the comedian. He came here in a chauffeur driven car. When he wanted to leave, the car wouldn't start. The reason soon became obvious to his driver, who discovered a slick of oil underneath it, whilst on his hands and knees.

A few days later I received a charming letter from Nobby trusting we had "an uneventful trip home." In recent years Higher Farm is said to have become known for growing 'Pimientos de Padron' chilli peppers. The peppers vary between one and two inches long and are very hot, some blisteringly so. Not that Theophilus could feel that.

However, his was not the only eerie story for Jane and me that summer. And like with Dave Allen, it affected the car. The Battle of Langport was not the only fight Somerset experienced that caused a large loss of life. Forty years later the last pitched battle in England was fought on flat peat moor between Chedzoy and Westonzoyland, on the way from Langport to Bridgwater. No film covering the history of Somerset could be complete without including the Battle of Sedgemoor and its consequences.

Having first been to Chedzoy church to see a copy of the battlefield map from the time, the original being in the Bodleian Library, Jane and I drove along a rutted old drove road to arrive at a granite memorial to both sides in the battle. Around it stood four staddle-stones and two large ash trees. Jane knew the history from her university tutorials.

The Monmouth Rebellion of 1685, also known as the Pitchfork Rebellion, was an attempt to overthrow James II, who had become King of England at the death of his elder brother Charles II. James II, though, was unpopular, because he was Roman Catholic and many people were opposed to a 'papist' king. Another James, James Scott, 1st Duke of Monmouth, an illegitimate son of Charles II, claimed to be rightful heir to the throne and attempted to become king himself. And so began the 'Pitchfork Rebellion'. Supported by a ragtag 'army' of untrained West

Countrymen, James Scott had the temerity to actually declare himself king in Taunton. Shortly after he got his comeuppence.

On an early July night, Monmouth's rebels advanced. However, they hesitated at the watercourse of Bussex rhyne and instead of rushing the royal army, took it on at a distance in a fire-fight. The forces exchanged musket and cannon fire in darkness, but at daybreak the King's army advanced, crossed the rhyne and forced the rebels to flee. Many were caught and killed in what is now Moor Drove rhyne. This was something discovered in 1858, when someone called Boyd Dawkins and his father tried to discover burial places and found a local whose great-grandfather had helped to bury the dead in moorland trenches, covering them with sand. Boyd found human bones and some coins that hadn't been worth much in a place of ghosts.

With my filming of the monument done, I was putting away my kit, when the two ash trees began to shake like they were in a gale. No other trees around were even having the slightest rustle. "Car," I said. We got ourselves and the camera clobber inside in a bit of a hurry. I turned the ignition key. Nothing. Not a sausage. Jane wasn't happy, and I empathised. Then, less than a minute later, the two trees became still. I turned the key again. 'Brooom'. We left a cloud of dust behind us that drifted over the fields that are never ploughed. There is nothing these days to indicate the site of the graves, just the occasional burned out car wreck in a field or a layby, modern statements to the abandonment of rustic hope.

Many stories exist of what happened to the rebels after the battle and they have beome the stuff of legend in many books. There are tales of trees used as gibbets and of ghosts outrunning horses. Five hundred rebels were held captive in Westonzoyland church, dying of their wounds without food, water or medical attention, as the bells proclaimed the King's victory. Elsewhere, the King's revenge was brutal. Colonel Kirke administered instant 'justice' with his regiment, ironically known as "Kirke's Lambs" that was later to become the Queen's Regiment. After over three centuries the extent of the "Lambs" atrocities is still remem- bered, with the Queen's Regiment only taking recruits from the south east of England. Until very recently it was forbidden for the regiment to recruit in Somerset - because of Sedgemoor.

Monmouth was discovered "hatless, haggard, hungry, and in his pocket the Order of the Garter and a handful of raw peas." He was executed for treason on 15 July 1685, but only after several chops to the neck, and many of his supporters were executed or transported into slavery in the 'Bloody Assizes' of Judge Jeffreys.

One story that seems to have affected me is about some of the unfortunate souls, told by a curator at Dunster Castle, a Glaswegian called Jim Smith. Possibly reared on tales of Culloden, he appeared to revel in excruciating English deaths. Four village men were taken up Gallox Hill and disembowelled, hanged, drawn and quartered. Their limbs were boiled, salted, pitched in tar and strung along gateposts all along the high street.

The television camera crews filming the likes of Agatha Christie's 'Poirot' that coo as readily as grockles at the aspic tranquility of Dunster's Yarn Market and 'olde worlde tea shoppes' might feel muted, if they realised that Somerset once didn't look so charming. During those few months of 1685, a larger proportion of the population was killed, executed or transported than was lost during the whole of the Great War.

At summer's end Jane decided that this wasn't the place for her to work, but said she was "grateful for the experience."

The last time I saw Clive Gunnell, he was red faced in the members' bar at the County ground with a G and T in hand. "Sorry about the film," he slurred. "I liked the end result. I once had a little incident after Chilton Cantelo. I must tell you about it sometime."

"I already know," I replied, and with mutual smiles, we turned to applaud Somerset taking a wicket.

LESSON TWENTY-FOUR
BATS, PADS AND PENGUINS

*"Last ball of the match. Three runs required. The last pair together.
If Colin Dredge bowls another no ball they'll hang him here."*
(BBC commentary, Taunton, 16th August 1978)

I've got it. I've got it. I've got it. My eyes were fixed on the plummeting ball, as I back-peddled as fast as my legs could carry me up Timberscombe's steeply sloping outfield.

No, I hadn't. I toppled over like a Falklands' penguin and bruised my bottom, convulsing my Wivey 2nd XI team mates into hysterics. I felt a prat in grass-stained cricket whites. To have tried one's best in true Somerset spirit and not to be appreciated was really quite galling. The thoughts of penguins lingered from a twenty-year-old memory and suddenly I felt my forty-something years.

Yet, I consoled myself, stiffly rubbing my backside with a flipper wing, colonies of Falklands' penguins had suffered before me, when fighter aircraft flew over their heads playing games of dominoes. A time when Margaret Thatcher had decided that Falkland islanders should never weary of eating mutton for breakfast, mutton for lunch and mutton for tea, and so put a stop to Argentinian ideas of varying the diet with tins of corned beef. Those woolly-headed battles for sheep were a sorry distraction from that 'Golden Era', when the spirit of Somerset had never been better and the County Ground in Taunton was the place for heroes.

So when I got offered a chance to make a film with the Somerset and England off-spinner Vic Marks in the 1990s about the exploits of Botham and Richards, 'The Dasher' and 'Big Bird', and the bowler called the 'Demon of Frome', I bounced like a Falklands lamb.

When I turned up at the County Ground with my camera, the first urgent images were not of anything Somerset, but of Warwickshire. Brian Lara was on the square doing a pre-match horseabout, pushing over Gladstone Small and jumping on the back of an unknown. Their hosts had returned to the trough of lean times.

Vic had to give me a nudge about the job in hand. He was keen to tell the background that had led up to one fondly remembered match played beneath Lara's feet fifteen years earlier. A match that got me blasting the Wurzels, 'Take me back to good ol' Somerset' from my dinky cassette player, as I became rather excited on Jeff White's farm where I then worked. All around me the mood was infectious. The cows tripped the light fantastic to the parlour and Jeff swore blind that the milk yield was up, as he uncorked another bottle of wine with his wife. Oh, to have actually been 'there' that August day. To believe everyone who said they were, the crowd would have been over a hundred thousand.

Looking the part for a success story was easy for Vic. All he had to do was smile a cheeky grin and put on his beloved creased brown leather jacket. Somerset had a reputation for being the scruffiest team around, although the stumper, Charles Carter, tried to address the balance by sporting a cravat whilst keeping wicket. Sadly, his tenure was for only a season or two. When Somerset won their first ever trophy a decade later in 1979, 'Dasher' Denning was happy in skimpy white shorts and T-shirt, and Nigel Popplewell started net practice wearing a crumpled raincoat in front of the old pavilion.

The rickety structure was brought in from the Taunton racecourse in the 1880s, when the athletics, the running, the cycling and the cricket clubs of Taunton all decided it was time to have a ground. The County Ground was bought from a farmer with some imagination, who went bankrupt trying to develop something to do with armaments and bullets. The ground was right on the outskirts of Taunton in those days. First it was Taunton cricket club, then it became Somerset cricket club.

After becoming a first class county in 1891, professionals and amateurs would take to the field through different gates. That was until the Second World War. The professionals used to change behind the old pavilion, where there's a little groundsman's hut now. And they used to have to hang up a towel, or a sheet, or something because all the members used to walk by. And all the amateurs, and there were quite a few because Somerset was poor in those days, would be called "Sir" by the professionals. The professionals did most of the bowling and the amateurs most of the batting, and for that matter, the captaincy. The county didn't have a professional captain until Maurice Tremlett in 1956.

For almost a century it had been a club composed of some yokels, some not very good players and some odds and sods, until the Australian Greg Chapell bought the element of world class into the club. He arrived at the end of the 1960s with Charles Carter and Brian Rose who would become the 'Captain Marvel'. He seemed a man of few regrets, although 'Wisden' recording his birthplace as Dartford in Kent, rankled. In fact he had only spent three weeks of his life there, having lived in Weston-Super-Mare ever since.

And that was the other thing. Brian was really miffed that his town was taken out of Somerset and incorporated into Avon. I caught up with

Brian, as he was walking his dog behind Burnham golf course:

"I had a difficult start to my career, when perhaps Somerset cricket was at its lowest ebb.

"My memories of Somerset must be playing with groups of individuals brilliant on their day sometimes awkward, sometimes churlish, many happy days, winning days, many more losing days." Cricket was a relaxed affair played by men from varied backgrounds.

If the truth be told, Arthur Wellard was said to be the best poacher in Somerset. And T.C. Lowry was a member of the elite Cambridge 'Hellfire' club. An honour bestowed on a man who could blow three smoke rings and spit through them.

Colin McCool, an Aussie before Chapell's time, used to sit in the dressing room in one of the big old armchairs the club once had when preparing to go into bat and he'd be puffing away on his pipe. Knowing his time had come when he heard the groans from the crowd, he'd get up and put his hand up onto the ceiling, where there was an old beam withered with age. And up on that beam were about twenty pieces of chewing gum. He'd just put his hand up, take a piece of chewing gum off, put it in his mouth, start chewing, go out to bat, get whatever were his runs of the day, come in, take the piece of chewing gum out and stick it back on the beam for the next time.

So it was unsurprising that with being so laid back, Somerset was still the 'Cinderella county' when Vic first pitched up at the County Ground on a cold and blustery day in 1974. He was wide eyed and couldn't wait to get started as a professional cricketer. In those days there was a little bit more respect from uncapped players to capped players and they used to have separate dressing rooms.

Vic joined other young pups sent to change in what was nicknamed 'the cowshed', a room of about twenty feet long and eight wide at the back of the main dressing room, because players felt as though they were herded in there like a herd of cattle. However, Viv Richards, who, Vic recalled, had been indroduced to Somerset by a Bath bookmaker called Len Creed, managed to get into the main dressing room. The 'other young pups', Roebuck, Botham, and Slocombe weren't exactly leaping for action. They were all huddled around an old gas fire in the home dressing room and didn't do a lot of cricket in the first hour or two. It was time spent discussing far more important matters, like how much petrol money they were going to get and whether their meal allowance was sufficient. Things became a lot more salubrious after the cowshed was turned into loos.

Conditions were worse for visiting teams. Something I found out when I drove up to Bristol to talk to the Test Match umpire and former county stalwart, Mervyn Kitchen. Here was a man whose jovial swagger spoke only of Somerset. "In the old days," he said jogging his memory, "when we used the old pavilion and it rained, the visitor dressing room always used to leak through the roof. And they always used to lump all their kit onto the table in the middle of the dressing room and as the rain came in one corner, they moved the table around, and as it came through the next corner they'd move the table around again. And those sorts of things were a regular occurrence, when the rain came down at Taunton."

Rain though wasn't the only thing to dampen the wicket. Sat in his comfy armchair, Mervyn turned his head to look lovingly at a photograph of his dog Thumper on the shelf behind him. He laughed as he spoke.

"At the beginning of the 1970s I went out with Roy Virgin to open the innings. Thumper was left on the concrete steps. My wife had gone up town shopping and she'd left the dog with a friend of ours. As I walked out the gate and on to the pitch, I heard a little chuckle. I looked over my shoulder and the dog was following about fifteen yards behind. So I turned at Roy and said, 'Bloody dog's following me out.'

'That's all right,' he said, 'You go up the top end and I'll go down the bottom end.'

I said, 'OK.'

So I walked towards the Riverside end of the ground to start the innings, and as I'm approaching the wicket up there, John Langridge, the old Sussex player who was umpiring in them days turned to me and said, 'Mervyn, is that your dog down there?'

And I said, 'Yes, I'm afraid he's followed us out, John.'

So he says, 'I think you'd better look round 'cos he's peeing all over the wicket.'

And I looked round and Thumper actually had his leg cocked over the stumps."

The decade had got off to an inauspicious start. Things could only get better. And to get better, the team had to get fit.

Players used to put more into the arts of bowling and batting than they do now. It became a different state of affairs, when George Lambert, a well-known Gloucestershire bowler came to Somerset as a coach. At the start of a season with April snow on the ground he sent the team out to the army camp at Norton Fitzwarren and had them doing rifle drill. A great big PTI instructor who was about fifteen stone and built like a battleship, then had them all running across country, carrying packs on their backs and lifting rifles up and down. Like it or not, it was the start of better things.

The 'Golden Era' began with 'that' game. The Gillette Cup Semi-Final against Essex at Taunton on the 16th August 1978. Before the game began, Gillette gave the teams free razors as corporate gifts. A shave if you win, cut your throat if you lose gesture. However, the game itself had the best finish of any match captain Brian Rose had ever played in, or ever seen. The excitement it generated was outstanding and the crowd was just unbelievable. Vivian Richards had hit 116, Ian Botham and the 'Big Bird' Joel Garner had chipped in, but it came down to the final ball bowled by Colin Dredge, 'The Demon of Frome', with the whole of his enormous family behind his arm. The Somerset songs 'Rosey's Army' and 'Cider Drinking' were hushed. Brian began to look haunted, as he relived the moment:

"I was actually praying at the time that the ball wouldn't come to me, and I think every other Somerset player was praying it wouldn't come to them either. I deposited nearly everybody, including the wicketkeeper Derek Taylor, on the boundary to stop the four or six obviously.

"I can remember people behind me were so excited. The whole crowd was in a state of anxiety and that sort of rubbed off on me, really. The bloke behind me was virtually dying of heart failure. Then all I could see, all I remember, was John Lever having a swish at the ball. I didn't see the ball. I didn't pick the ball up for what seemed an eternity and could see Viv shouting and yelling at me to run. My legs felt like rubber. My chase was like slow motion to get to this ball. I was very lucky to pick it up at the first attempt."

What Brian omitted to say was that his throw was poor. However, Peter Roebuck in his book *Slices of Cricket* was too much of a gentleman to call it that. Merely that Brian "hurled the ball in first bounce, a yard off target." Taylor, keeping wicket, collected it in a glove and dived at the wicket. The rest as they say is history. With runs all square Somerset had won, albeit just, by losing fewer wickets. Sadly, Cinderella's glass slippers missed the ball again and the team lost the final. The stage, however, was set. Between 1979 and 1983 the county won the Gillette Cup twice, the Benson & Hedges Cup twice and also the 'One Day' League.

Brian always was a man to do his best in the true spirit of Somerset. As an eighteen year old pup Peter Roebuck remembered the "colossus that was 'Rosey" wandering down the wicket to have a word during an innings. Peter had been scoring freely and Brian was struggling. Looking baleful he said: "Cricket's a funny game, isn't it, lad? They're bowling some right rubbish to you and they're bowling right well to me." And then he went up the other end again.

Vic liked that last story told in the new pavilion, watching it back in my small home studio before glancing down at the transcript. "There's an 's' in fascinated," he said, peering at a page. Did it matter? This was unsubtitled video film footage. But who was I to argue, when someone had read Classics at Oxford, spun a cricket ball devilishly slowly and batted when it mattered both for Somerset and England. He had been one of the heroes and was rightly proud of it. But he's still a pedantic old whatsit, I thought.

After tea in Timberscombe my penguin impression turned into one of a duck. On a radio beside the boundary edge, Justin Langer and Marcus Trescothick were trying their best to bring a glow to the early evening at the County Ground, where Brian Rose was now Director of Cricket. Perhaps tomorrow would see another golden dawn, as spectators would file in through the Sir Vivian Richards gates and sit in the Sir Ian Botham stand. It will be fascinating to find out and Vic, sitting with his microphone on BBC Test Match Special, will be first with a cheeky grin.

**GILLETTE CUP SEMI-FINAL SOMERSET V ESSEX.
16TH AUGUST 1978.**

SOMERSET

B.C. Rose	c East b Pont	24
P.A. Slocombe	lbw Phillip	0
I.V.A. Richards	c Denness bGooch	116
P.M. Roebuck	c Lever b Phillip	57
I.T. Botham	b East	7
V.J. Marks	not out	33
G.I. Burgess	b Lever	5
D. Breakwell	not out	17
Extras		28

Total (6 wkts, 60 overs)   287

Did not bat: D.J.S. Taylor, J.Garner, C.H. Dredge.
Fall of wickets: 1-2, 2-86, 3-189, 4-208, 5-247, 6-255.

Bowling: Lever 12-0-61-1; Phillip 11-1-56-2; Turner 8-6-22-0;
         Pont 6-1-35-1; Gooch 12-0-42-1; East 11-1-43-1

ESSEX

M.H. Denness	c Marks b Dredge	3
G.A. Gooch	c Taylor b Garner	61
K.S. McEwan	b Burgess	37
K.W.R. Fletcher	c & b Botham	67
B.R. Hardie	run out	21
K.R Pont	run out	39
N. Phillip	run out	1
S. Turner	b Botham	12
R.E. East	b Dredge	10
N. Smith	run out	6
J.K. Lever	not out	5
Extras		25
Total (60 overs)		287

Fall of wickets: 1-9, 2-70, 3-127, 4-166, 5-246, 6-248, 7-248,
8-266, 9-281.

Bowling: Garner 12-1-46-1; Dredge 12-0-60-2; Botham 12-1-48-2
Burgess 12-1-43-1; Breakwell 2-0-11-0; Marks 1-0-13-0;
Richards 9-1-41-0.

Somerset won by losing fewer wickets.

LESSON TWENTY-FIVE
HAVING A FLUTTER

"Somerset is an old and proud county, and people in Cornwall and Devon which are also old and proud counties, they have their own flags. I think it only right we have our own."
(Ed Woods, Somerset Flag Campaigner from Langport).

For five hundred years Chewton Mendip had been reknowned for its 'frid stool' in the old church. It's a stone seat for a criminal, said to be one of three seats of refuge in England, for those who claimed sanctuary. The other two are at Hexham and Beverley. Any violation would be met by hellfire and endless damnation. Such rhetoric could only be character building for a local boy.

Somerset suffered a tragic loss in summer 2007. Peter 'Dasher' Denning had been a specialist in the 1970s. A one day mumbling wonder. Lovingly remembered for his country yokel image of unruly blond hair, white floppy hat and adoration of the Wurzels, he died from cancer aged 57.

He was the Chewton Mendip butcher's son who invented the Chewton chop. Healthier than the Barnsley chop, unless an unfortunate happened to be dozing in the field anywhere from cover point to slip, Dasher's chop was an ingenious cut of a cricket ball rather than a greedy cut of lamb. Choosing cricket over school-mastering, he was a rarity of a sportsman, being disinclined to boast. Once, having removed his seemingly over-sized pads after another innings of propelling balls niftily into boundary boards, he was asked to do a BBC radio interview.

"Well, now, after this great, great performance today, you'll be looking forward to greater things."

(Indistinguishable mumble.)

"D'you expect to be in the England side soon?"

"Er, no."

"But why do you say that?"

"Not good enough."

Dasher could only have played for Somerset. He may never have worn the badge of the three lions, but he always battled his best for the dragon beast that flew from the pavilion flagstaff. It meant everything. Somerset had a thing about dragons ever since St Carantoc had led one by a neck halter across marshes to play with the village children and to light the cooking fires of Dunster. It is understandable that folk want to see a dragon on the county flag. And there is the rub. Believe it or not, the county does not have an official flag. For that, Avon must take the blame, when between 1974 and 1996 it swallowed up North Somerset, Bath and North East Somerset. Indeed, the councils in Weston and Bath still fly their own flags. Politics, don't you know, although it has to be said that on the day of Avon's creation some people hoisted some flags and they were black ones.

It is a rumpus that caused Councillor Alan Gloak, Chairman of Somerset County Council in Taunton, to call the renegades "lost tribes," saying they would be welcomed back and that their seats still wait for them in the Taunton council chamber. Sumorsaete Ealle?

Not surprisingly, many Somerset folk think that it is high time that we got our act together, got ourselves a flag fluttering to express countywide unity and put a dragon on it. The beast motivated 'Dasher' to valiant deeds and many believe it has had the same effect on Langer's modern army, so why not on everyone else? Action is pressing, particularly as Exmoor is causing worry by now raising its own flag, one that reverses the colours of Saint George's Cross, having been a law unto itself in the past. There are people alive who remember the rhyme,

"Steal the sheep and burn the wool
Goes the bells of Withypool."

Once, when a policeman was sent from Dulverton to investigate sheep stealing, the wild independent and spirited men of Withypool flung him into the river and stoned him.

They flatly refused to accept anyone looking into their affairs, except the parish constable, a man who they personally elected. These days, folk are kinder to visitors and the trophies on the local pub wall are just the heads of fox, stag and that of otter paw. The flag, though, remains a problem - despite reassuring the pilgrims lured to Lorna Doone that they are in the right place, Exmoor has a third of itself in Devon. One writer says the Exmoor flag is the "true flag of Somerset." Time then for a dragon to get its own back on St George and put the house in order.

What it should look like though, is a question for debate. Obviously, there is nobody still around old enough to have actually seen a dragon, except of course Harry Patch, and I'm sure he hasn't. So what to do? BBC Somerset Sound expressed an interest in staging a competition to decide on a flag for the county, but the competition was never held. And this was despite that stalwart of local broadcasting journalism, Clinton Rogers, stopping people in the street outside Taunton's Café Nero to get their hesitant opinions for 'Spotlight.'

So instead, the answer was to plump for something 'dragony' and not too Welsh and, like the cricket club, call it a wyvern. Sadly, this has only created argument, the gist being that both the existing county cricket club and county council badges have not got a wyvern on them, despite it often being said that they do. It is very confusing and probably the fault of the stop-start campaign running since 2006. The Lord Lieutenant of Somerset, Lady Elizabeth Gass, has shown her support, as has a local MP and the local TV, radio and newspapers.

In September 2006 the *Somerset County Gazette* ran an article head-lined "The County Flag – Dragon, Griffin or Wyvern?"

"For several years after the creation of Somerset County Council in 1889 they had no official coat of arms. In 1906 the council unofficially adopted a variation of the Wessex wyvern, in this instance a four-legged dragon, as their crest. The dragon was golden on a red background, just as the old wyvern of the Saxon Kingdom of Wessex had been. The motto Sumorsaete Ealle means "All the people of Somerset" and is a line from the Anglo-Saxon Chronicle of 878, when they rose up under King Alfred the Great, to liberate Wessex from the Danes. The creature is a dragon both in the flag and the coat of arms. A Griffin has an eagle's head, whilst a wyvern only has two legs and a fish's tail."

My good friend Phil had started to guddle in a 'Bearin' Up' moment. "Oh, for heaven's sake!" He folded the paper in half and with a clenched teeth "Gerrrr," slammed it down onto the small pub table, wobbling his half full pint glass. To argue over the mythical was something annoyingly ludicrous and so very Arthurian. So very Somerset.

Every flag should have its day. There is a body of opinion saying any chosen Somerset flag should be flown in Taunton on St Botolph's Day on the 17th of June, a date hearkening back to when a fair was once held there and could be again. As he is the patron saint of farmers and travellers, perhaps it should be flown in Glastonbury anyway, at festival time at least.

Alternatively, there is the 19th of May, the feast day of St Dunstan, born just east of Glastonbury in the Mendip village of Baltonsborough, anciently known as Ballsbury. Once a Glastonbury abbot, he was canon-ised for nailing a horseshoe onto the devil, which earned him a place as a patron saint of blacksmiths. Still, despite the balderdash, he's the nearest thing the county has to show as its own patron saint.

"A Langport bloke is campaigning for what looks like a chilli red dragon on a field of yellow custard, even got his own Somerset flag website asking for other suggestions," said Phil rereading the article. "Daub me a mug of cider on a old sheet and I'll fight for a rag on a pole, just see if I don't. Dragons aren't everything. It's what's in the heart that matters."

With that I went to the bar for replenishment, confident that 'Dasher' would have probably agreed.

LESSON TWENTY-SIX
STICKS AND STONES

"I was very into Arthurian myth.
I had always read all the White stuff, devour the stuff."
(George A. Romero, American director, writer, editor and actor).

"You can feel the vibes."
(Youth with a digeridoo, Glastonbury Tor, 2005)

When two related things happen within a short time of one another, they can cause comment. That morning I had walked past the Palace Theatre in London's West End and had seen that Monty Python's 'Spamalot' was on. That evening, back in West Somerset, I sauntered with two friends carrying rods, a box of fish bait and 'munchies' and passed a young lad claiming that he was Sir Lancelot. Clacking away with a plastic sword at a metal National Trust sign above Bossington beach, he was part of the new generation lost to make-believe, as his parents watched adoringly from their French-made 'people carrier'. The clack-clack-clack noise annoyed shelduck snoozing in the marsh samphire that grew beside a pool, where Horner Water's flow to the sea is slowed down by the high shingle bar.

I voiced thoughts on Camelot irreverence before refusing to put on a flotation suit, judging that it wouldn't have looked becoming on me. However, my friends Paul Wylie and Tom Potts were happy in theirs. With Tom wittering on about 'The Land Girls' and 'Killing Me Softly' being filmed on Bossington beach and the village having had a walnut tree that was "five yards around the trunk when it died in 1918," they were soon standing on the tideline of Bossington's shingle casting out to sea. Behind us was a sea-smoothed tree trunk that a storm must have thrown ashore. It was a good place for me to sit during the hour that passed, before the evening's first sea bass and line of mackerel. Time enough for me to aim pebbles at driftwood sticks and have the germ of a new story, and also to discuss whether folk cared about the caddle caused by Somerset legend. Paul, a spectacled 'sparky' whose currents of interest lie mainly in Porlock Bay and the waters of Europe, thought not. Whereas Tom, once a Royal Marine, and now a builder with a head full of factual trivia that has earned him the nickname 'The Walking Wiki' felt the need to test the water.

Did Paul and I know about the Essenes? No, we didn't. They turn up at Glastonbury on Midsummer night to watch the angels, who have guarded the earth over the past year, fly back to heaven from the top of the Tor, while those taking their places fly in. And the Wallies, did we know about them? Paul and I shook our heads. It was a religious sect founded by a London motor mechanic called Wally, and they loved Glastonbury, too. What about the abbey monks finding a tree-trunk coffin with Arthur and Guinevere inside? Of course we knew that, everyone did.

So we decided to set ourselves digging at the nonsense, and Tom was the one best suited. With a smile he turned to his i-Pod. It wasn't that we wanted to be killjoys, far from it. I especially loved the idea of fairy kings having realms under Glastonbury Tor. No, as we tucked into chorizo sausage and ciabatta rolls filled with mozarella and tomato, with basil leaf garnish drizzled with balsamic vinegar and olive oil, the three of us felt compelled to dig, knowing Somerset wasn't an isolated kingdom, but part of a European union. This is something that hasn't really been acknowledged for centuries. Once we put our oars in, others would surely disagree.

Local folk are possessive of good King Arthur, he's important to the local economy, particularly for the peddling of candles and crystals, books on angels and spells, wizard hats, resin cast hares and a plethora of Arthurian paraphernalia from the many magic shops.

With Dunster having an old yarn market, it's unsurprising Somerset folk like to weave a story or two. Good tales prove to be both romantic and lucrative. I don't want to sound pedantic, but when it comes to telling the truth, folk can sometimes be naughty. It's what makes local history so interesting. The gift of the gab can be as convincing now, as it has been over the centuries. Say 'Camelot' and thoughts turn to chivalry or Richard Harris trying to sing in the 1967 film. Me? I think of Cadbury Castle and being stung by a horsefly, making me sceptic rather than septic, knowing others think the hill was Arthur's court and has knights sleeping in a hollow beneath it. They are said to ride out by moonlight to water their horses at the well in Sutton Montis.

Whisper the word "Avalon" and listeners go positively weak kneed. Legend has it that the dying King Arthur was borne to the Isle of Avalon by weeping maidens. History is fairly clear where the word Avalon comes from. A Celtic tribe called the Belgae crossed from France to the Solent and made their way inland and westward to the sea in the neighbourhood of Glastonbury Tor. They settled themselves on what was then an island peninsula, which began to be called Avallach, the name of one of their chieftains. Becoming Avalonensis in Latin, it led to the variant Avalon. 'Excalibur' it's said, was wrought at 'Afallach'. Curious. In contradiction, John Hillaby reckoned 'avalon' was just Saxon for apples.

And then there's the power of suggestion. Plonk a sword in a stone outside Taunton Museum and the wishful think "Oh, King Arthur, goody. Let's go have a look!" Sadly, they'll find no Excalibur. It's a delicate issue, I know, and I'm sorry to disappoint the Gandalfs and Pendragons of solstice, but the 'Sword in the Stone' is Italian. This is a story born in Tuscany and later adopted into British 'history' from an isolated valley among Siena's hills. The ruined medieval Cistercian Abbey of Montesiepi owns a religious relic, the sword in the stone of Saint Galgano, a knight who became hermit. The sword has been in its stone now for eight hundred years. Both the Cistercian Abbey and the chapel dedicated to Saint Galgano are of the same time period as King Arthur's tomb in Glastonbury. Reputable historians are now saying the myth of the sword in the stone, although tied to the saga of King Arthur, originated in Tuscany and was later exported to France to become the famous Arthurian legend sung by troubadours. These lyric poets would surely never let the truth spoil a good story, if it meant they could earn silver and get fed.

And that's not the half of it. Merlin is the fictional creation of Geoffrey of Monmouth who was writing in the mid twelfth century. The wizard was a meld of earlier historical and legendary figures. Old stories of Myrddin Wyllt, a northern madman having nothing to do with King Arthur, were combined with tales of Aurelius Ambrosius, a fifth century warrior famous for leading a mixed force of Romans and Britons successfully against the Anglo-Saxons. The result was the made up character Geoffrey called Merlin Ambrosius.

Then, obviously, there's Guinevere, Arthur's queen. She is most famous for her love affair with Sir Lancelot. However, this story is the invention of Chrétien de Troyes', a French poet and troubadour who flourished in the late twelfth century with his poem 'Lancelot, the Knight of the Cart'. Cart? Having seen lots of horsedrawn carts, some with tyres and others with wobbly wooden wheels in Romania and Moldova, my mind boggles what Guinevere could have seen in Lancelot. Heigh ho. Love it's said is in the eye of the beholder. Troubadours must have thought it profitable to give the common touch.

Chrétien, in turn, may well have been inspired by Caradoc of Llancarfan, a Welsh monk who had written the largely fictional life of Glastonbury's St Gildas the Querulous a couple of decades earlier. In it Caradoc was the first to write about that big episode in the Arthurian legend, the abduction of Guinevere. There is the possibility that Caradoc was a playful romantic at heart. The name 'Guinevere' translates from the Welsh 'Gwenhwyfar' as 'The White Fairy' or 'White Ghost.' So, in other words, she did not exist as a mortal soul. Looking back at my university rag weeks I remember that it was invariably the Welsh students who were best at jolly japes, which were mostly at the expense of the English. Those from Cardiff were positively a pain in the rear. Enough said.

With Llancarfen opposite Watchet, doubtless the story of the white fairy soon crossed the water from Wales into Somerset and it came at an opportune time.

The 'black monks' of Glastonbury were seeking funds to rebuild the abbey after the original wattle and mud one was burned down in 1184 and the relics of St Patrick, the Irish patron saint who had ended his days at Glastonbury in 461, were not the draw they hoped for. Perhaps it was the idea of a bright spark Benedictine with his eyes on the ledger accounts, but whichever way one looks at it, in 1190 the monks claimed they found Guinevere lying dead with Arthur in the Lady Chapel. It was a certain 'porky pie' and not very Christian. They also gilded the lily a bit by 'finding' an oddly shaped cross with a Latin inscription naming Arthur and Guinevere. This, too, was said to be in the grave. The fibs, though, turned the monks into fat cats, made wealthy from gullible pilgrims, who in believing monks spoke the word of God, gave large donations. And Glastonbury has remained famous ever since.

Far be it from me to point the finger, but Chrétien also spent nine years trying to write 'Perceval, the Story of the Grail', but he never finished it. No wonder then that the Grail seekers are still about today and many come to Glastonbury, believing the sacred cup was hidden in the Chalice Well.

There is little doubt, though, that the Tor has always held the greater magnetism.

Certainly it attracted men from Spain, in days when the Brue estuary was open water near the west of the Tor. They came and they settled. These men were Iberian miners and knew the Tor as the 'Isle of Mictis'. In the second century BC it was the centre of the British metal trade.

Pliny recorded: "Six days sail inland from Britain there is an island called Mictis, in which white lead is found, and to this island the Britons come in boats of osier, covered with sewn hides."

Only a few miles north of the Tor is Wookey Hole. Here the stalactites are deeply stained with red, blue and green from the iron, lead, and copper in the soil above. Proof, if need be of an abundance of valuable ores in the district iron that made mining worth the trouble. Professor Boyd Dawkins has said the mineworkers "were short in stature, about five and a half feet in height, with brown skins and dark hair." Derek

Sharland, who lives the other side of my garden fence, fits this description. Knowing his family has lived in Somerset for generations and he has a hankering for Barcelona, I must remember to offer him Thorne's home-made pork sausage and chorizo and tell him to take his pick.

A standing stone at Priddy makes it clear that the Iberians worked at the local lead mines long before the Romans came to the Mendips. All this history has sadly become suffocated. Better this folk believed than for Glastonbury to be known as anything other than a mining town. Today there are more novel attractions.

As Hinkley Point has its power lines, so Glastonbury Tor has its ley lines, although a chap with a Y-shaped hazel twig told me off not long ago saying they aren't the same things at all, despite them both being lines of energy. I have tried very hard to understand his point of view, yet people are drawn here in the guise of earth mystery researchers, folk-lorists, dowsers and youths with digeridoos. Indeed, there is a common thread among these people in believing that Glastonbury is their Avalon on ley lines and has a "very holy vibration." For them it's one of the most powerful energy centres on the planet, playing an important role in New Age spirituality. Not surprisingly, it was a 1960s' phenomenon.

During that decade of England's cultural revolution, John Michell, an English antiquities expert, found evidence of an alignment of Neolithic sacred sites in the Glastonbury region. The Tor, he believed, was linked with such respected ancient holy places as Avebury stone rings and St Michael's Mount. Alternative folk rather liked that idea. More recent research by Hamish Miller and Paul Broadhurst, featured in their book *The Sun and the Serpent*, has revealed this mysterious alignment runs all across southern England linking hundreds of Neolithic, Celtic and early Christian sacred places.

Miller and Broadhurst are a pair of dowsers working in a world of sceptics. Indeed, even many of dowsing's supporters believe that dowsing apparatuses have no special powers, but merely amplify small imperceptible movements of the hands arising from the expectations of the dowser, who has a subliminal sensitivity to the environment. Let it be said that recent in-depth German research at the 'Society for the Scientific Investigation of the Parasciences' in Kassel debunked dowsing as 'chance'.

However, both Miller and Broadhurst believe they are very sensitive and have brought to light matters of great importance. Laboriously dowsing the entire alignment over a period of years, they discovered there are actually two distinct parallel lines of energy flowing for nearly three hundred miles that they have called St Michael and St Mary despite claiming the lines are older than Christianity. After following these lines up the sides of the Tor, the two dowsers made a remarkable discovery.

"The two lines appeared to mirror the ancient landscape labyrinth as it winds its serpentine way to the summit. Even more astonishing, the two lines move in a sort of harmony with one another and, at the very peak, interpenetrate as if they are ritually mating. The female, yin or Mary energy line encloses the masculine, yang or Michael energy in the form of a double-lipped cup. It is a most evocative image. The configuration of the Mary energy line, containing the phallus-like mediaeval tower of St Michael, seems to portray a chalice or grail and is thus a potent symbol of the alchemical fusion of universal opposites."

The discovery of this symbol on the Tor, created by a positive and a negative current of energy, confirmed to them that Glastonbury Tor was indeed a centre of the ancient mysteries. A theory reinforced in those of like mind, when strange balls of coloured lights were 'seen' spiralling around the Tor. In 1970 it's said, a local police officer reported having seen eight egg-shaped objects "dark maroon in color, hovering in formation over the hill," and ten years later a witness saw "several green and mauve lights hovering around the tower, some smaller than others, about the size of beachballs and footballs."

I can't possibly comment other than to say policemen, like sea fishermen at Bossington, have been known to exaggerate sometimes and that a phallus isn't complete without balls. Putting aside sexual symbolism and alarming imagery for a moment, it's nice to think that Glastonbury may have a deeply rooted and ordinary meaning.

A footnote in an old book from 1829 titled *North-West Somerset* reveals something quite interesting, an unusual derivation of the name Glastonbury. It says 'Glastan-byrie' means the 'Hill of Oaks'. A name that is perhaps a little less romantic than the 'Isle of Glass' that many writers say is the origin of the name, alluding to the Tor once being an isle and lapped by water or owned by a Somerset farmer known as Master Glass. I like 'Hill of Oaks' best. It ties in nicely with another legend, that of Joseph of Arimathea.

There were once two ancient trees called 'The Oaks of Avalon' that had been under the stars since the birth of our desert religion. Singularly, they were known as Gog and Magog and they grew with other oaks in a grove from which an avenue of oaks ran up towards the Tor. The year Somerset County Council unofficially adopted a crest of a four-legged dragon in 1906 and mistakenly called it a wyvern, Gog and Magog were cut down, as was the rest of the grove and the avenue, to clear the ground of a farm. Perhaps that farmer had wanted to landscape a Jerusalem in England's green and pleasant land, but it was surely others who muttered the word 'Jesus'. Magog was an immense tree eleven feet in diameter and had more than two thousand season-rings making it a sponge of myth.

Writing in 1714, the antiquary Eyston in *A little Monument to the once famous Abbey and Borough of Glastonbury* tells a story gathered from the landlord of the 'George Inn', who rented a large part of the Abbey enclosure.

The story went "that St. Joseph of Arimathea landed not far from the town, at a place where there was an oak planted in memory of his landing, called 'The Oak of Avalon'; that he and his companions marched thence to a Hill, near a mile on the south side of the town, and there being weary rested themselves, which gave the Hill the name of Wearyall Hill; that St Joseph stuck on the Hill his staff, being a dry hawthorn stick, which grew, and constantly budded and blowed upon Christmas Day."

About the same time as Eyston was writing his piece, Daniel Defoe wrote, "Of the Holy Thorn many absurd accounts have been given." The best that can be said is that the facts were very subjective.

What Joseph was supposed to have brought with him was a pair of cruets, containing a relic of the Holy Blood and of the sweat of Christ. He can be seen carrying these cruets in the fifteenth-century glass in the east window of Langport Church. Again, Joseph's arrival in Somerset is a fiction. His name was first introduced into the Glastonbury story in the thirteenth century by a deliberate borrowing from French romances and from the Cornish. The major twelfth century historian, William of Malmesbury knew nothing of him.

After Gog and Magog went under the farmer's axe, they were sold to Messrs J. Snow & Son, Glastonbury timber merchants. A Mr Curtis who worked for the firm remembered five boys standing in the one called Magog, when he was a lad. Magog was turned into bowls, candlesticks, picture frames and a Glastonbury chair. The oak's wood was said to have an extraordinarily red and unique grain.

Nasty things have happened on the Tor. The Dissolution of the Monasteries at the order of Henry VIII saw the end of Glastonbury Abbey's wealth and power. The story of the last abbot, Richard Whiting, is one too sad to dwell upon. He refused to surrender his abbey to the king. On 15th November 1539 he was tied to a hurdle, dragged up the Tor and hanged, drawn and quartered. Whiting's execution was on a trumped-up charge of embezzlement and treason. The jury included his treacherous steward called Horner. Following the destruction of the abbey, the steward was rewarded with the Manor of Mells. His treachery is remembered in a nursery rhyme first published in 1725, that I learnt as a small child:

Little Jack Horner sat in the corner
Eating his Christmas pie,
He put in his thumb and pulled out a plum
And said "What a good boy am I!"

Mells was certainly a plum.

A survivor of the Reformation was the Levantine thorn tree in the abbey ruins. Its claims to sanctity awakened the ire of an unhappy Puritan, who felt the need to diligently and impiously cut it down. For a thorn it was gigantic, and was in two parts. One part he demolished, the other he mortally wounded. The tree, though, revenged itself. A splinter flew into the Puritan's eye and finished him.

The wounded tree lingered another thirty years before dying. But in the meantime various thorns were budded from it. One is in the abbey grounds, a better one in the parish churchyard of St John the Baptist on Glastonbury High Street and another in the vicarage garden. They keep the habit of blossoming in May and again at Christmastide, but more freely on old Christmas Day the 6th January. Nearly always on Christmas Day morning flowers from one of the thorns are placed on the altar of St John's and on the Royal Breakfast Table. A sprig was even sent over to Washington for the funeral of President Kennedy. And that's the truth of it.

Having scrambled back up Bossington's shingle, without a fish, but with empty sandwich bags stuffed in my pocket, I saw the people carrier was gone. There was just a crow giving me the eye. Chucked in the bambles was a broken length of hilted plastic. They don't make swords like they used to.

Paul carried a sea bass, mackerel and cod while Tom was still hooked to his i-Pod, immersed in Roxy Music's 'Avalon'. I watched them both leave eagerly to get to 'Darts Night' at their local. Then, in the twilight, I sat in my car and tapped into my laptop the story that had formed in my head. There was a Glastonbury enchanted lady I knew, whose eyes had caught the interest of 'Mister Cadbury' of chocolate fame. She would relate to the whimsical tale, I knew that, yet I was sure it was something she wouldn't mind. The character I was inventing was as real as Guinevere.

The Healer of Bossington

At a time when folk denied that iron boats could float, Hettie the healer bottled nature and believed that love sailed through the rainbow. So they whispered that Hettie was "hare-mad" and "pickled on apple-brandy."

"Who're they?" you ask. Well, some people in Porlock Vale. Those with the nervous laughter of ignorance. They didn't understand Hettie was different. How could they?

But the wizened lady did. She understood her daughter, born of a father Hettie never knew.

A daughter born in the place of siskin and peregrine, and the all knowing black-eyed crow, where the pretty stream that's Horner Water burbles through Bossington village; past Hettie's home, to where the Marsh Samphire grows and Horner Water becomes a mirror pool because a shingle bar prevents the stream from meeting the sea.

The wizened lady had seen Hettie's likeness before in her own reflections of memory.

Oh yes, it's easy to forget the wizened could once have had beauty even though sly winds cause ripples of distortion.

Oh goodness, Hettie was radiant; beautiful. But she was also impatient and easily irritated. People irritated Hettie. A screw her eyes up, grind her teeth, fingernails clenched into the palms of her hands irritated.

But impatient and irritable though she may have been, Hettie had the light. Her body was surrounded by it. A sphere of light. An aura of brilliant white. At its best when the moon was full and Venus bright. An aura only her own mother could see. Then of course, even flowers had their own auras. Auras that heal. Her mother knew that, too. What else did that wizened lady know? Oh yes, of course, that love sails through the rainbow. What Hettie had was a gift. A healing gift as rare as happiness. "Impatiens, impatiens," her mother would mutter under her breath. Such care the wizened lady took in nurturing the Busy Lizzie flowers in her cottage garden. From them would come the drops added to the water-cup by Hettie's bed. It was the only help this mother could give.

The other village women scorned Hettie. Jealous. Scowling. What could Hettie do, though? It was their men that annoyed her. From the muscular to the frail. From teacher to idiot, blacksmith to parson. Her breath-catching beauty aroused batchelors, marrieds and widowers to cheek-blush. Made them fawn. Made them irritating. Men did her head in.

So Hettie sought to heal. O yes, she'd purge men of their irritations. Each and every one. Instinctively. From self-pity to piety, indecision to despair, dalliance to being just too nice.

Out into the wild Hettie went, withy basket in hand, to smile at stoats and skip with hares, to gather her remedies on the heath of adders and the slopes of scree. Remedies of heather and holly, wild-oat and gorse.

Tiny bottles of this and tiny bottles of that were Hettie's creations. Trace dilutions suspended in apple brandy. The healings were subtle. Hettie though, was not. She'd cry, "honkers-ponkers!" at the merest hint of bad-breath and "yuckity-doo!" at dandruff. To Hettie no one was perfect, except him. The man she loved. All she had was never enough.

Although her sleep was dreamless, when the moon was full and Venus bright, Hettie lay awake lonely. Lost. Aura shining. Chaste. Sipping from the cup by her bed. Yearning for the rainbows that could only come betwixt sun and rain. On such days she'd walk in shawl-wrapped slenderness between fields of barley, on the path that changed from dust to mud, mud to dust, to gaze at herself in the shingle-trapped pool of water. Were they ripples or wrinkles she saw?

Then up the shingle bar she'd climb to become as one with her Bay of the Sickle, where the winds cut clean. Winds that billowed sails. In the distance, embedded leech-like on Hurlstone Point was the sailors' beacon light. A useless light. Never had it drawn him to her. Impatiens, impatiens.

Wearily treading on the shifting smooth pebble-hardness towards the beacon, Hettie would reach the seat where once her mother sat. A worn tree trunk, storm-stripped of bark. Wave-borne flotsam. Stranded.

Where had that tree grown? In what place had it flourished green? Had it come from his country? Surely he'd come for her, sail-wind seeking. Appearing through the arch of a rainbow. She just had to believe it. Spirit knowing. Cosmic called. Bringing his love to Hettie. A love over lifetimes reincarnated again. She sang sad elegies to ease the yearn and heart-pain as she watched the black-eyed crow. Impatiens, impatiens.

It was the crow that had shown Hettie the rainbows. Sitting as a girl on her wave-borne seat. Lonely. Damp with rain, yet sun drying. The bird alighted open-beaked and staring upon the pebbles between Hettie and the waves.

"Show me joy," she had said. So the bird did. A black feather of portent dropped, quill pointing out to sea, as the horizon became a vision blessed. A profusion of colour. Glorious. Ethereal arches one above the other. Beauty greater than heaven itself, or even an aura reflected in a mirror pool.

Hettie though never saw the like again. Neither did her love sail through the rainbow. Only her mother had that joy. The joy of a love meant to be, to cherish until the last day of her Bossington life. The day that left Hettie alone. Alone with her aura. Alone to bottle nature, because men did her head in.

As time passed Hettie conceeded that they were wrinkles she saw in the pool where the Marsh Samphire grew. But whenever rain poured through sunshine, she would still gaze out to sea, calling to the bird that knows everything.

"Can you see my love? Can you see his sail?" A voice forever snatched away by the sly wind before reaching the black-eyed crow circling high and tumbling low above the sickle shore.

Impatiens, impatiens.

LESSON TWENTY-SEVEN
MAY BEES AND HANKIES

"Nemo enim fere saltat sobrius, nisi forte insanit."
(Cicero)

("Hardly anybody dances sober, unless he's completely mad.")

The two honey bees had sought shelter from the rain and had managed to get stuck in the dining room. Now that the sun was out, the bees were head-buzzing against the window.

The first day of May was not the time to be indoors, with or without a headache. The world outside was exciting. The Minehead 'Sailors' Horse' and 'Town Horse' had already joined in a dance together at sunrise. Cattle were being let into Tatworth's watercress beds. And with the virgin plonking her naked foot down onto the grass and flattening seven daisies, it was officially spring. Elsewhere, in Manganese de la Povorosa a live goat had been chucked from the church belfry to hopefully be caught in a tarpaulin. Not kidding. And on the subject of kids, at Castrillo de Murca men dressed as devils had taken running leaps over babies laid out on matresses in the street, in a fertility rite where, unsurprisingly the village population is falling. Time then, in the new-build sprawl of Cotford St Luke, for Reg Gutteridge to iron his white hankies.

Reg has an eye for detail and a certain panache. If something's worth doing, he'll set about doing it with his heart and soul. It was an early observation made when we were 'boat buddies' together, creating a model ship out of newspaper and sellotape, part of a team building exercise during our teacher training. His felt-marker penned pirate flag stuck to a toothpick flying from the mast made of yesterday's *Sun* was a gesture of flamboyance. Here was a man who hankered after silliness.

The problem was he looked so sensible. Despite sporting a beard, the trend of many a Somerset 'character', he looked every bit the I.T. nerd. He had trained as an architect and in computer-aided design, had a patent pending on a disability vehicle he'd invented, was a whizz at making model sand-yachts and had created some animated butterflies to edit into a short fairy tale film about a witch, some cowslips and a young mother who stuck pins into a sheep's heart that I was making. Nothing untoward there, then. However, in Somerset nothing is ever quite as it seems It was the butterflies that gave him away. Reg wanted to be sure I was Okay with the CGI'd wing beats of a tortoiseshell. This meant going to visit his brick box of a home crammed with hundreds of others into what used to be the grounds of Tone Vale Mental Hospital. A promising address that the planners thought would be better served with an alias or two. The odd lost looking souls with droopy jowls in raincoats and plimsols that still wandered about didn't seem to be affecting sales. It just added substance to the time-misted reasoning that every village needs an idiot. Cotford was dutifully offering the rural package.

"Come into the doctor's surgery," said Reg, opening the back door to me. Not that his house was a surgery, only that both he and his sensible looking wife, Sue, felt it had a rather right-angled, featureless feel. It did, but there was a lot to see and hear, that more than compensated. With Reg distracted by kettle and teabags, Sue was soon confessing that she believed in fairies, which must have been a relief to the plastic ones she had stuck into the pots of houseplants and flowerbeds and left to play flutes and fiddles.

I asked her, if she knew that any man who stands under an elder tree on Midsummer Eve can see the fairies and get the wish of his heart. But he will die within the year. No, she hadn't and was very pleased Reg had proposed to her beneath an oak.

She was interrupted by the frantic yappings of a tiny hairy Yorkie turning circles. Muffin was the house boss determined to show me her butler's favourite things. Being an innocent at most times, she lured me with her adorability from kitchen to sitting room. Reg's shout came too late.

As with Sue's fairies, so with Reg. He obviously liked his instruments. Accordions, recorders and penny whistles were in cases and boxes on sofa and floor. On a chair were a neat pile of white hankies and hanging from the chair back were what appeared to be a couple of belts coloured purple and gold, and some black leather straps with bells on. Good God, I realised, Reg is a Morris Man.

His other life no longer secret Reg picked up an accordion and played. This man of secrets was very, very good and was without doubt a folkie to the core.

Me having to go abroad for ten days a few weeks later, Sue volunteered that Felix, my youngest, could stay with them. He thought it a grand idea. "I could teach him the penny whistle," Reg offered. Felix gave me his hopeful look.

"You'll become what I've always wanted," I said to him.

"Wot?"

"A Morris Minor." When I returned from foreign shores Felix had apparently spent all his spare time on his Game Cube.

As I opened the window giving freedom to the bees on that May Day morning, Reg would be preparing once more to come out of the closet.

Ever since being outed by Muffin, he has claimed that it was Exmoor real ale that first got him talking to the bagman and squire of the West Somerset Morris Men. His ears had pricked up when he heard a squeeze-box being played in the back room of a pub in which he had already downed four pints. Enchanted, he left Sue with half a large glass of Pinot Grigio in her hand, and weaved off to investigate. By the time her glass was empty, Reg's was refilled and he had been enlisted with much thigh slapping and merriment as the newest and youngest recruit. He had stumbled upon his destiny to wear the motif of the stag and baldrics inspired by the colours of heather and gorse, and upon the concerted joy of waggling his legs to the jingle of bells. As if this wasn't enough reward for Reg's guddled impulse, there was more. He had acquired the right to a second home. One of curious gargoyles, battlements, pinnacles and a 'goodly bell-cot'. The eccentric fifteenth century Quantocks delight of Halsway Manor is the rustic pad adopted as base camp for the West Somerset Morris and now England's only residential centre for folk dance and music.

When Sue caught up with her beloved rascal, not even a wagging finger could pull him out of slurred tongued giggledom. He was happy being regaled with stories about Morris Men landing on people's dogs when jumping over hay bales and falling off toilet roofs.

The bagman, who is to all intents and purposes the secretary, had done his job well. Something appreciated by the squire, who has the role of chairman. He admitted to Sue that finding young blood was getting harder nowadays. In his mid-forties, Reg was a mere colt and at least twenty years younger than the rest.

Morrising seems to have been a sixties thing, not so much with age, but with decade. Reg's troupe first formed in 1966. In the year England won its only football World Cup, Halsway had a ball with bells on. Some with an odd disposition felt there had to be an alternative sound to the Beatles. Certainly locally there wasn't much on offer, just a few local jigs and hornpipes for the mainstream music lovers. The more adventurous danced along a broom laid on the floor or on top of a haystack. To all intents and purposes, that was it. The Victorians had put an end to fun, if it descended into drunkenness, bawdiness or anything un-Christian. This meant that Morris dancing with its lack of temperance, humorous indecency and roots in pagan fertility rites and ritual sacrifice was firmly knocked on the head, having earned the 'full house' of iniquities.

New to the fun, the bumped and bruised Taunton Deane Morris have taken the precaution to practice their own take on Rap music by wearing motorcycle and cricket helmets until their stick dancing proficiency is fine tuned, allowing A&E at Musgrove Park Hospital to save on the Witch hazel. Their motto 'alterum trahe tintinnabula portat' meaning 'pull the other leg, it's got bells on' is all very well, but doesn't get around the fact the story of the helmets is true.

A close neighbour of Reg's West Somerset bunch are the floral and pheasant feather hatted, blue-green ragged Exmoor Border Morris. They are a mixed bunch of men and women and their blackened faces, bells and sticks give a clue where Morris dancing originally hailed from. The Crusader knights away in far off lands, it's said, were so impressed by dancing Moors that they brought notions of the dances back to England. The bells and sticks had the job of frightening away evil spirits and ensuring that crops grew to be bountiful.

Reg avoids short measures and yearns for the harvested product of barley and hops, real ale. They are such wonderful incentives to nimbly tinkle away whilst flapping hankies with the rest of the lads. However, on May Day, Reg and the rest must wait their turn. Etiquette has it that the Minehead Sailors' Hobby Horse must have both the first and second dances of the day. Age before beauty. With an entourage of white-peaked, sailor-capped money collectors carrying buckets and of musicians with drums and accordions the Hobby Horse embarks on three days of chasing laughing children, accosting grumpy men and catching playful women in Minehead and Dunster to the sounds of the Hobby Horse song:

"The Hobby Horse was crowned the King of May
A shrine for us to live on the Minehead Bay
The Sailors Horse will dance and bow and play
In the old traditional way
Hail for the ancient King of May."

Sometimes in the past things have tended to get a little raucous and out of hand. And on a few occasions the police had goes at trying to stop the festivities. Hilda Parham who owned a sweetshop shop with her husband in West Street still giggled when she talked to me about her childhood memory of a killjoy of a new police inspector who had arrived with several vans of constables.

"We were going a bit wild about the Hobby Horse, mind," she laughed. "When the police came, all us children and many grown-ups raced away down the alleyways and hid behind gates. Tons of people were running down our lane. I don't think the police caught anybody, except those too drunk to move their feet. It was great fun."

Historians of the biddling sort are adamant that the Hobby Horse is older than Morris dancing. There has been a May festival in Minehead since 1465 and the Hobby Horse earned a reputation not so much of leaping over babies, but of making them under the cover of canvas. The horse is a large wooden frame carried on one man's shoulders. His head pokes up in the centre, wearing a mask with tall, red-dyed ostrich feathers on top. The sides are made of canvas painted with coloured circles, the top is decked out in ribbons and a tail of rope, also ribbon tied, has a bruising knot on its end.

The horse demands money like an outlaw, as it dances and prances with abandonment. In the past, a refusal to pay led inevitably to a booting. The horse kicked out at the miser's nether regions. Booting has died out, but a similar action, tupping, has not. In pagan times, this may have formed part of a fertility rite. Nowadays, it is just harmless horseplay, although the tupping of pretty maids is understandably frowned upon, although watered down to mere simulation. "A-one! A-two! A-dree! A-vour! A-vive! A-zix! A-zem! A-eight! A-nine! A-taine!" Some Victorian blood remains resilient to dilution. It even affected Vaughan Williams. He was so enamoured that he composed a folk dance in honour of the ostrich feathered one in 1912. Sadly, propriety saw to it that it was never published. Still, anyone failing to pop a contribution into a bucket these days runs the risk of a 'praper tail lashin'', however broadminded they may be.

The hobby's ancestor, legend says, scared the marauding Danes away to Watchet by prancing around on the beach. Either the Danes feared being devoured by whatever the great feathers belonged to, or they were on dried fly agaric mushrooms and hallucinating an amazing technicolor paddling dragon. It's not all as daft as it sounds. A performing hobby horse from Suffolk went by boat over to mainland Europe in the Normandy landings, in a sneaky ploy to put the Germans off their guard. Nazi officers must have wasted valuable time checking both their own and their machine-gunners' water bottles. Every soul inside a frame covered in canvas and rags must do his duty and England owes them.

Whatever might have happened in the case of the Minehead Hobby Horse, it's definitely traceable back at least to 1792. Having now become the adopted face of the town, it has to be better than that other face of Minehead, the one of a local sailor that appeared on the packets of John Player cigarettes, said to be responsible for the premature deaths of thousands.

When the Hobby was first recorded in the ledger at Dunster Castle, it must have already been part of the local scenery. For dancing in front of Lord and Lady Luttrell it was paid five shillings, then the best part of a week's wages. And so began the custom of the Hobby Horse dancing dervish twirls on May Day evening outside the castle's front door before 'tupping' the May Queen in all her prettiness and false modesty beneath her floral crown. The Hobby Horse has true star quality and it knows it. Too much for the Morris Men to compete with, and a quality Reg really wished he had.

He was chuntering that he had been elected bagman and after several months he still hadn't managed to enlist any new recruits. The responsibility of keeping the West Somerset Morris Men going was getting too much for him. The worry was putting him off his ale. Before joining his aging comrades for a dance at sunset outside the 'Old Ship Aground' on Minehead harbour, emotion broke like a ripple-wave over his small sandwormish ego.

"I'm going to resign," he said before wiping the corner of an eye and blowing his nose with a white hanky before skipping off on jingle-jangle legs. Across town in the yard of the 'Queen's Head', a legless Hobby Horse snoozed for the night and doubtless in a house somewhere nearby the young May Queen was adjusting her ruffled skirt, forgetting her floral crown was more askew than straight. In two Spanish villages a goat and a number of babies were perhaps suffering from disturbed dreams. A good thing, I thought, that the Iberians who once sought iron, lead and copper from the rich, red soil below Glastonbury Tor's terraces didn't bring their May Day customs along with their digging tools.

Try as I might, the honey bees trapped in my dining room ignored my encouragements and refrained from leaving. They seemed determined to miss all the fun.

The following month a letter appeared in *The Times* newspaper written by Paul Reece, the Squire of the Morris Ring:

"The upsurge of interest in our folk traditions and the ability of the performers of the Morris dance, in its different forms, to put on large-scale, colourful and moving performances is achieved largely through self-financing in order to keep these traditions alive at a time when regional cultural identity is increasingly being eroded. As we enter the four-year period of the cultural Olympiad, its planned regional events and the opening and closing ceremonies of the London Games in 2012, there is a strong case to be made for featuring one of our most enduring traditions: the Morris dance."

There you go, Reg, I thought, something to strive for. And if the Hobby Horse gets to dance before events and steps on some Suffolk toes, perhaps the good men and women of Somerset could sweep the gold medal board.

LESSON TWENTY-EIGHT
HOLES AND SQUEALERS

"A sly rabbit will have three openings to its den."
(Chinese Proverb).

Sometimes, just sometimes, somebody is born to make England smile. Chris Rawles used be a bare-fist boxer, became a builder and foster parent, has a voice loud enough to be heard between Wivey and Norton Fitzwarren, swears to make the air blue and has the kindest heart in Christendom. He can be heard from the touchline of the rugby pitch, shouting at his teenage son Dean. "Come on, Deano, bite their legs!" And a few seconds later, "Oh no, Deano's been hurt, Deano's been hurt!" before running on with a crate of water bottles and a sponge. In the rugby club bar he will order, "A pint with a dash but quicker than that," or call out, "Ouzes this scrum pee?" when confusion reigns over the owner of a half drunk pint of the rough stuff. Chris has been doing it for years.

At a time of daffodils and shrinking violets Chris called at my home, as the light was going from dimpsey to dark. He had come to measure for a porch over the blue, warped front door that was too old to cheat the wind driven rain and so full of character that a replacement had never entered my mind. He told me that he had come by some bricks originally from Thailand that would do the job nicely; that he would find some 'suitable' slates from some reclamation or other; and would also haggle for a couple of oak posts, but "they would be a bit dear, mind." And then he told me the story of his day.

He was on his way to help a friend in need living in the back of beyond on the Brendon Hills. Whilst driving his transit van down a rutted lane between hedgerows, he saw two rabbits running across a field in his direction, only to see them disappear from view. Then, hearing a hell of a thud on the side of the van, he stopped, thinking that he must have caught a stone. But it was not a stone. It was a groggy, dazed doe rabbit. Before Chris had time to do one thing or another, a buck rabbit shot from the hedge and mounted the doe to do what rabbits do best. Chris took his mobile phone from his pocket and called his friend and mine, Phil. "I'm just watching a rabbit being raped," he said.

For its part a rabbit consumes about a pound in weight of green stuff a day. Edges of cereal fields can be demolished. Turnip tops are gratefully munched. Cabbages and Brussels sprouts are well liked and complete garden crops in Somerset can disappear overnight. Seedling trees get ring-barked and killed by the gnawing of rabbity teeth, so white plastic protective tree guards are now common. They also eat their own poo inside their burrows. A rabbit's stomach can't cope with cellulose in one sitting; so redigestion is a needs must, a bit like cows and sheep chewing the cud. A rabbit, though, is cruder. The burrow dung is nice and soft, ready to pass through the tummy a second time. The small pellets that lie in quantity near rabbit holes are the 'finished article'.

I asked Chris, if he was fond of rabbits. He told me that he was. At a pinch he could teach me how to catch them, what with the cost of living being so high and bunnies being bountiful. What I needed, he said, was two small sticks and some copper wire. He even thought that he had some in his van.

A snare had to be set up in the paths used by the rabbits, but that needed a practiced eye given that rabbits didn't often use pavements, there are simply not that many about in the countryside. They only used tarmac if feeling suicidal.

What you had to do, Chris showed me, was find an ash or hazel tree and cut a length of stick the width of your little finger, below where the stick branches. Then cut the stick into two, just below the branch itself. You have a longer stick and a shorter one that branches. Split the longer stick at one end and poke the other end in the ground. Trim the shorter one into a V- shape to form a rough hook and poke it into the ground a hand's breadth behind the other one. Tie your copper wire around the hook to prevent the wire slipping free when time comes to wriggling and tugging, then pass the wire through the split and make a loose noose. Then leave it alone to catch a rabbit. Simple.

How many have you caught over time, I asked. "None" he said. "Can't do with the squealing."

That reminded me of a secret that I just had to share. Once, when I had visited Phil at his home down the end of the same bumpity-bump track where Chris had witnessed the rape of the rabbit, I showed something to Phil's son, Roger. Freckled and red hair in dreadlocks, Roger was seeing huge potential in what looked like a piece hazel wood. I had known the lad for several years, but only now was it dawning on me that he was a fox murderer. The piece of hazel now in his hand would be bringing them to the slaughter. And it was all the fault of 'Ivor the Engine' and wind.

I had earned my keep for a while doing some television wildlife film work. It had obvious difficulties. Not only did you have to find your animals, they also had to be obliging enough to wander into frame. And even if they did that, the pictures would look rubbish if out of focus or wobbly. Wobble is caused either by the lack of a tripod, or a muscular spasm, or wind. I used to use a sock filled with green lentils instead of a tripod to get low shots, and with the lens on full zoom I would get camera shake if a flea farted.

I was trying to film foxes in and around a Somerset wood without much success in getting 'close ups'. Then, as chance would have it, I had a conversation with Eddie who helped out with a Dulverton GP's pheasant rearing. What I needed to do, he said, was to sound like a rabbit. Foxes would come so close I'd be able to stretch out my hand and stroke them. I stuck two fingers above the sides of head and did a Bugs Bunny impression. I thought Eddie was talking rollocks.

"Not like that," said Eddie. "Like this." What he then showed me, he had made himself. From out of his pocket he took a piece of wood and blew on it. The sound was just like the eerie squeal of a rabbit in pain. Every fox wants an easy life. Somewhere they can feed with as little effort as possible, as well as having a nice safe haven to bed down. Any place where Man breeds tasty pheasants is like Sainsbury's for a fox. Eddie provided armed shop security. On the occasions he caught a thief, there was no slap on the paw, but instead a coup de grace from close range with a shotgun. All very sporting.

Eddie's rabbit squealer was a wonder and like Chris, he showed me the 'Blue Peter' way of making one for myself. By whittling with a sheath knife at a piece of hazel stick, then adding a length of old video-cassette tape and some electrical insulating tape, you have it. A bit like blowing on a piece of grass held between your thumbs.

The secret of rabbit squealing is not to blow too hard, Eddie warned, otherwise you just sound like a rabbit fed on Indian takeaway. Also, the mouthpiece should not be too large, as a good seal was very important; and I should be careful the tape did not tear under tension. Still, making one was very much trial and error for me. I had replaced a fuzzy and temperamental VHS copy of 'Ivor the Engine' with the DVD, so I pulled a length of tape from the cassette and snip-snipped at it with kitchen scissors. The tape had been the inspiration for my children's love of the West Somerset Railway and had prompted my daughter Ez to ask a driver whether he had any dragons in his firebox.

Now, finally after having the success of making a squeal, it allowed me to film fantastic fox footage including a vixen who left the den with her cubs to play for the camera at dusk, thinking that they were out rabbiting. I was very proud of my squealer.

Where had Eddie learned of such a thing? I was curious to know,

171

having had a vision of an old gamekeeper on his deathbed, imparting a rich memory into Eddie's ear. "Oh, some website or other", Eddie said. The last I heard of Eddie was he had been caught by police hunting urban foxes around dustbins in the St Paul's district of Bristol.

And now I was showing my squealer to Roger. I was a fool. Poor foxes. "You could double your chances, said Roger in bouncy mood, "if you laid out a few whiffy bunny-hopper road kills at the same time." He had taken country living into his soul and went off to play.

A few weeks later I asked my son about the fox population, now that Roger had 'discovered' the squealer. He was sure to know, because he and Roger were at college together. "Fine," he said. "Roger's making himself a lot of money."

Roger had been selling squealers around college for a fiver a time. There was a rumour going around of rabbits being heard in the Nationwide Building Society, Starbucks and amongst the lingerie in Marks and Spencer all about the same time.

"Anties in the panties," said Chris with a laugh. Wherever there are rabbits nibbling, there are ants loving the short grass. So good advice is not to go having a picnic by a rabbit hole.

Fried, stewed or stuffed and roasted, Chris loved his rabbit. On Sundays his Mum used to roast a couple. "She stuffed them full of sage and onion and put little strips of bacon on them to keep them moist. And if we got the very young ones, they were particularly nice, jointed, dipped in flour and fried."

Then again, even I knew that a saddle of rabbit gently braised with cep mushrooms was a dish for early autumn that was hard to beat. But you had to know where to look in the early morning, when out cep searching, otherwise the maggots got them first.

Folk had been catching rabbits in Somerset since Norman times. The hill in Dunster called 'Conygar' means rabbit warren and it was made to provide food for the priory monks. By the thirteenth century the rabbits preferred the taste of freedom rather than warren grass and so made their escapes to decimate village gardens. The Mohuns who were Lords of Dunster at the time permitted the villagers to catch and kill the culprits on condition that all rabbit skins were taken to the castle. Even in recent times there had been a ready market generally for rabbit meat and the skins for glove making. Indeed, anyone could buy a rabbit for 1s 6d on a Saturday and the next week get 3d or 6d back for the skin.

In the days of charabancs a resourceful woman called Bessie Langdon collected the rabbits that weren't eaten locally and sent them from Wivey station in their hundreds to London on the Rabbit Train. Before Beeching did his nobbling of the railways, the train began its journey in Barnstaple and stopped at stations on the way. Sadly, rabbits have fleas, and fleas bite. Myxomatosis, the viral infection the fleas transferred, wiped out most rabbits to destroy Bessie's trade in the mid 1950s.

The humble flea has a lot to answer for, and it should be in for the high jump, because rabbiting was fun in Somerset. Rabbiting parties were popular and intense occasions. Dogs quivered with excitement, when the rabbit wranglers strung long nets across fields or when ferrets scurried into burries. The dogs were the rabbit chasers, a job that kept them fed. Harvest time was best. Word would go around that some field or other was near to being finished, as the threshing machine bound the sheaves. In Taunton Deane families stood listening on their doorsteps. Then they would hop on their bicycles to arrive just as the last patch of corn shrank to the size of a postage stamp. Out would pop the rabbits to be pursued by screaming men and boys and, of course, very excited dogs who would never see a lead or a pooper-scooper.

Dogs were never idle. As well as rabbiting, there was also mole and badger catching to be done. Badger digging was the work of terriers that chased the badger out of its sett to be caught with tongs. Badger hams were a delicacy for a few.

I asked Chris whether or not he knew of Radley Greenslade. He did. Radley was a character, one of the last of the breed who seem to grow organically from the soil. He lived at Upton, the place where the church became two halves. Nave, chancel and seats were moved a quarter of a mile away up the hill, but the tower and the old churchyard were left to the wiles of ash, sycamore and ivy in the valley. The Norman font stayed behind, too. Money was to blame.

Often found outside the 'Blazing Stump' pub in Luxborough, Radley would be hitting car bonnets with his walking stick and startling drivers and passengers, many of a frail disposition. "I've seen the dancing of the summers!" he would shout repeatedly.

In explanation, what he claimed to have seen were two hares run into Upton's old churchyard on a golden evening and turn themselves in a gentleman with top hat and tails and a bonneted, finely dressed lady. The magic couple then danced and danced before turning once more into hares and vanishing. "It was the most beautiful thing I ever saw," he would say with tears sparkling his eyes.

Visitors, although there were apparently not many, often found a stew-pot bubbling away on Radley's kitchen stove. One Dunster chap I knew stole a taste by sticking his finger in and licking it when Radley's back was turned. Not only did he think the stew was beef, he also thought it was rather good. Radley caught him wiping gravy from his lips. "Tis old badger, 'tis badger for the dog," laughed the old so-and-so.

173

When he died, he was greatly missed. There was not enough room in Upton church at his funeral for all the mourners. The large overspill paid their last respects solemnly outside. Afterwards the countryman was buried in the company of moles that perhaps sought sanctuary from the trappers in the fields around. I have never tried his cure for inflammation from an infection on the leg or nose. "Eat a bowl of stewed slugs, boy," he told me with a twinkle in his eye.

Moles themselves were normally caught at night by traps in their wontwiggles, the lovely Somerset word for a mole tunnel. These can be over two hundred yards long. The power of a mole to shift soil is amazing. It can disappear underground in fifteen seconds. In twenty minutes it can move thirteen pounds of soil, which I am reliably told is the equivalent of a person moving four tonnes.

The secret of setting good mole traps, Radley had once confided, is to ignore the molehills. These just show where the moles have been digging for worms. Look instead for small depressions in the ground indicating a wontwiggle beneath. To tell whether a wontwiggle is still in use, squidge a heel into the ground, then look at the squidge mark the next day; if it shows any signs of messing, the flat muscular hands of the little gentlemen in velvet are still down there happily wontwiggling.

Six moles a night was good work, and it would go on in the fields throughout the year. Once the skins of short silky fur were dried, they were sold for 6d each. Dried moleskins and badger pelts were often sent to Wisbech in Cambridgeshire. Payment for them came by return of post. Somerset moles and Somerset badgers would then end up as fashionable fads on ladies' toques and wide-brimmed hats, pelerine collars, stoles and muffs in London and New York. The old mail order catalogues, however, are hard to come by.

A slightly alternative local lady, who shall remain nameless, has convinced those willing to listen that she can talk to animals and in particular can speak Mole. Over time she has learned that a mole is an unsurprisingly grumbly, mumbling, timid creature of brittle mortality whose spirit can leave its body if it suffers even the mildest shock. So when Phoebe, the lady's Border Collie, had the fortune to catch a mole in her mouth, it was a bad thing to have happen. The nano-second before the spirit departed, the lady's scream, which was loud enough to give a crow a heart attack, made Phoebe drop the mole. The lady tells how the mole scrambled back into its wontwiggle chuntering "shitty dog, shitty dog", which to my mind is proof of modern vocabulary in a toughie. I feel both the lady and Phoebe will one day be prompted to find happiness in Glastonbury, among the folk of alternative persuasions.

The tale of Phoebe's mole and of bunnies and badgers set me to philosophically think out loud that Somerset is a place of holes, little ones and bigger ones. I had a little one in my shaggy lawn, where a bumblebee nested as a self-invited guest, resenting the childrens' stick prods. Catching my son Felix giving the hole a focused poke one weekend, I called him 'a little Slytherin'. This was harsh and he went straight into a mush. Countless evenings I had sat on Felix's bed, reading him Harry Potter books from cover to cover. We made up accents for the characters and absorbed every word. As each day came, my lad would live his life in Gryffindor, wishing himself at Hogwarts instead of Wivey Primary.

The evening of the stick poking I sat with Felix on his bed and explained the good things that bumblebees did; and if the bee in the hole stung him it would really, really hurt and the bee would die, because its insides would fall out. But all Felix wanted to know was why I had called him a Slytherin. I told him he had not been very nice and said that Harry's creator, Miss Rowling might just have come across a book of old Somerset dialect and found 'dumbledore'. It means bumblebee. The next day Felix was flicking a stick like a wand and doing battle with the garden wizard. And he was struggling, or should I say, 'mugglin'.

Back on the subject of holes, there were really big ones at Cheddar and Wookey. But I agreed with Chris that probably some of the bigger holes in Somerset weren't that far away from Wivey and the Welsh took the blame for them.

A ten-minute uphill drive brings you to where Raleigh's Cross looks down onto Blue Anchor Bay and across the Bristol Channel to South Wales. Nearby, the holes are dark-looking and fenced-off. The travel writer John Hillaby came by them in 1968 and felt compelled to give them book space in his *Journey Through Britain*. He noted that a notice board announced that they were not only dangerous, but also private. And that they had been sold. Who on earth, he wondered, bought holes in the ground? The holes belonged to the abandoned shafts of iron ore mines excavated by Welsh miners who had floated into Watchet from their distantly visible homeland. Having had their heyday in the 1870s, the mines have been defunct for the past hundred years.

What drew us to them was not so much an interest in industrial history, but more a liking for the wonderful field mushrooms that grow in the fields round about. Their lusciousness is well worth the cost of diesel, even in these hard times, especially when fried in butter with a little pepper and garlic and served beside Mike Thorne's grilled back bacon.

It is very easy to distract oneself from holes by the pleasures of the kitchen. But one can provide a service for the other. A survey from a few years ago has shown that the iron ore mines were 'extraordinarily deep and capacious enough to hold the combined municipal garbage of the neighbouring towns'. This includes Minehead, Taunton, Bridgwater, and amazingly Bristol; though I hope not, in our ecologically friendly age, the hot air of government. Whoever it was who had bought the holes at the time Hillaby first jotted his notes, sold the concession. Instead of throwing it away, I now put my bacon fat out for the birds.

"I'll make your porch look as old as your cottage's bird table." Chris said, when he eventually left in the moonlight. Soon I heard the first bangs of 12-bores being fired by the night lampers out in the fields. It used to be a man and dog thing, lamping. An excuse for going walkies with a torch. If caught in the spotlight, a rabbit's eyes would light up and it would take-off as fast as its little legs could carry with only a short head start in a race with a lurcher. First to a hedge with holes won and a beaten rabbit would mean 'one for the hot pot'. To hear the sound of guns, however, was a different matter. Guns meant light in a fox's eye. I wondered if Roger was still selling squealers.

To distract myself I googled 'Holes' and found that the work of the 'iconic German artist Joseph Beuys' was being exhibited at London's Tate Modern. Beuys apparently had also been ecologically engaged, but in a manner that had nothing to do with bacon fat. "His masterpiece 'The End of the Twentieth Century' could be found", the review said, "in a room with some blocks of basalt scattered around. Into each of the slabs, Beuys bored a conical hole to create a metaphorical 'wound'. He then 'treated' it by smoothing and lining the hollow with insulating clay and felt, before re-inserting the plug of stone. These plugged cavities imply the potential for healing, suggesting the possibility of renewal and regeneration at the end of a violent and destructive century". Beuys holes, I went on to read, were insured for thousands and thousands of pounds.

What would John Hillaby have made of that? I wondered. And for that matter, the same could be asked of bees and badgers, rabbits and moles.

How to make a Rabbit Squealer
Cut a length of hazel approximately 15-20mm in diameter
Cut the hazel into 100mm lengths
Split the 100mm lengths down the middle
Cut a 30-40mm groove no more than 5mm deep in each half
Place a length of VHS tape between the two halves and carefully tension it
Secure the two halves tightly together with insulating tape.
Check for pitch
If it doesn't work, make another. With a bit of luck, practice makes perfect!

Rabbit Hot Pot

1 saddle of wild rabbit
300g potatoes peeled and finely sliced
300ml chicken stock
1 large onion, peeled and sliced
2-4 cloves of garlic sliced
1 large carrot peeled and sliced
1 stick of celery peeled and chopped
A cupped handful of cep mushrooms de-maggoted, washed and sliced (optional)
A good glug of grapeseed oil or 25g of lard if you don't give a damn
1x15ml spoon flour
1-2x5ml spoons mustard
1x15 ml freshly chopped parsley
Salt
Course ground black pepper

Method:
Season the flour with salt and pepper and coat the rabbit saddle. Place it in a casserole dish. Add the onions, garlic, carrot, celery and the stock, then add mustard and parsley. Cover with the sliced potatoes, then brush over the oil or melted fat. Cover and cook in a preheated moderate oven (150c /325f or gas mark 3) for 1 to 2 hours. Baste rabbit occasionally until cooked thoroughly. Divide saddle into two portions. Sumshus and recommended by an Exmoor gamekeeper as the perfect candlelit dinner.

LESSON TWENTY-NINE
THE BIG BANG THEORY

"Remember, remember, the 5th of November
Gunpowder, Treason and Plot
I see no reason
Why Gunpowder Treason
Should ever be forgot."

The big green papier-mâché crocodile and large red alarm clock beside the long trailer the other side of the hedge made a mental connection. For a few moments I felt a bit giddy and tried not to show it. My mind a blur of engine noise, loud music, odd names like Devil's Disco, Yán Huó and Umoja, strobe lights and gyrating dragons, vampires and fairytale visions, before I was carried back to Frankfurt airport and the secure windowless room with one chair and one table, with a burly German policeman standing guard by the door.

It was me sat in the chair. I had been on my way to Bologna to film a launch of a new IBM ticketing machine. The day before I had foolishly strayed from Somerset into Devon to cover a massive blaze with whizz-bangs, crackles and pops at a firework factory in Uffculme. This was the joy of freelancing. When my TV camera went through the German airport scanner, there was rapid beeping and an Alsatian went woof. Strange how dogs speak the same language, wherever you are.

My camera, as I found out after two hours in the one chair room, had specks of gunpowder on it. However, calls had been made and I was free to go. An important looking German in a tie smiled, apologising that he had only been doing his job, as I could have been a terrorist. I kept to myself the small observation that technology seemed to be more sensitive in Frankfurt than in London, as it wasn't reassuring to know. Gunpowder is problematic. I blame Roger Bacon. He invented the stuff. Born in Ilchester in 1214, he was the towering genius of Middle Ages Europe.

But what was my mental connection? What linked the crocodile with gunpowder? It was one word, 'Carnival'. The phenomenon that has become Somerset's Carnival season began with a priest called Robert Parsons, who lived four hundred years ago in Nether Stowey, home to Barbara and Barnaby and famous for a plague of mice in Coleridge's cottage. Born in the village in 1546, Robert became a Jesuit and one of the most enigmatic figures of late Tudor England who spent his life in a notable endeavour to bring England back to traditional Catholic faith.

He had hoped for a swift conquest of England by the Spanish Armada and suffered greater and more bitter disappointment than any local cricket fan never seeing Somerset win the County Championship. However, Robert should not be confused with the stalwart county crick-eter who has the same surname. Keith is totally unrelated. Yet as Keith did his best to bang a cricket ball and bowl a maiden over, Robert had wanted to bang gunpowder and put a Bohemian maiden on the throne of England. In the end, the only Bohemians out and about locally frequented Dunster's 'Stag Inn ' and Barbara certainly hadn't treated them royally.

Those with their heads turned to Rome described Robert as a man of great parts, eloquent, influential, zealous, spiritual, disinterested and fear-less. To others he was a big rascally-roodle, if ever there was one. It is now thought that Parsons was the mastermind, or at least the inspiration, behind the 1605 Gunpowder Plot, and his burning ambition to blow up parliament with a mine "to open up a new road of hope" was for the one good reason that Protestants were being nasty to Catholics and James the First did not appear to care. It was a tense situation for which Guy Fawkes, amongst others, took the rap. When things went pear-shaped, Robert made for Rome like a rat up a drainpipe. He had been doubly disappointed.

With me having had a few years primary education in Lisburn in Northern Ireland, I have experienced sectarian unhappiness first hand. On my seventh birthday party my mother leaned out of the car window outside the school gate and told my friend Raymond, a wee lad from the Catholic estate, that he could not come. "But sure I've bought him a present and everythin'." My mother wasn't for moving and I've seldom been more embarrassed. Raymond just looked sad. Then the 'Troubles' began. Religion can be a pain and prejudice hard set.

Four hundred years ago an irked King James decreed that the whole nation should remember the 5th November by lighting bonfires. There was no town in all of England, let alone Somerset, that took this to heart more than Bridgwater. Like most West Country towns Bridgwater was Protestant and 'Bridgwaterers' they say were also pyromaniacs. Bonfire night was their excuse to enjoy an evening of heated fun, as roaring flames staved off one of the long, cold nights of winter. Robert Parsons really was a fish out of water.

A bronze statue called 'The Spirit of Carnival' was unveiled on the Cornhill in Bridgwater on the 28th October 2005 to commemorate the

400th anniversary of the 'Gunpowder Plot.' Created by the Chilton Polden sculptor Dave Faulks, the figure is an early seventeenth century 'squibber'. Dressed in cloak, breeches and a brimmed high hat, the bearded, gloved figure holds above its head what the uninitiated might think is a broom handle. It's not. Instead, it's just a long wooden pole attached to a solid block of wood called a cosh. Strapped to this is a squib, a large firework; expelling a fountain of steel stars. Although easily mistaken as being Guy Fawkes, the statue is a reminder of Bridgwater's Carnival tradition. The religious origins of the event are almost forgotten and far less significant today.

Where the squibber now stands on his plinth, the original Bridgwater celebrations had a large bonfire. A large leaky wooden boat was sacrificed, onto which went a hundred tar barrels and almost anything else burnable that could be scavenged. Eventually, due to lack of boats, the tradition stopped. This didn't mean just old wooden wrecks, but also several river worthy ones being chucked onto the fire by the over-enthusiastic.

Home made 'guys', effigies of the gunpowder plotters, began to be created and added to the fire by local gangs. It was those gangs parading the guys towards the bonfire that started the years of processions that were to follow. Now the 'Bridgwater Guy Fawkes Carnival' is the oldest event of its kind in Britain, with the Victorians being instrumental in establishing today's format. They got a grip on things after 1880. That year the usual good humour and excitement gave way to ill temper and acts of violence, leading ultimately to serious disorder and riot.

Even when there were no parades during the Second World War, a local carnival fanatic, Ted Lockyer, strolled the two and half mile route for six years to keep the tradition going. And it has evolved, becoming more and more elaborate in both costumes and music. Thousands and thousands of people now annually fill the grandstands or line the route, braving wind, rain or frosty chill, to absorb the procession that takes over a couple of hours to complete.

From spring onwards look behind hedges and into rural barns, or peep into urban warehouses and garages across Somerset and it's likely you'll be surprised. Gremlins, Harlequins and Masqueraders, as well as many other local carnival committees from Bridgwater to Castle Cary and from Templecombe to Chard will be welding and doing carpentry, painting and wiring. Troughs of papier-mâché and bucket loads plaster of Paris are mixed and moulded. Floats, or 'carts' as they are known, are fantasies on wheels. Some take thousands of hours of craftsmanship and can cost anything in the region of £20,000.

The goal is competition. Pirate ships will take on vampire castles as carts vie for the top awards of the autumn's carnival parades in each town and form the largest light festival in Europe. However, in truth, there are no losers. The purpose of the events is to raise thousands of pounds for local charities. Folk are encouraged to chuck coins into nets on collection carts.

First modernised in 1881, the Bridgwater carnival parade was originally lit by lamps, with electric lights being introduced in 1913. These days there are over a hundred carts up to hundred feet long, each decorated with as many as twenty two thousand light bulbs.

It was my next-door neighbours, Jeremy and Jill, who enticed me to my Bridgwater carnival baptism in 2007. Arriving from London they had bought their first house in Wellington in the summer of 2004. Neither of them had ever seen a carnival parade of any description before, so they were looking forward to the local one. Their house set behind railings and beside the undertakers was on the parade route, so they had a prime view. Jill opened a bottle of wine in readiness and Jeremy put on BBC Radio 3. Nothing. Zip, except for an unpleasant smell. There had been a gas leak and the carnival parade was cancelled.

Three years later and for Wivey residents there was nothing for it but to go and see the 'biggy'. Jill, as with so many other people, liked the idea of the Squibbing more than the parade of carts. Although I also decided to join the crowds, I was a tad wary. And it wasn't just because of my Frankfurt experience. Parish records of St Mary's Church in Bridgwater show that a John Taylor and his two children were killed in a gunpowder explosion in their home in November 1716. It is said that they were early casualties of making the old home-made squibs that culminated with a loud bang, as each squib extinguished itself.

These days squibs are safer, there is only one factory in the world that makes them for the carnival and it's in Peterborough. The Carnival Committee is quick to say their event "is well organised and nobody has been hurt to date." To be on the safe side, my son Lawrence, bless him, home on army leave from the Royal Engineers, offered to lend me full body armour for the evening. Feeling brave, I declined him, saying that I would 'busk it'. At about 11.30, after the thump-a-thump music and lights had trundled away with my £1 coin in a net, everyone looked on with the thrill of expectancy. The two lines of squibbers stood along the High Street and the Cornhill readied themselves, some with fluorescent plastic jackets and hard hats, gloved like 'The Spirit of Carnival', others foolishly bare-handed, wearing blue flame resistant overalls and woollen tea-cosy hats. In a few blinks a hundred and seventy sky facing squibs, on the end of red, white and blue poles, were lit at the same time. For more or less a minute I was awed by trails of fire that can best be described as a Dante-esque inferno. KFC, illuminated by showers of sparks, looked more foreboding than ever. An Australian, who said his name was Jol and was holding a can of Fosters, happened to be standing next to me. "Strewth, I thought Sidney harbour bridge millenium fireworks were pretty wicked, but this lot were spectacular. Those dudes are a load of bloody nutters!" he observed, as the last squib fizzled and died in the night.

When I got to ask Jeremy and Jill what they thought, Jeremy just shrugged and said "Um," and Jill was dubious. The first twenty minutes or so of the procession had been great, but soon one tableau began to seem much the same as another. Then there was all that waiting around, feeling cold until the squibbing. Eying her empty flask of tea wistfully, she said, "I wish they could put the two things closer together for those of us who are only visiting."

Reading about the events a week later, I saw that the Bridgwater Carnival Committee had put out nine hundred and fifty marked traffic cones. Many of these had ended up on people's heads. Some, I noticed the following summer, were even being worn as rain hats at Glastonbury Festival.

LESSON THIRTY
DOG, CANDLE AND SADDLE

*"… court members are forbidden to rise from their seats
(except on payment of a fine) until the candle wick finally
collapses and is drowned in the hot tallow."*
(Rules of Stowell Mead Court, Tatworth)

My friend Lisa had denied all knowledge of the dog and candle despite her having lived in Tatworth for years. Well, you never know in life what's just around the corner. However, I didn't labour that point. Having worked with her halfway across Egypt and her refusing to do the other half, she knew my liking for shaggy dog stories and may have thought this was a wind up. Although to be fair, what had caught my interest was more about a waggy dog tail. Honesty and old-fashioned values can cause the gentle-hearted to become quite dewy-eyed.

I stood in a Chard car park with the mobile to one ear, my index finger stuck into the other, as a canine foursome fell into a snarling dogfight. The heat of the early summer afternoon must have frayed tempers. The dogs made as much a racket as their owners, who were shouting and swearing profanities, as they tugged and yanked on leads. It was hard to hear the voice in my ear that belonged to Lieutenant Colonel Michael Davies, an ex-gunner who had retired. Now he had the quieter job of being Clerk to the Stowell Field Charity, whose candle auction is believed to be the last surviving such event in England to be held every year.

The previous time we had spoken, we had waxed lyrically about the Vienna opera. I was about to have a week in that city of 'The Third Man' and arias, intending to write some more pages about Somerset, knowing that a Starbucks latte tastes the same whether it's bought in Sterling, Euros or Baht. Hearing the sounds of the Chard car park, Michael must have thought I led an eclectic life.

"I've got a guest today, so I can't come with you," he said raising his voice to the level of mine. "You can go and have a look by yourself. Have you got wellington boots? You'll need wellington boots." I glanced down at my bare feet in sandals. 'Fudge', I thought.

"We can meet up another day and have lunch in the Pop."

"Thank you, that'd be lovely." Pop? What in God's name? Then it dawned on me that he meant 'Ye Old Poppe Inn', as in 'pop in for a snorter', beside the A358, not a million miles from where I was standing. Folk say calling it 'Ye', as opposed to 'The', has made the pub one of the oldest in the country. In a deed dated 1838, it's called the 'Country Inn', and in another dated 1792, it is called 'Culverhay'.

"And you can even try some watercress," he concluded just before my battery ran out.

Watercress. This is what the fuss of the dog and candle was all about. And watercress was what I had convinced myself I wanted to see and taste. I was on an outing of nostalgia. From an early age my godmother drummed into me that watercress belonged to the mustard family and had a reputation as a cure all for everything from lethargy to baldness. I remember a very small me helping her pick the wild stuff from a stream for teatime sandwiches. But that was in Hampshire, where pure spring waters from the chalk downs make watercress whoopee. And folk over that way still revere and tend oodles of the cultivated stuff. It's in their psyche. How would it be in Somerset?

After 'bottoming out' my car exhaust several times, driving gingerly down the rutted and primrose banked lane, I found the closely guarded secret of Stowell Field. The word 'field' suggested cultivation. Wrong. Due to springs rising on its fringes, the few acres that run down to a stream are better described as a dog-legged, water-logged mead. It is the last part of the vast common land enclosed in 1819. Within a year or two, with too many farmers having grazing rights, the meadow suffered from overstocking. It was best to find a way to give it to one farmer alone and the inch of candle was lit.

I watched airborne goat-willow catkin fluff float over marsh marigold and meadow sweet, bogbean and dropwort. Some got trapped in the spikes of soft rush and quaking grass, the rest drifted away over a profusion of watercress that grew everywhere, even escaping 'en masse' through the metal barred gate that was the way into the field. This was watercress 'au naturel' and what Michael Davies was clerk to. My sandals took me only as far as the squelch that began car-side of the gate. I picked and nibbled an escapee leaf. Such pepperiness. No cellophane-bagged watercress from Tesco or Sainsbury's can match it. I popped a couple more leaves into my diary for later.

Every year in April the tenant rights to the watercress beds of Stowell Field are bought at a candle auction held in 'the Pop'. The old custom called Stowell Court requires Michael to light an inch of tallow candle burnt over a wooden platter that's dated 1832. Then the bidding for the field begins. It's a very private affair. Only people who own or tenant certain properties have the right to bid or be present. New members to the court are called 'colts' and have to pay Michael 'a colting fee' on their first attendance.

The last bidder before the candle gutters and dies is the tenant for the ensuing year. But win or lose a supper of bread, cheese and Stowell watercress follows the successful final bid. Stowell Court has an old set of rules, which inflict fines payable to the Clerk on those who break them. The custom itself is a lot older than the dated platter. Exactly how long cannot be traced, as the earlier books have been lost. In 2008 twenty court members came along, but only eight bid with the successful one topping £300, before everyone adjourned for a game of skittles.

Every custom seems to have a good story attached and so it is with the Stowell Court.

The story goes that many years ago a farmer, who was quite long in the tooth, had fallen into penury. It was said he was a man of integrity and too proud to accept charity.

What to do? His neighbours got their heads together and decided that the obvious way to help would be to allow him a successful bid at a very low price. So only two other people declared themselves as bidders at the auction and they had jobs as stooges. Their function was to 'accidentally' blow out the candle as soon as the old farmer's bid reached a credible amount.

At the clerk's signal, one of the stooges staged a coughing fit worthy of pantomime towards the candle. Quicker than a rat up a drainpipe the farmer was on hand to shield the flame with his body. This prompted the second stooge to wind himself up for an almighty sneeze. "Aaaah...Aaaah...Aaah...Aaaah..." By the end of the fourth "Aaah" and before the "Choo," the farmer had pulled a crusty handkerchief from his pocket and thrust it over the contorted nose. Things were not going according to plan. Help though, if not at hand, was on the other side of the door and came from a cold-nosed friend. A sheepdog was said to be telepathic to its master's wishes. And so it was that evening. Having succeeded in being let into the auction room by some exemplary whining, a couple of tail wags were all that were needed to blow the candle out. The result was a pat of the dog's head from the stooge who had ceased his coughing and the tenancy of the watercress beds declared for the old farmer.

It's said that this event caused the platter and candle to be suspended by link chains from a hook on a beam in more recent times, out of the reach of even a gale from a wagging tail.

"Felix, try this," I said, opening my diary and passing across wilted watercress leaves that must have been at least a couple of hours from freshly picked.

"Eeurrgh!"

Enough said. The thought then occurred to me that perhaps, like my son, the old farmer just didn't enjoy the strong taste of pepper, or for that matter, getting his feet wet. You can never quite read some Somerset folk. Which maybe is a good thing, because dewy-eyes might soon dry. Then it resurfaced that at my godmother's tea table I'd asked in a small, unheeded voice for Marmite between my slices of bread instead. Watercress was what I had and watercresss was what I got. Funny thing is, even in muddling middle age, I still have all my hair.

With the foxgloves tall and pink-purple, I took up Michael's offer of a Poppe lunch. My pint of draught cider and a plated puddle of steak and ale topped with a suet crust were placed before me by a smiling young woman wearing an orange T-shirt and jeans. As she disappeared off to find the mustard, Michael said none too quietly "She used to work for NATO." What is it with this village, I thought? Michael loved it, though. So much so that he has no intention of leaving, and is adamant that he never need renew his passport. His travelling days are over.

"More time to watch cricket," I suggested, only to learn that he loathed the summer game. I could see by his eyes that the hard cherry of a ball had hurt him more than once.

As I battled to open the small yellow sachets of mustard that were the Poppe's contribution to the modern world, Michael talked about his old army life and how during 'Suez' he had a part in organising the defences of Malta, in case the Egyptians decided to invade. It turned out that they were too busy fleecing tourists and documentary filmmakers, or persistent in tugging shirtsleeves for baksheesh, to bother receiving anything more dangerous than streams of invectives, particularly as the Mediterranean was a bit more than a stream to cross swords with. Michael ended up taking Jimmy Edwards, of handlebar moustache fame and come to bolster troop morale, out to lunch at the comic's expense.

Today, Michael was paying and I was grateful. He had a small moan about army pensions and I parried with a winge about the artistic life. Perhaps we should take lessons from Egypt and exert a little more pressure on the grockle. On the other hand, I've a fair idea that saying "baksheesh, baksheesh" to a bull-necked Midlander would only lead to A&E. No, it's best to stay polite.

Leaving the pub I couldn't fail to notice a giant Fresian cow propped against a low load trailer. "Oh, that's 'For the Udder One', last year's Bridgwater carnival entry. The Poppe got ninth best 'Comic Feature Cart'." said Michael knowingly. Way to go, I thought.

"I was there," I said, not admitting to having missed it passing by, probably when I was in the half hour queue for an indigestible hotdog.

We both agreed that keeping up the standards in Somerset was getting harder and that we needed a constitutional to work off the suet crusts. So we ambled back to Michael's home to pick up his best friend. On the way Michael confided that the cow cart wasn't the only exhibit for Tatworth to have been proud of. In 1851 John Phillips, a local clothier who owned the Perry Street factory, made a piece of linsey for the Great Exhibition in Hyde Park, London and won a prize. The late Mrs Stevens used to tell folk that she had had a linsey petticoat when she had been a girl. Her mum had told her it was practical; however, the strong, coarse fabric with linen warp and woollen weft made her itch to bits.

And then we were there, at Michael's back door.

An exceedingly loud two-fingered whistle in my right ear was followed by a high-pitched shout. "Maisie!!!" Together they brought forth an excited rush of youthful wag-tailed Springer spaniel. As a wet nose sniffed my trouser legs I caught a glimpse of a sitting-room mantelpiece chocker with horsey photographs showing point-to-pointers and presentations of silver cups. Clearly Maisie wasn't Michael's only delight.

Another look at Stowell Field seemed like the order of the afternoon. The mead is now managed as a Site of Special Scientific Interest under English Nature, as meadow land untreated by fertilizer, pesticide or herbicide. However, DEFRA sees fit to interfere with grants and Michael views them as an "embuggerance". It was only a couple of meadows away down through the garden gate.

The rabbit just sat there in No Man's land and continued to nibble. Maisie ignored it. This surely wasn't a proper spaniel. Then the rabbit gave Maisie a knowing wink to give the game away. There was obviously a mutual understanding. Rabbits would be left unchased, as long as they left 'Master's' vegetable patch alone. Life, she had been taught, was all about having good manners.

"Rabbits nest in trees round here, you know," said Michael.

"Pardon?"

"Honestly, we've got high-rise rabbits. There's a chap called Peter Bell, out Misterton way. A retired agricultural journalist, he calls himself. He's into his eighties now and has a moustache like Jimmy Edwards', although Peter's much smaller and wirier. He wrote in his parish magazine that he'd been told of a rabbit's nest ten-foot up in a tree. A doe had liked the look of an old willow leaning at forty-five degrees, offering a useful hole high above the ground. The trunk was easy to climb and so she made a nice warm nest for her babies. Mind you, it would have been a better place for a pheasant, with Maisie around."

In that moment Maisie was off in pursuit of a large cock bird making for a sanctuary in the watercress with a kerfuffle of wings. She was a proper spaniel after all.

Ankle deep in a field of forget-me-nots, dandelions and sorrel, as Maisie returned panting without a feather to her name, I asked Michael the question that was on my mind. Did he own a horse? I detected a slight hesitation before he nodded and said "A racehorse."

"Oh, what's it called," I asked with enthusiasm and then hedged my bets whether I should have done.

"'So Wise So Young'."

This did not augur well. I recalled the wisdom of the 'thirds'. Shakespeare's put the words "So wise so young they say do never live long," into the mouth of Richard III and from a dark corner of my brain I dredged up the nous of the American Dr Franklin J. Wise III, "You aren't a racehorse just because you can outrun a cow."

"Have you had much success?"

"He came third at the beginning of last year at Wincanton in the novice hurdle at a hundred to one." I kept my mouth shut, but my expression seemed to prompt Michael to a resigned shrug, "He was first past the post and looked very pleased with himself, until he realised he still had to go all the way round again. Still, it was his finest hour."

I gathered the horse was given its name by some ITV producer involved with the Morecambe and Wise Show. 'So Wise So Young', Michael said, was accident prone, had a funny tail and was sired by a stud stallion called 'Little Ern'.

Michael had decided he didn't much like Wincanton's racecourse, not because of his horse's mistake, but because it wasn't dog friendly. Taunton's was much better. He could park in the middle and watch horses and riders gallop by with Maisie at his side. Man and dog can get into the habit of becoming inseparable. These days, however, he prefers to watch events unfold on television, although he misses the atmosphere of actually being there. As for betting, he still gets the odd bit of good advice from friends at William Hill. This is more sensible, he thinks, than the method adopted by a mutual friend who dowsed for winners with a pendulum. Something he was inspired to do from his wife's father who was a retired Royal Engineers officer. Apparently he is very good at dowsing with hazel sticks for underground water. And yes, he lives locally, too.

Pointing at the watercress mead in which cows were conspicuous by their absence and in which cow parsley now flourished, he told me that they did graze a horse in it not so very long ago. In 1990 a local fellow called Jeff Townsend fronted a horseracing club at the Poppe. A group of a dozen or more biddlers paid a small amount of capital and a pepper-corn of a weekly fee. It was enough to buy a nag of a mare by the name of 'Malborough Lady', who until that time had been a flat disaster. The question was where to put her. The answer was simple. With the highest bid of £155 the candle went out after only fourteen minutes. Jeff had secured the mead for the Poppe's new Lady. Then a local trainer was found to raise Poppe hopes. The trainer suggested that Lady took a running jump.

Entered in a small race at Taunton, she took several, all over hurdles and every one witnessed by the Poppe hopeful, fortified by goodly quaffs of beer. To everyone's amazement their Lady won. Easily. Ecstatic, Jeff was soon being interviewed by BBC Radio 5 Live who happened to be at the track that day. "Your horse has little past form, what do you put this sudden improvement down to?" Before his brain cogs turned, Jeff's voice went national. "It's all thanks to the grazing at Stowell Mead and the magic mushrooms she has been eating." The Lady was quickly dope tested and the Poppe hopeful held their breath for the second time in an hour. She tested negative and became an instant celebrity. The same cannot be said unfortunately of 'So Wise So Young'.

As the salmon with lemon and dill cooked its seventeen oven minutes that evening, I did a web search. In 'the-racehorse.com' I found what I was looking for: 'Stallion fees 2008 - risers and fallers'. There, amongst the £300,000 stud fees was 'Little Ern' coming in last at six hundred quid, the cheapest chap on the block up a whopping twenty percent from 2007. 'So Wise So Young' coming third at Wincanton must have made a difference. The success of the Somerset stables of Martin and David Pipe and Paul Nicholls with their respective Grand National and Gold Cup victories are a world away from Tatworth. Somebody must be having a chuckle whilst Michael holds the short candle.

LESSON THIRTY-ONE
MUSIC AND MUD SLINGING

*"It is universally acknowledged that Glastonbury Festival
brings in considerable income into an area which extends
beyond Mendip and brings in several hundred acts which
would otherwise never set foot in rural Somersetshire."*
(Graham Jeffs, Chief Executive, Mendip District Council)

*"I have never been to the Glastonbury rock festival and I never will go.
I do not want to be in a field full of ********* who work for the BBC
and the* Guardian *and the British government, temporarily decked
out in casual gear while pretending to be counterculture fellow
travellers for the weekend."*
(Glastonbury web blog, 2008)

In 1940 Arthur Mee visited Pilton, a Mendip village looking across the fields of Worthy Farm to Glastonbury Tor. The village, he wrote, "is part of the pride of old England, a lovely place full of beauty and kindly old folk when we called. A youngster of 84 took us around his garden, touched by no hands other than his, with two huge apple trees in bloom which he had brought under his arm from Shepton Mallet. The old vicar was 88, and was writing his story of Pilton." One shudders to think what that vicar would think of Pilton these days with Worthy Farm owned by one of the best-loved figures in the music industry, the Glastonbury festival founder Michael Eavis.

At first glance the farm appears pretty normal, but a closer pry reveals a surreal landscape. Weird skeletal structures share space with fields, cows and trees, whilst formidable telecommunications infrastructure is hidden under the sod. The most impressive visible framework sits on the ley line running between Glastonbury Tor and Stonehenge. Over the weekend nearest to the summer solstice this largest of frameworks becomes the Pyramid stage, the centrepiece on the thousand acre site for the seething horde of 105,000 expensive ticket holders and 35,000 pass holders that include performers, traders, children, stewards and security.

Life has moved on from 1940. One morning before a breakfast of bread, tomatoes and cheese handmade by a shepherd, I resorted to drawing a picture with a biro on scrap of lined notepaper as a means of explaining. "Medusa?" said Ionica scratching his head.

"Medusa," agreed Romi.

"No, they're dreadlocks, not snakes," I said rather too quickly for the two men to follow.

"Dreadlocks," Alina said more clearly and slower than me, translating my English into English. Describing herself as a European mongrel, a mish-mash of Romanian, German and Hungarian with a smidge of French, she was a Somerset doctor and had become my wife. This was cultural chit-chat whether it was preferable to face mud or bears.

It was June and the weather outside was typically Glastonbury, torrential rain and thunderstorms. A few miles away cars were being washed away by floodwaters. But I wasn't in Somerset. I was on the fifth floor of a 1970s built communist block of flats on a Brasov estate in central Romania. Against a wooded backdrop of the Carpathians I was with friends, trying to describe the sort of folk who wanted to experience the great wet outdoors of England's largest music festival. What was the hype about, they wanted to know?

Back home the debate was raging whether the festival should even continue. On web blogs feelings were running high. Once there seemed to be two distinct camps separated by pronunciation. As a generalisation, those for the festival said Glastonbury with an 'ass' as in donkey, Gl'ass'tonbury. Those against said Glastonbury with an 'arse', as in bottom, Gl'arse'tonbury. Now in a manner of speaking elocution has become muddied and an ass or an arse can be on either side. Ionica rolled 'Glarsetonbury' around his tongue a few times and definitely preferred it, but wasn't sure which side it was on, before he reached for the afinata, his fortifying home-made whortleberry brandy.

Both Ionica and Romi, Alina's father, were engineers, stubbled and still in their white vests. They were quick to understand why people made a fuss about having bears on their top floor landing. It had happened the day before in the adjacent block. Bears should obviously keep to the street and know better.

Folk thereabouts are resigned to the company of the wild bears who wander around, bin raiding under streetlights like outsized versions of Weston-super-Mare's urban foxes These rummage through hotel garbage from grockles that take their bare skins off to the beach. Brasov's residents have no choice other than to put up with things as they are - their bears, like the bares in Weston, are protected by law.

With all that Somerset has to offer, to choose to live outside their comfort zone and spend a week camping in mud with running rivers of pee was strange to Ionica and Romi, and much worse than having a big furry brown bear on the landing outside your door. Personally, I also thought it was barmy. Young people these days spent a lot of money beforehand, not only on tickets, but also festival wardrobes of designer sunglasses, torpedo shorts and perforated leather jackets hopeful for sex, shrubs and rock n'roll.

Thinking that comments on 'rites of passage' and 'the great unwashed' might offend my friends in vests, or at the very least get lost in translation, I wished my friend Mark Reynolds was there to give his opinion. He had done Glastonbury and in 2003 had played the same stage as 'Kings of Leon', 'Goldfrapp' and John Cale. From the time he and his playing partner Wes Ellis, who called themselves 'Steve', had their application for a gig accepted, months were spent practising in Nynehead village hall. It became filled with nervous bum guitar notes. 'Mic'ed up' on the big day they came across as true professionals to a crowd of over 500 mud-caked souls. Afterward there was only one question, which out of Mark and Wes was "Steve?" "Which was kinda good," Mark still reflects as he tells of the hive-like backstage efficiency of military proportions engendering a lack of camaraderie or even contact with the other bands. The kudos has kept him in with the odd free pint at his local ever since.

He is very much aware of the how things have changed. On the 19th September 1970 the Worthy Farm venue was a small affair of big hair and the Afghan coat. Tickets for the festival cost £1 and offered "Pop, Folk and Blues, sheltered fields for camping, all food at fair prices, ox roast, and all farm's milk free." The festival was sparsely attended due to being badly advertised and poorly organised, but the site was nice. The decision to change the festival date to summer solstice was to prove a good one. 'Stackridge', a band of quirky humour and rhythmic catchy sing along tunes had kicked things off. On the bill were Marc Bolan, Ian Anderson, Keith Christmas, Quintessence, Al Stewart, Sam Apple Pie and Marsupilami, whose lead guitarist Leary Hasson lives near Wivey and still waxes lyrically of "freaky times, man."

By 1989, when Mark first braved the mud as a teenager, it was still a hippie festival of bean curd, cider, dogs on strings and kids with rainbow jumpers, dirty faces and, of course, dreadlocks. There was a sense of a coming together. People listened to the music of the Waterboys and the Levellers and there was space to enjoy an alternative lifestyle. Camping under canvas and plastic was a social thing. Wild characters wearing beads arrived with more solid roofs in ex-Post Office Commer vans with sliding doors and Ford Ivecos with little chimneys coming out of the top.

The early Nineties saw change with the coming of the scallies, Northerners in tracksuits who walked on the sides of their trainers in the mud. People's possessions began to disappear. A man stood outside the main gate whispering "E's, trips, whizz, black 'ash, Man," or "Ten Pounds for a stamp". The queue for the man became longer than the queue to get in with legitimate tickets. Festival-goers were happy to pay the man's friend for a little of what they fancied and for an ink stamp on the back of the hand, a pass for 'free' entry. Security had to get tighter. And it did.

Young people began to make their own free parties at Steart beach and on the Blackdowns, as Glastonbury went commercial with multinational sponsors. A fence constructed around the site provided a challenge to the 'impecunious ingenious' whose choice of free entry became the rope ladder buoyed up by 'illicit substances'. By the turn of the millennium fence climbers pushed the venue well beyond its licensed capacity, Eavis incurred a fine and the future of the festival was thrown into doubt. The reputed events company Mean Fiddler became involved to reassure Mendip Council that it was safe to issue future licences. Security was tightened further and a million pound double fence and sniffer dogs made the ingenious impossible. The festival was made bigger, but lost its spirit despite the 'ass' take on events:

"Over one weekend 140,000 people gather creating a 'Global City' overnight. In this tiny space in rural Somerset, festival-goers are exposed to a programme so culturally diverse one would more usually associate it with sprawling urban centres. The programme offers a huge variety of choice from the obvious rock, jazz, dance and acoustic music, to contemporary dance and theatre, street theatre, global music, circus, new age, film, children's festival, participatory workshops, poetry, healing arts, alternative technology and cabaret. People from hugely different backgrounds and of all ages rub shoulders for three days. There is something for everyone."

However, these days the wild characters with their chimney vans are gone. Now it's girls applying hippie war-paint in the vanity mirrors of their new style VW beetles and Golf cabriolets. Glastonbury has become a fashion parade, a place to spot Kate Moss and get text updates on personal mobile phones. Like mornings on a South East commuter station platform, people camping think 'wall and window', protect their own space and don't talk to their neighbours.

It used to be a place where the normal rules did not apply, where many a blind eye was turned and you could succumb to most indulgences safe in the knowledge that no-one was looking over your shoulder. That, too, has vanished into the ether, as overbearing security guards whip spliffs out of the mouths of anyone daring to light up, having survived the sniffer dogs on the buses en route and the bag-searches at the gate.

Despite this there still is the occasional Section 136 issued against the ingenious where a person can be detained by police without charge for their own safety or to protect the safety of those about them. But one has to ask whether comments like "In a former life I killed you, because you were a flea and I was a leopard," actually warrant it. Gone is the Glastonbury folk had come to know and love.

Mark feels jaded and doesn't want to go anymore. Camping, he says, is for the South of France, not for the fickle Somerset weather at equinox. Anyway, he has major bugbears. Thinking back it was the cacophony of recorded noise from the many C-shaped four-foot long brass Kombu horns that had distorted the sound coming out of the studio speakers that got us onto the subject. That and I suppose the discussion we had about the accompanying images for our newest documentary of gold decorated festival elephants and sacrificial chickens carried above the heads of blue painted Keralan men. Glastonbury has become too big, Mark thinks. "There's a twenty minute walk between stages," he said to me as we gazed out from his garden bench across the growing vegetable beds, "If you time it wrong you could spend all day walking and see nothing. When wet, it's simply miserable. You can't sit down and you have to be on your feet all day." He was sure that sunny days were great, but they were a far off memory.

In the year of 'Arctic Monkeys' thousands of people were delayed leaving the 2007 festival site because of bad weather. There was mud enough to give Somerset's oldest man, Harry Patch, nightmares of Passchendaele. Cars and camper vans got stuck in mud soup as the rain hammered down and tractors were drafted in to tow vehicles out of the car parks. Police handed out 3,000 space blankets to those trying to get home and the Red Cross treated queues at Castle Cary railway station. It was reported that many buses failed to turn up. A concerned mother rang the BBC. "My son was on a combined ticket with coach and has spent nearly seven hours waiting in the cold and rain without shelter for a coach back to Colchester in Essex."

When the BBC investigated unfolding events, no one from the 'Festival Office' was available to comment. Speaking at the time to a reporter, one reveller said she had only moved 200 yards in more than eight hours, trying to drive off the site. "No one has told us what is going on and we've only had one burger and a bottle of diet coke all day." Bring back the days of bean curd.

The following day Michael Eavis praised festival-goers' spirit and said the weekend had "gone very, very well, in spite of the rain and mud". What he failed to mention was the mess. From the mud obviously, but also from the 'bomb-site' of tins, wrappers and other discarded rubbish that in its amount is always quite gobsmacking. Especially given the background of those who dropped it.

Sadly, Glastonbury has a discriminatory feel, and cynically, one might be forgiven to think, only attractive to middle class 'Q' readers. A bibbler friend of my eldest son went for the first time at the age of 29, not only because it's something he must do before he's 30, but because this is the first year he's been able to afford it. Food and drink prices have become extortionate, worse even than the motorway prices at Sedgemoor and Gordano services. More importantly, people have to have computer access and be prepared to give away their identity as well as having the money in the bank for a ticket three months before the event. To actually get a ticket, one has to pre-register with one's bank details and also provide one's name, address and a personal photograph. Civil liberties are a worry to Mark and I can see his point of view. If a government can lose your personal identity on trains and on misplaced computer discs, what will corporate hippies do with it?

In 2008 there was a problem selling tickets at £164 with unavoidable booking fees and postage, whereas in previous years they had been over-subscribed. It seems people had been priced out. Michael Eavis told BBC reporter John Kay that he had "lost half a stone in weight through worry," and things got "a bit scary for a while." The good news was that there were going to be two and half thousand portaloos and twenty thousand bins.

As the 'Kings of Leon' were headlining on the Pyramid stage 'Steve' played the 'Foresters Arms' raising funds for the charity Leuka beside the disused Dunster animal pound. Perhaps, like Ionica, I too, prefer to say "Glarsetonbury" and avoid the mud slinging by watching it with Alina on our Wivey telly. Far away in Eastern Europe bears distracted by bins would be unknowing of richer pickings elsewhere.

LAST THOUGHTS

"The Future is something which everyone reaches at the rate of sixty minutes an hour, whatever he does, whoever he is."

(C.S. Lewis).

I was introducing Alina to the wonderfulness of whortleberry picking. Hunter gathering is an addictive habit come the August end of July. A group of Exmoor ponies in the company of sheep scratched their bums and noses on hawthorn trees. We were the only ones visible under the wild acres of summer sky. I was not complaining, but with my mouth and teeth purple with whortleberry juice, I wondered where everybody else was.

At the last census in 2001 Somerset had a population, including me, of 855,697. Now it has risen by another 30,000 and although not exactly bulging the borders, the numbers are still going up. However, with Somerset folk established and new tending to stick to the towns, it was not really this news that perplexed me. The question was, where were the grockles? Over nine million tourist nights are spent in the county each year. God alive, they can't all be stuck on the M5. This was summer and there was not a grockle to be seen. Certainly some would have got no further than Bath to buy a teddy bear, expensive shortbread or see where the Romans shed their togas. But the rest?

The answer came later that day, after Alina and I had driven up Minehead's North Hill to park the car. We planned to take the steep sheep path down to Burgundy chapel, an overgrown ruin with a cute hobbit-sized stone arched doorway.

Looking back down from North Hill through the black fire-frazzled gorse stumps was the bay that the science fiction writer Arthur C. Clarke, Minehead's most famous son, likened to the Moon's 'Bay of Rainbows'. At the far end was the futuristic seafront skyline pavilion world of Butlins. That's where the grockles were. They were there fun-seeking, burger-munching, playing bingo and torturing karaoke under the gleaming white sails, only to occasionally venture out, before being bussed home. I took my excited children there for a day once. For me, that once was enough. At the gate some lad in a cap with his T-shirted bull-necked father was gazing in the direction of where Alina and I now stood. "Cor Dad, are those mountains?" "Nah, thems 'ills." Dad was a clever grockle.

These days the red coats are worn by Poles and the camp itself is very different to what it used to be, when it first opened in 1962. Within the first three years Francis Rossi and Rick Parfitt, who were both working there, became friends and decided to form Status Quo. Also in that period the peace of Minehead station was shattered by the screams of hundreds of schoolchildren and teenagers. The Beatles came by steam train on the West Somerset Railway to shoot scenes for their first movie 'A Hard Day's Night'.

On a day of piercing wind and slate-grey cloud early this year, a new Minehead attraction was launched by Titan, an eight foot tall, talking, dancing, robot, and breakfast television's Lorraine Kelly who cut the ribbon with a glitzy pair of garden shears. Butlins calls its new asset 'BlueSkies'. No, this is not a state-of-the-art rollercoaster, but an art deco-style apartment block. Built as time-shares at the cost of £4 million, the architects think it's their new Miami. Butlins is keen to change its image and reach out to the sort of people who might normally turn up their noses. From my viewpoint, mine gave a compulsive twitch.

But that was all yesterday. Today I was back in Jonathan Farey's kitchen at 'Folly Farmyard', sitting at the table beneath bunches of herbs hanging from nails banged into a ceiling beam. I still had whortleberry stains on my fingers as I opened my laptop. Distracted from his weaning piglets, Jonathan poured me a mug of homemade scrumpy from an old whisky barrel. It sat under last season's brittle dry nasturtium flowers twined along a hanging porch string, left there because he liked them.

He saw they had attracted my interest. "Do you want some nasturtium plants? I've got so many."

"Thanks anyway, but I've got loads clambering out tubs on my patio. The dumbledores love them." His limping lurcher lapped twice at a little puddle of spilt cider.

I showed Jonathan what I had written about the farm a couple of months earlier. "He's still with us," he said, "Hairy John."

Maria, his primary school teacher wife, put down the laundry basket and picking up a Leonard Cohen songbook, sang a few impromptu choruses of 'Hallelujah' with Jemima and Lily, her eldest and youngest daughters. The other two, Otterly and Polly, blew soap bubbles at my laptop. Once more collecting up the laundry, Maria went upstairs saying "We must practice that at the school for Christmas."

"k.d. lang's live version's best," I offered.

A tractor horn in the road summoned Jonathan. I followed him as he went to say hello to Richard, who had been farming for fifty-three years. He was a man who apparently worried more about other folk than himself and had never killed an animal in his life. Despite this he had "muddled through." Certainly he had done so with his tractor, as it had new patches of black and red painted over heavy rust. As he and

Jonathan talked of the exhaustion of haymaking, I noticed Hairy John, Jonathan's shaggy blind Highland steer, across his field content under a crab apple tree. After my having strolled across to get a photo and getting caught up in the live wire of the electric fence, Jonathan introduced me to Richard. "Meet Charles, he's writing a book about how to survive in Somerset."

Richard looked down at me from his cab. I was still feeling a little tingly around the seat of my chinos.

"Is ee? Glad ee's survived 'Smoky Bottom'. If ee's writing a book ee should go and see Robert over at Pitt Farm in Culmstock, ee's got a lot old tools for winnowing and what not. There's nothing ee' don't know. Tell 'im 'Richard sent 'ee.' Have you told Charles about the 'Golden Calf' and the 'Clump', Jonathan?"

"No."

So I listened to two tales of strange phenomena. Firstly, a bright apparition appeared on Christmas Eve about thirty years ago when Water Board workmen were busy repairing a pipe in a nearby field. They dropped their tools and did a runner and never returned.

"'Tis true, I saw the light over the hedges" said Richard. Another farmer who had "gone on", had got a closer look and swore it looked like a giant golden calf.

And up the top of Folly Lane and through the gate on the other side of the main road is 'the clump', an oval piece of raised ground within a stone wall that was used as a Blackdowns' cattle pound. Trees have taken it over, and roots forces are crumbling the walling. Both Richard and Jonathan agreed that no birds or animals ever go near it. Why, they don't know. However, they both seemed very thankful that these days the 'clump' is owned by the County Council. The stories were proof, if proof was needed, that there is so much more to discover. I had only just scratched the surface, when I thought I had known a lot.

The good news was that my green Peugeot was still going thanks to Terry, Wivey's magician of a mechanic who was adamant "she'd be good for a little longer." Saying my goodbyes at 'Folly Farmyard' and thinking the likes of winnowing would have to be for another day, I headed home with the established order of priorities to feed the cat and give Alina a hug and then make Hairy John my screen saver, all behind the blue, warped front door.

As I passed by the Buddhafields music festival where tickets are handmade clay pendants, a BBC voice on the car radio told me Somerset had thrashed Kent by over two hundred runs at Taunton and were only a point away from the top of cricket's Championship table. Could this be an historic year?

Life in Somerset goes into the future, ever hopeful. Amor meus Somerset.

APPENDAGE ONE
LOCAL WIT

New Romantics

Matty and Charlotte parked the rusty car up an old drove road near Westonzoyland after the Young Farmers' disco. It was a moonlit summer's night in the early hours and very quiet. Matty became passionate and after a while suggested Charlotte get into the back of the car. She resisted.

"Come on," he pleaded, "Please get in the back."

"'No," said Charlotte.

"Oh, why won't you get in the back?" he asked.

"Cos," said Charlotte, "I would much rather stay in the front with you."

Feeling Needled

Milly lived alone and felt bored. There was not a lot to do on an Exmoor winter's night. So she taught herself to knit. She became so keen she spent all her time knitting. She even did it while driving her little red Fordham tractor, which she steered with her knees. A local policeman peddling his bicycle noticed her doing just this and waved Milly to a stop.

"Pull over," he ordered loudly.

"No, socks," called out Milly waving back.

Numb Thumb.

Linda was a barmaid in a Highbridge pub. One evening a hiker walked in with a limp and asked for a pint of cider. He explained he had turned his ankle and been trying to thumb a lift for hours.

"Highbridge must be the bumhole of Somerset," he complained.

"Oh, what a shame," said Linda, "and you are just passing through?"

Hot Head.

Ted turned up in A&E at Taunton's Musgrove Park Hospital. His right ear was blistered, red raw and weeping.

"What happened to you?" said the nurse in triage.

"Blime-o'-Blinkin'-Riley," moaned Ted, "There was oi just ironin' m'jeans when the phone rang."

Bird Watching

Somerset has a wonderful variety of wildlife. Red kites soar over from Wales, deer wander Exmoor and the Quantocks, dormice doze in woods, otters enjoy the river valleys, eels are plentiful and an egret is seen outside Dunster. So when it comes to creatures that run and creep and weave and fly, keeping an open mind means you will never be surprised. One day Stan came home to his wife Shirl in Chard, with two rockhopper penguins on the back seat of his car.

"Where in God's name did you find they?" asked Shirl.

"Just walking along the Crewkerne road," Stan replied.

"You had better go back the way you came and take 'em to Cricket St Thomas zoo."

Stan nodded his head in agreement and set off.

Later when he returned home the penguins were still on the back seat.

"I thought I told you to take them penguins to the zoo," exclaimed Shirl.

"I did," said Stan, "And we had a lovely time. We're going to Butlins tomorrow!"

Country Report

The good air of the Quantocks helps make Crowcombe a healthy place to live. A number of summers ago Sam Scroggins had exceeded even local expectations and had just celebrated his 106th birthday in Honeysuckle Cottage. The family felt rightly proud and Sam's grandson contacted a tabloid newspaper, giving rough directions to the cottage. Thinking it had been gifted a wonderful 'human interest story', a young reporter was dispatched from London. Although having got close to Tom's cottage, the reporter became lost in the maze of Somerset lanes. Forced to stop at a crossroads where the roads dwindled away in three directions to winding sunken lanes unsuitable for cars, the reporter was near despair. There was no signpost. Then he saw Zac Tribber hedge laying.

"Do you know the way to Sam Scroggins's?" asked the reporter.

"Aye, I do," said Zac.

The reporter felt light-headed with his luck.

"Which way do I go?"

"Well, which ever way any you loike. All three lanes go passed Sam's door, but you'll 'ave to walk mind."

So the reporter abandoned his car, gave his thanks, turned right, and after a two hour yomp found himself outside Honeysuckle Cottage. The door was ajar and the reporter heard a familiar voice inside. It was Zac's. And he was sharing a cider with Sam, and what must have been all of

Sam's family. Red-faced and sweaty, the reporter gave the door a knock and was beckoned in.

"So you got 'ere then?" said Zac, as the reporter stared at him bemused. "No good you lookin' at me loike that. You never asked me how far it were each way, did ee? I've been telling Sam here that I was scratchin' me head about you wanting to walk eight mile and all. But then again had you gorn left, you wouldn't 'ave got 'ere for tomorrow's breakfast. Gorn straight ahead, mind, this cottage would've been just around the corner." Sam and his family were all nodding agreement. Still feeling his aching legs, the reporter suppressed a weary sigh, and introduced himself.

"Find yerself a pew, lad" said Sam, a grinning face of wrinkles. "Zac's an ol' bugger."

"Are you really a hundred and six?" the reporter asked him.

"Yep"

"And have you lived here all your life?"

"Not yet," said Sam.

Tip-Tip-Tapping.
When Robbie Richards decided to have a go there were to be no half measures. He was a stubborn soul. Being nothing short of ambitious, he would go the whole hog, even though he had made a complete pig's ear of his first try in evening class, at the Rural Education Centre, in Winsford. Once his mind was made up, that was it. He was going to buy himself his own PC. This is what modern Somerset farmers did; he had read it in the *Farmers Weekly* magazine. A PC got you organised, and organisation was what Robbie needed. He had the full support of his wife. His accounts were a mess. Bills and papers filled random boxes that spilled over under the bed, behind the sofa and on the kitchen table.

To make a start, the first thing that Robbie did was convert his chicken shed beside the log store into an office. This was a hassle because his chickens kept forgetting they no longer lived there anymore. By having to keep the chicken-wire over the two windows, and dropping cornflakes from his breakfast bowl onto the floor, he confused them even more. Robbie left it to his wife to inevitably solve the fowl problem over several Sunday lunches. Despite having to peer through the window wire, the view he had was distracting, to put it mildly. He could see right down into the valley below, where the River Barle churned and bubbled, and where fish swam.

As autumn turned to winter the chill set in, as did Robbie's reluctance to even switch on the new PC. What he needed was a log burner, his wife told him. So Robbie had one installed. Unfortunately, the whoozy warmth tended to send Robbie to sleep and to attract mice. Consequently, he sought the company of the obliging farm cat.

With the coming of spring and the lighter evenings he much preferred a spot of trout fishing in the River Barle to tip-tip-tapping at his PC. By the time the hay was up again, he had made so little progress that a spider had made a home in the PC's keyboard. Family and friends had yet to receive an email, and the only thing he had downloaded was a brochure for a new hen-house. One evening Robbie's wife caught him ferreting through a box behind the sofa, swearing and blinding. This finally made her go off to find a pen and some paper.

Next morning Robbie found a note pinned to his office door. It read:

'Robbie's Computer Manual':

Boot up =	When Robbie puts his wellies on in the morning
Broadband =	The fan-belt keeping the tractor going
Burner =	What the logs go on
Chip =	A kitchen snack
Cookie =	An out of kitchen snack
Crash =	The type of course Robbie needs to use his computer
Cursor =	Robbie when swears a lot
Downloads =	Getting the hay bales off the tractor
Floppy disc =	What Robbie gets lifting too many hay bales at once
Hard Drive =	Getting home during bad weather
Hardware =	The gurt immovable nails that keep the chicken-wire on the windows
Keyboard =	Where Robbie hangs his keys
Laptop =	Where the cat sleeps
Log on =	Make the wood stove hotter
Log off =	The time to reach for the fire tongs
Megabit =	What Robbie takes out of a Cox's apple
Megahertz =	What Robbie gets when he's not careful downloading hay
Microchips =	What's left on the plate when the big chips are gone
Microsoft =	Robbie's tickly bit
Modem =	What Robbie did to the fields
Mouse =	What eats the cornflakes on the floor now the chickens are gone
Network =	When Robbie has to repair his fishing net
On-line =	Where Robbie hangs his fezzies
Off-line =	When a fox steals away Robbie's fezzies
RAM =	What's needed for the spring lambs

Shut down =	What will happen to the farm if Robbie's doesn't sort his flipping accounts out
Software =	Robbie's favourite pair of underwear
Upgrade =	The steep hill home
USB =	A bee useless at making honey
Web =	What the spider makes
Windows =	What Robbie wants to shut when it's cold
Wireless =	What Robbie wishes his windows were
Word =	The rude thing Robbie says when he hurts his thumb.

A Matter of Understanding.

As farms go Tom Godney's place outside Priddy was not the biggest. Yet for Tom the few sheep and apple trees were his life and soul. One day Tom found himself leaning over one of his gates, having a conversation with an American grockle who had wandered up the lane.

"You sure do have a pretty place here. How much land do you have?" asked the grockle.

"From the apple tree with the mistletoe you can see over there, roight aways round behind the barn and away to that gurt oak tree on top of the hill," said Tom proudly.

"That's not a lot," figured the grockle, "Back in the States I farm some land and it would take me best part of a day to drive around it."

"Well m'dear, oi used to have an ol' car like that too," sighed Tom sympathetically.

Informal Education.

Big Josh Jenning took his ten year old son, Adam, out fishing in a boat last summer on Clatworthy Reservoir. It was a grand day for it. While they paddling about and trout were biting, Adam suddenly becomes curious about the world around him.

He asked Josh, "Dad, how does this boat float with you being so gurt?"

"Don't rightly know, son," Josh replied.

Five minutes later, Adam looked at his father and asked, "Dad, how do fish breath underwater?"

Giving this a little thought, Josh again replied, 'Don't rightly know, son.'

Another five minutes passed. Then Adam asked, "Dad, why is the sky blue?"

Again, Josh was flummoxed. "Don't rightly know son."

Finally, Adam said, "Dad, do you mind my asking you all of these questions?"

Josh was quick to reply, "Of course not, son. If you don't ask questions, you never learn nothin'."

Wishful Thinking.
Thomas was such an enthusiastic Somerset farmer that he had little time to think of anything else. As the years passed however he felt a little female companionship would be 'a proper job'. He wondered how he could meet the woman he yearned for, and eventually settled on an advertisement in the *County Gazette*: 'Man, 48, wishes to meet woman, 33-40, owning a tractor. Please send photograph of tractor.'

APPENDAGE TWO
KEEPING UP APPEARANCES

"If the sea stands for everything that mankind cannot control,
then the pier – as potent a phallic symbol as any skyscraper – was
a daring protrusion into that dangerous, boundless realm. It
invited those who stepped on to it to cast off the usual
constraints of polite society."
(Richard Morrison, *The Times,* 29th July 2008)

I'm not sure who the bright spark was in the 'Bearin' Up' who began the singing to which a number of bibblers joined in. They should be ashamed of themselves, I thought, it's too soon. However, I could not suppress my chortle. Bad taste can have that effect.
"Bob the builder
Can we fix it?
Bob the builder
Yes we can!"

The incineration of Weston-super-Mare's one hundred and four year old Grand Pier from a fire that started in a deep-fat fryer was not the sort of end of July heat wave anyone could have wanted. A Grade II listed building many believe represents Weston. It is iconic, perhaps more so than the M5 Willow Man, that has also had fire trouble, or the camel at Bridgwater. However, the entire wooden structure at the end of the mile-and-a-quarter pier was gone in the time it takes Yeovil Town to play a football match.

Firefighters could do little, their access along the narrow pier was difficult and there was a shortage of water for the pumps, which for a seaside resort is something of a paradox. The Somerset summer weather of hail and torrential rain was as ill timed as ever, coming an hour or so too late. The pier was already a steel skeleton of tangled girders.

Anne Magor, who has a fire engine daily in the pier's shadow, could do nothing. Her husband's family has had the donkey-ride concession since before the pier last burnt down back in 1930. Then children ran beneath the pier gathering handfuls of pennies dropping from melting slot machines. These days, ironically, Anne offers children rides in a horse-drawn fire engine. Hers, though, has Fireman Sam written on the sides.

205

With no pier to attract people other than the voyeurs, a hot summer could only benefit her.

Tim Phillips, chairman of the National Pier Society, had said only a few weeks previously on a visit to Weston that "it is a quirk of piers that they seem to catch fire." Well, the fire at Weston was the largest on any pier. It was seen as far away as Devon, South Wales and Gloucestershire.

The pier was bought earlier in the year for a staggering £10 million by brother and sister entrepeneurs Kerry and Michelle Michael who are Weston people born and bred. Kerry spoke for them both when he said, "When we purchased the Grand Pier we regarded ourselves as custodians rather than owners. For this tragic event to have taken place on our watch is truly devastating. I feel very sorry for our dedicated staff, many of whom have been on the pier all their working lives. We will work tirelessly to restore this magnificent structure to its former glory."

Faced with the true spirit of survival, the bibblers in the 'Bearin' Up', as with everyone else of true Somerset heart, can only wish them well. However, where would the grockles buy their candyfloss in the meantime? It was a question muttered by a bibbler, or two. After a pause for thought, the answer was probably Butlins.